D1625005

drink·ol·o·gy
EATS

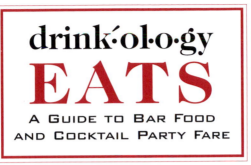

drink·ol·o·gy
EATS
A GUIDE TO BAR FOOD
AND COCKTAIL PARTY FARE

JAMES WALLER
AND
RAMONA PONCE

Illustrations by
GLENN WOLFF

stewart, tabori & chang
NEW YORK

Published in 2006 by Stewart, Tabori & Chang
An imprint of Harry N. Abrams, Inc.

Text copyright © 2006 by Thumb Print New York, Inc.
Illustrations copyright © 2006 by Glenn Wolff
Apologies to Sir John Tenniel for the drawing on page 131.

Library of Congress Cataloging-in-Publication Data

Waller, James, 1953–
  Drinkology eats : a guide to bar food and cocktail party fare / James
Waller and Ramona Ponce ; illustrations by Glenn Wolff.
     p. cm.
  Includes index.
  ISBN-13: 978-1-58479-529-2
  ISBN-10: 1-58479-529-8
  1. Appetizers. 2. Cocktail parties. I. Ponce, Ramona. II. Title.

TX740.W24 2006
641.8'12--dc22   2006018540

Editor: Marisa Bulzone
Designer: Jay Anning
Production Manager: Devon Zahn

The text of this book was composed in Adobe Caslon.

Printed and bound in China

10 9 8 7 6 5 4 3 2 1

HNA
harry n. abrams, inc.
a subsidiary of La Martinière Groupe

115 West 18th Street
New York, NY 10011
www.hnabooks.com

For our mothers,
DOROTHY KEMSTEDT
and
PATRICIA PONCE

'A little red wine, I think, for me.'

'And for me,' said Thorin.

'And raspberry jam and apple-tart,' said Bifur.

'And mince-pies and cheese,' said Bofur.

'And pork-pie and salad,' said Bombur.

'And more cakes—and ale—and coffee, if you don't mind,' called the other dwarves through the door.

'Put on a few eggs, there's a good fellow,' Gandalf called after him, as the hobbit stumped off to the pantries. 'And just bring out the cold chicken and pickles!'

—J. R. R. TOLKIEN
The Hobbit

ACKNOWLEDGMENTS

W E COOKED AND COOKED AND COOKED. WE ATE AND ATE AND ATE. We mixed drinks and we drank them. And we had some help.

An incalculable debt of gratitude is owed to our life-partners: Ramona's husband, Eric Mueller, and James's companion, Jim O'Connor. Without their steadfast love, their unflagging support, their imperturbable patience, their discerning palates, and their insatiable appetites and unquenchable thirsts this book could never have come into being.

Next, we thank all of those who were subjected to our culinary and mixological research over the eight months spent developing the recipes for this book—especially the cocktail party guests who, interrogated by Ramona following *Drinkology EATS*'s parties, responded to her queries with frank—sometimes brutally frank—assessments of our menus. (Don't worry. You'll be invited back.)

Ramona's sisters—Lorenza, Patty, and Rachel Ponce—merit lifetime achievement awards for having been, for so long, such willing and enthusiastic guinea pigs for her experiments in the kitchen. Others deserving special thanks include Joe Ligammari and Frank Verlizzo, for their tireless pursuit of the outlandish cocktail (and for our scrumptious frozen Margarita recipe); Chris March, for his always gracious culinary advice (and for our San Francisco chicken wings recipe); Ken Frederick, for his assistance with the essentials of Maryland crab cookery; Betsy Keller, for investigating the subtleties of crab imperial; and Jane Cohn, for digging into her file of tried-and-true cocktail party recipes just for us. James sends his thanks and his love to his Aunt Babe (Mrs. Amelia Earley), whose eponymous hot-milk cake (page 179) has been enjoyed by guests at his parties for years and years.

We're grateful, too, to a number of professional acquaintances. Thanks to Bob Ransom and Susan Wine for letting us play hosts at a cocktail party at the Vintage New York wine shop in SoHo, Manhattan. And James is deeply grateful to Debra Argen and Edward Nesta, of LuxuryExperience.com, for their tireless support of the Drinkology series. It is very nice indeed when professional "contacts" become good and true friends.

Hosannas flow to *Drinkology EATS*'s designer, Jay Anning, and illustrator, Glenn Wolff. You've done it again, and a very large measure of the Drinkology series' success is due to the elegant look you've created for these books. As always, the staff at Stewart, Tabori & Chang have been greatly supportive; particular thanks go to our editor, Marisa Bulzone (who also supplied a finger-licking wings recipe); to STC's publisher, Leslie Stoker; and to Steve Tager, who gets things accomplished. Liana Krissoff was one of the most astute and meticulous copy-editors James has ever worked with.

Finally, James reserves a special note of thanks for Mina Hamilton, Al Sbordone, and his Thumb Print colleague Areta Buk, all of whom contributed in indirect though essential ways to this book's realization.

—JAMES WALLER AND RAMONA PONCE
New York City
June 2006

Contents

Indexes

Drink Up, Chow Down

A "To-Your-Health Foods" Cookbook

I F YOU'RE GOING TO DRINK, SHOULDN'T YOU HAVE A LITTLE SOMETHING to eat, too? Well, yeah, you definitely should. All the scientists who study this stuff agree that eating while drinking slows down the absorption of alcohol into the bloodstream—substantially. Eating while drinking does *not* mean that you won't become intoxicated. (That, finally, has to do with the amount of alcohol you imbibe.) But it does mean that you won't get drunk nearly so quickly as you will if you drink on an empty stomach.

But this rationale for eating while drinking leaves out the *pleasure* part. Everyone takes it for granted that the pleasures associated with one alcohol-delivery medium—wine—are enhanced when wine is drunk with a meal.

The truth, though, is that all kinds of alcoholic beverages—beer, hard liquor, mixed drinks, saké—are more pleasurably enjoyed *with food.* And, no, that doesn't mean that you have to worry about whipping up a three-course dinner every time you feel like cracking open a cold Bud. A fistful of roasted, salted nuts might do you just fine.

Don't leave out the pleasure part

As with so many things in life, *appropriateness* is key. Beer simply tastes better when accompanied by certain foods. (One food that *really* goes with beer—although we'd bet you've never thought of it—is cake, so long as it's cake of a plain-ish, not-too-sweet variety.) The enjoyment of aperitif cocktails is heightened when they're served alongside simple salty/savory snacks. The *ne plus ultra* delights of Champagne are, in fact, ultra'd by eggs—whether those eggs are fish roe or the kind that chickens lay. And so on and so on.

CONVIVIALITY

But appropriateness alone isn't the whole story. The art of pairing certain foods with certain drinks, however important, can become a dry, persnickety, and flavorless science if one forgets about the essential reason for eating and drinking (aside from satisfying hunger and quenching thirst, that is). And that reason, of course, is *conviviality.* Animals eat alone (well, except for when they're feeding their young). Even when they're forced by human "masters" to eat side by side (think of cattle at a common trough, or two cats at their respective food dishes), animals don't *share* their meals. They don't really *want* company while eating.

We humans do. Sure, there are times when all of us would rather do our eating by ourselves—and our drinking, too, though that's an awfully slippery slope to set your little sled upon. But, in general and for the most part, we feel a deep and abiding need to have friends and family close by, partaking along with us, as we drink up and chow down. A meal consumed alone is usually a lonely meal; a drink that's drunk alone seems happy-sad, at best. Let's just face it: As a species, we're genetically programmed to *party*.

And that's what this book is about: not just the putting together of food and drink in gustatorially interesting ways, but also (and every bit as important) the creation of experiences that make eating and drinking more fun for everybody involved.

Eats and Drinks

As you make your way through this book's pages, you'll notice that it's a highly unusual cookbook, in that it includes recipes for drinks as well as for eats (nearly fifty drinks recipes in all, the great majority of them original to this book). We believe that skill in the kitchen easily translates into skill at the bar—after all, good cooking and good drink-making both have to do with putting together the right ingredients, in the right amounts, in the right way. But we further believe that in planning menus for celebrations and for ordinary meals, it's a salutary idea to pay as careful attention to the beverages as to the food. And though James and Ramona don't pay too much obeisance to the golden calf of Fashion, it pleases us that we seem to be on the cutting edge in this regard. Witness the phenomenon of the "bar chef"—a professional mixologist who, at a growing number of fashionable restaurants, is responsible for designing the bar menu and coordinating the drinks offerings with the dishes prepared by the other chef (the one in the kitchen).

You'll also doubtless notice that this is *not* a book for dieters of either the low-carb or the low-fat persuasion. Nor is it a health foods cookbook, though we occasionally offer some nutritional pointers. We prefer to think of *Drinkology EATS* as a "to-you-health" foods cookbook, and we apologize (disingenuously?) to those readers who don't share Ramona and James's passion for sugar, cream, butter, bacon, and, yes,

Dieters beware liquor. Our extravagance has its limits, however. It should go without saying that you should approach both your drinking *and* your eating with an eye toward moderation: Eat, drink, and be merry, *not* scary.

Finally, a word about how we think *Drinkology EATS* can best be used: In compiling it, we tried to be as comprehensive as possible, given the book's small size. To that end, we've included recipes and strategy notes for convivial gatherings small and large, for impromptu get-togethers, and for meticulously planned parties. We've developed menus for various times of day and for different seasons. But these distinctions aren't meant to be utterly rigid. Many of the bar foods discussed in the book's earliest chapters would, for example, perform handsomely on a cocktail party bill of fare. Likewise, many of the recipes presented in our afternoon tea chapter, or the Mexican-themed buffet chapter, or the wintertime brunch chapter—or, indeed, the long chapter on mounting a "do it yourself" cocktail party for scores of guests—would be appropriate in a variety of contexts. So we advise you to mix and match, to happily experiment.

And, of course, we hope you enjoy yourself mightily. Bon appétit. Cin-cin.

CHAPTER ONE

Eat, Drink, Men, Women!

BAR FOOD BASICS

W HATEVER HAPPENED TO ALL THE GOOD BAR FOOD?" RAMONA asks. Whereupon she and James spend a few melancholy minutes meditating on its disappearance.

It wasn't too long ago, we seem to remember, that many bars—humble hooch hovels and exalted cocktail-cult temples alike—made it their business to nourish their clienteles as well as to get them tanked. Fondly do we recall the mixed-nut medleys, the barbequed chicken wings, the salami-and-cheese platters, and the groaning, chafing-dish laden sideboards of the taverns of the day before yesterday. (And James never ceases yearning for the pickled eggs and pigs' feet available for the asking at the proletarian dives that he spent all too much time in during his dissipated youth.) Nowadays, even at the toniest gin joints, you're lucky if you manage to nab a few goldfish crackers as the single, small bowlful makes it way down the bar, reluctantly pushed by one hungry (but polite) patron on to the next.

Oh, alright, we're overstating the case—but not by much. Good, substantial bar eats, even at happy hour, seem a rarer and rarer amenity. Which, when you think about it, is doubly weird. First off, many traditional bar foods—especially salty snacks—whet the thirst. Feed your customers, and (or so we imagine) you stand the chance of selling them a few more drinks, so where's the marketing logic in being stingy with the vittles? Second, depriving bar-goers of some nice, toothsome munchies makes it likelier that they'll get too drunk too quickly. In an age when bars (and bartenders) are increasingly held legally accountable for monitoring their customers' level of intoxication, it strikes us as lunacy not to offer the folks at the bar something to nibble on.

PUTTIN' ON THE DOG

Drinkology EATS can't hope to counter this inhospitable trend in the so-called hospitality industry, of course. And, anyway, that's not our purpose. What we aim to do in this chapter is to reacquaint American boozehounds with the concept (and reality) of great old-fashioned bar food, so you can serve it up yourself when puttin' on the dog for friends and relations at your own home bar.

The principles of good bar food are pretty straightforward. It should be relatively easy to prepare—and to prepare ahead of time, so you're not caught slaving over the stove while your chums are downing collinses in the rec room. And for the most part it shouldn't be too perishable, so that you can keep some on hand (for a few days or even a week or two) for impromptu get-togethers. Meat- and seafood-based bar snacks—covered in chapter 2—are the obvious exceptions to these rules.

Protein, carbs, and (yes) fat

Protein-rich foods, foods with lots of "nutrient-dense" carbohydrates, and—especially—certain kinds of fatty foods (because fat inhibits alcohol absorption so effectively) make for the best bar fare. Salty foods encourage thirst, and—so long as you don't take the thirst-quenching to extremes—there isn't a damned thing wrong with that. Hot 'n' spicy foods are OK—that is, as long as you don't overdo it in the eating or drinking department, since too much *picante* fare might make your morning-after stomach upset all the more miserable. Highly acidic foods are generally a no-no, since alcohol, all by itself, acidifies the system, and acidic edibles may magnify the damage. (Having tendered this warning, we do offer a recipe for pickled eggs in which, of course, vinegar's one of the preservative agents, but we still advise you to be judicious and to limit your intake of very acidic foods while drinking.)

In the smorgasbord of bar-food recipes that follows, you're likely to notice one glaring omission: the unglamorous-yet-glorious baked snack known as the pretzel. There's a logic to this lacuna. To make pretzels properly, you've got to immerse the shaped dough, ever so briefly, in an extremely dilute (though piping hot) solution of *lye* before baking. That's right: It's that extremely caustic alkaline compound that's essential to creating the polished, crunchy surface that makes pretzels—both the hard and the soft varieties—so appealing. We don't know about you, but we at *Drinkology EATS* are a tad reluctant to use lye in our cooking. (We're even afraid of using Drano to unstop a clogged sink!) What's more, baking hard pretzels requires an extremely high temperature that most home ovens can't achieve. We love pretzels, but the limitations of our oven and our aversion to lye convince us that they should be left to the (commercial pretzel-baking) experts, not homemade.

Nutty (Drinking) Buddies

When it comes to that trifecta of fat, protein, and nutrient-dense carbs, nothing outperforms the nut. Nuts also contain loads of potassium and other necessary minerals, as well as folic acid (vitamin B9) and, depending on the variety, other vitamins, as well. (Good things all, given alcohol's tendency to purge your body of electrolytes and vitamins—one of drinking's less salutary side-effects.)

Just about any kind of roasted and salted nut—from the humble peanut to the semiprecious macadamia—partners smashingly with alcoholic beverages, whether you're guzzling cheap beer or sipping a single-malt scotch. (James lived for a while in Turkey, years back, and the memory of the elegant little dishes of toasted hazelnuts that were always presented alongside cocktails in the bars of Istanbul still brings tears of gratitude to his rheumy eyes.)

Your buddies will be in awe of you

Even better than a plain salted nut, to *Drinkology EATS*'s addled-though-still-discerning tongue, is a nut that's been decked out in some salty-sugary or salty-savory coating. We're not alone in our craving for such confections. After all,

one of America's favorite commercial bar snacks—Beer Nuts—is nothing other than peanuts swathed in a salt–and–caramelized corn syrup glaze. We like Beer Nuts just fine (though we're a tad leery of that high-fructose corn syrup), but we also know that it's a snap to make some much more interesting sorts of coated nuts all by yourself. Your lazier-than-thou drinking buddies will be in awe of you, believe us.

Here are four of our favorite recipes. (Take note: If the amounts seem overlarge, not to worry. In our experience, coated nuts tend to get scarfed up as soon as they're set out. If you have leftovers, seal them in an airtight container. Coated nuts will stay fresh for upwards of a week or more.)

SWEET GLAZED PECANS

The unusual ingredient here is five-spice powder, a premixed Asian combo of cinnamon, cloves, fennel seed, star anise, and Szechuan peppercorns that's available, these days, in most supermarkets. It—along with the cumin, black pepper, and cayenne that the recipe also calls for—adds complexity and a little fire to the caramelized pecans.

½ cup (1 stick) unsalted butter
1 cup brown sugar, packed
½ cup water
2 teaspoons salt
4 teaspoons five-spice powder
1 teaspoon ground cumin
1 teaspoon freshly ground black pepper
¼ teaspoon ground cayenne pepper
8 cups pecan halves

Preheat the oven to 350° F. Melt the butter in a large, heavy nonstick pan over low heat. Add the brown sugar, water, salt, and spices. Heat, stirring occasionally, until the sugar is dissolved. Add the nuts and stir as the sauce thickens and coats the nuts. Turn out onto a couple of buttered jelly-roll pans, and spread the nuts out evenly. Bake for 10 to15 minutes.

Let cool on the pans, breaking up any clumps. (Stored in an airtight container at room temperature, the nuts will keep for up to 1 week.)

HOT AND SPICY WALNUTS

The hot pepper sauce that we prefer to use in this recipe is Tuong Ot Toi Viet-Nam Chili Garlic Sauce. (No, we can't pronounce the name, either, but the popular sauce—which is made by Huy Fong Foods, of Rosemead, California, and sold in most Asian-foods markets—is immediately recognizable by the container's bright green lid and the company's rooster trademark.) Tabasco sauce makes a perfectly acceptable substitute.

½ cup (1 stick) unsalted butter
1 tablespoon Worcestershire sauce
1 teaspoon hot pepper sauce, such as Asian chili garlic sauce
5 cups walnut halves
1 tablespoon sweet paprika
1½ teaspoons salt
1 teaspoon garlic powder
1 teaspoon onion powder
¼ teaspoon freshly ground black pepper
¼ teaspoon ground cayenne pepper

Melt the butter in a large, heavy nonstick pan over low heat. Add the Worcestershire and hot pepper sauces and mix well. Add the nuts and stir to coat. Cook for 20 to 25 minutes over low heat, stirring frequently, until the nuts are lightly toasted. Remove to paper towels to drain. In a large, resealable plastic bag, mix the paprika, salt, garlic powder, onion powder, black pepper, and cayenne and shake to mix well. Add the still-warm nuts and shake until well coated. (Stored in an airtight container at room temperature, the nuts will keep for at least 1 week.)

GINGER ORANGE NUTS

Adding an egg white to the mix—as this and the following recipe do—gives the nuts' coating a crusty, crunchy, batter-like quality.

1 egg white
5 cups pecans, walnuts, or roasted unsalted cashews (or a mix)
1 tablespoon finely minced ginger root
1 tablespoon orange zest
1 tablespoon fresh orange juice
2 tablespoons orange liqueur, such as Grand Marnier or Cointreau
½ teaspoon salt
¼ teaspoon ground ginger
1 cup granulated sugar
2 tablespoons (¼ stick) unsalted butter, melted

Preheat the over to 275° F. In a large mixing bowl, beat the egg white until stiff peaks form. Add the nuts, ginger root, zest, juice, and liqueur and toss to coat. In a separate bowl, mix the sugar, powdered ginger, and salt; sprinkle this mixture over the nuts and stir to coat well. Pour the melted butter into a jelly-roll pan, making sure that the surface of the pan is entirely coated. Spread the coated nuts across the pan in a single layer. Bake for 45 to 60 minutes, stirring every 15 minutes, until the nuts are a rich, medium-brown color.

BOOZY SPICED NUTS

Our nearly boundless affection for liquor means that *Drinkology EATS* is especially fond of bar snacks in which booze is a prime ingredient. Several rounds of experimentation demonstrated that several different kinds of hooch—from beatific Benedictine to humble rum—lend themselves well to this recipe.

1 egg white
5 cups walnuts or pecans
2 tablespoons Benedictine, bourbon, cognac, or dark rum
1 cup sugar
¾ teaspoon freshly ground nutmeg
½ teaspoon cinnamon
¼ teaspoon ground allspice
⅛ teaspoon ground cloves
⅛ teaspoon ground ginger

BAR ASSOCIATIONS

WE'RE NUTS ABOUT . . .

. . . classic cocktails paired with coated nuts. Sugary coated nuts make us thirst for bourbon's dusky pleasures; savory coated nuts for the sharper, cleaner thrill of a Martini. Here are two variations on time-honored drinks that, we think, make more-than-compatible partners with coated nuts.

BOURBON SIDECAR

Traditionally, the Sidecar is a brandy-based drink, but bourbon—especially a good small-batch bourbon like Knob Creek or Maker's Mark—makes for a potent counterpoint to the Cointreau and lemon juice.

lemon wedge
superfine sugar
2 ounces bourbon
1 ounce Cointreau
¾ ounce fresh lemon juice

¼ teaspoon salt

2 tablespoons (¼ stick) unsalted butter, melted

Preheat the oven to 275° F. In a large mixing bowl, beat the egg white until stiff peaks form. Add the nuts and liquor and toss to coat. In a separate bowl, mix the sugar, spices, and salt; sprinkle this mixture over the nuts and stir to coat well. Pour the melted butter into a jelly-roll pan, making sure that the surface of the pan is entirely coated. Spread the coated nuts across the pan in a single layer. Bake for 45 to 60 minutes, stirring every 15 minutes, until the nuts are a rich, medium-brown color.

Rim a chilled cocktail glass with the lemon wedge and sugar. (Discard the wedge.) Combine the other ingredients in a cocktail shaker, with ice. Shake well, then strain into the prepared glass.

"Pickled" Dirty Martini

Face it: If you have more than a couple of Martinis, you'll end up pickled. Here's a tasty way of fighting fire with fire, and pickling the Martini before it returns the favor. (Feel free to substitute vodka for the gin, if you wish.)

1 small gherkin, halved lengthwise

2 ounces gin

½ ounce dry vermouth

1 teaspoon pickle juice (from the gherkin jar)

Drop the gherkin halves into a chilled cocktail glass. Combine the other ingredients in a cocktail shaker, with ice. Shake well, then strain into the glass.

Eggs—Unscrambled

Back in the day before a rack of Beer Nuts was to be found behind of the bar of virtually every downscale American watering hole, another snack—this one of a decidedly humble, homemade kind—reigned supreme in neighborhood saloons across these United States: the hard-boiled egg. In many an establishment, the eggs, offered free of charge or for a few cents apiece, would be displayed in an egg tree—a Christmas tree–shaped wire apparatus that holds a dozen eggs, with a crow's-nest basket for the salt shaker and a circular bin ringing the bottom for stowing the peeled-off shells. (Still popular in Europe, egg trees of French make are sold stateside in some specialty housewares shops and online cookware emporiums. Visually quirky, emotionally comforting objects, they make great gifts.)

Touted in TV commercials of several decades ago as "nature's most nearly perfect food," the poor egg took a tumble from gastronomic grace during the anti-cholesterol hysteria of the 1980s and '90s. Luckily, one can sometimes put Humpty-Dumpty back together again, and—now that we know that those horrid trans fats are the real cardiac culprits—the egg has regained much of its former (and legitimate) standing as a superbly nutritious and, yes, healthful food. When it comes to what to eat while drinking, the egg has few competitors. Egg whites are virtually pure protein, and the yolks are chock-full of (good-for-you) fats and harbor a multivitamin-long list of essential nutrients. (Eggs even contain an amino acid, called cysteine, that offsets some of the deleterious effects of a hangover, making eggs one of the very foods with some scientifically demonstrable value as a hangover remedy.) And it's probably not even necessary to mention the egg's extraordinary versatility and popularity. Human beings have been chowing down on this avian reproductive apparatus since—well, since before we *were* human beings—and virtually every culture has produced a range of egg dishes for every sort of meal and culinary purpose. (It should come as no surprise, then, that you'll find quite a number of egg-based dishes in this book.)

Humpty Dumpty's been put together again

The simplest egg dish of all, of course, is the hard-boiled egg. Simple to eat, that is. As it turns out, the hard-boiled egg is not so simple to cook, *if* what you want is an egg that remains uncracked during cooking, one whose shell is easy to remove cleanly, one that's cooked through without being rubbery, and one whose yolk is an even, golden yellow— unblemished by that ugly, bluish/grayish/greenish caul that's a sure signal that the egg stayed in the pot too long.

Drinkology EATS is gonna give it to you straight. Despite multitudinous claims to the contrary, there's just *no* method of hard-boiling eggs that's guaranteed to produce the perfect result every time. Hard-boiled eggs that don't come out right are a major annoyance—and one that every cook, no matter how meticulous and skillful, will experience a dismaying number of times over the course of a lifetime.

RAMONA'S ALL-BUT-FOOLPROOF HARD-BOILED EGGS

With that caveat out of the way, let us clue you in on the method that we believe promises the greatest chance of success. It's the method that Ramona's been employing for years, and it performed best when tested against the several others we experimented with when conducting our research for this book.

13 or 14 eggs

If you want to be reasonably sure that you'll end up with a dozen flawless eggs, start with thirteen or fourteen, since it's almost inevitable that one or two will crack while cooking. (*Drinkology EATS* prefers organic eggs from free-range hens, which, besides their health-related virtues, tend to have sturdier shells than the factory-farmed variety.) Do *not* use extremely fresh eggs, which, even when expertly cooked, can be difficult to impossible to peel; so try to plan ahead, and to buy the eggs at least two days before you intend to boil them.

Keep the eggs refrigerated until an hour or two before you intend to use them. (Allowing them to achieve room temperature before boiling can help ensure thorough cooking.) Examine each egg carefully, making sure it's free of cracks. (Discard cracked eggs, which can be risky to eat.) Carefully place the eggs at the bottom of a large pot, and cover them with cold water to a depth of about 1 inch above the eggs.

Set the pot on the burner, and turn the heat to its highest setting. After a few minutes have passed, make sure that you check the pot once every minute or so, since it's essential that you be there, ready to act, the moment the water comes to a full boil. As soon as it does, turn the heat down to its lowest possible setting. (Achieving a rapid shift in temperature is, of course, much easier to do on a gas stove than on an electric range. If your stove is electric, you may want to transfer the pot to another burner, preset at the lowest setting, as soon as the water's begun boiling.)

Now we come to the finesse part: The length of time you should allow the water to remain at this vague simmer depends on the size of the eggs. Medium eggs should continue to cook for another 8 minutes; large eggs 9 to 10 minutes; extra large eggs 10 to 11 minutes; and jumbo eggs about 12 minutes.

As soon as the requisite amount of time has passed (set the timer!), remove the pot from the stove, place it in the sink, and run cold water into it, allowing it to overflow until the pot is filled with cold water. (You may even want to throw a couple of trays' worth of ice cubes into the pot, since it's crucial to cool the eggs down—and halt the cooking—as quickly as possible.) Let the eggs sit in the cold water for 5 minutes, then drain them and allow them to dry.

If you're serving the boiled eggs in their shells, that's all there is to it. If you're making deviled eggs (see pages 316–320), an egg-mayonnaise topping (see page 331), or pickled eggs (see page 29), you've got to peel them, which it's advisable to do as soon as possible after they've cooled. (If you are going to peel the eggs, Ramona advises plunging your hand into the pot as soon as the water's cold and knocking the eggs around a bit, cracking them slightly to permit the water to penetrate the shells, which she insists makes the peeling go easier. James isn't convinced it makes much difference, so follow your own instincts on this score.)

When peeling the (cool and dry) eggs, crack the shells *all over* before commencing the peeling. Utter a heartfelt prayer to the god of the kitchen that the shells will come away smoothly and cleanly, without interference from that tenacious little membrane, just beneath the shell, that can wreak such havoc on the peeling process (and the chef's nervous system).

If left in their shells, hard-boiled eggs can be safely kept unrefrigerated for 2 to 3 days.

FLAVORED SALT MIXES

In truth, the only thing a hard-boiled egg requires by way of accompaniment is salt. But if plain old salt is too humdrum for you, you might want to tart it up with some herbs and spices. There are lots of flavored salt mixes on the market these days; buy one at your local gourmet boutique, and you'll shell out a few dollars for a couple of ounces. But realize that you're paying for the packaging (and for your own laziness), since the ingredients inside the tin are so cheap. *Drinkology EATS,* ever thrifty, suggests that you might want to try your shaky hand at making your own. We encourage you to experiment, and to create your own salt mixes. But take it easy on the nonsalt ingredients lest their flavors overwhelm the mix.

Here are three possibilities; each small batch is plenty enough for a dozen or more hard-boiled eggs.

- **Pizza Salt:** Mix 2 tablespoons fine sea salt with ½ teaspoon garlic powder, ½ teaspoon dried oregano, and ¼ teaspoon hot red pepper flakes.

- **Celery Salt:** Mix 2 tablespoons fine sea salt with ¼ teaspoon celery seed. (This is much more flavorful than the premixed celery salt on your grocer's spice rack.)

- **Curried Salt:** Mix 2 tablespoons fine sea salt with ½ teaspoon hot (Madras) curry powder, ¼ teaspoon Old Bay seasoning, and a pinch of ground cayenne pepper.

PICKLED EGGS

In this simple, traditional bar-food recipe, the eggs are pickled in beet juice, vinegar, and sugar. The dusty-rose shade the eggs acquire will appeal to sophisticated eaters but may repel your more puerile acquaintances. Expect comments like, "Yuck! Eggs aren't supposed to be that color!" And be forewarned: Heating the vinegar will stink up your kitchen mightily, so turn on the exhaust fan.

2 (14½-ounce) cans sliced beets
1 cup cider vinegar
1 cup dark brown sugar, packed
1 dozen hard-boiled eggs, peeled
1 medium red onion, sliced into rings

Drain the beets, reserving the liquid. Pour this "beet juice" into a large saucepan and bring to a boil. Lower the heat to a simmer, add the vinegar and brown sugar, and stir until the sugar is dissolved.

Place the eggs, beets, and onion slices in a large, wide-mouthed, heat-proof glass jar, layering them to ensure even distribution. Pour in the hot vinegar mixture, adding water, if necessary, to make sure all the ingredients are covered.

Let cool, the cover the jar, and refrigerate for at least 2 days before serving. (The pickled eggs get darker—and better—as time goes on, though we're loath to keep them around for more than 2 weeks or so.)

CHIPS OFF THE OL' SPUD

Potatoes aren't just "comfort food." These humblest of vegetables—originally cultivated by Andean Indians during pre-Columbian times—are also chockablock with stuff that's good for you. The egg may lay claim to nutritional near-perfection, but of all the world's foodstuffs it's probably the potato that deserves the top award. Packed with vitamins, minerals, complex carbohydrates, even a surprisingly large amount of protein (about four grams to the average spud), the potato has just about everything—but not quite. The one thing it hasn't got in any significant quantity is fat. That's the reason that potatoes, despite their bad rep among the nutritionally innumerate, aren't high in calories: A medium-size potato has only about a hundred.

Without fat to slow your body's metabolism of alcohol, the plain potato falls a bit short as a bar food. But, y'know, there's an easy way to rectify that deficiency, which (you guessed it) is to *fry* the potato in oil.

Let's put Mr. Crum on the dollar bill

Every culture that's adopted the potato has invented ways of frying it, producing numerous dishes that all share that crispy, nutty, toothy (and usually salty) savor that just about everybody loves. But it's America that holds the honor of being the birthplace of one of the fried potato's simplest and best forms: the potato chip. It was in 1853, in the resort town of Saratoga Springs, New York, that a chef named George Crum created the first potato chip. It's a crying-in-your-beer shame that his contribution to world civilization has gone so unsung. For *Drinkology EATS*'s money, they oughtta get rid of that other George and put Mr. Crum's picture on the dollar bill.

Drinkology EATS is well aware that you can buy a bag of potato chips at your local convenience store, and we're not about to dissuade you from doing so. (We like the sour cream–and–chives versions, ourselves.) But making your own potato chips isn't as much trouble as you might think—*if,* that is, you have a deep fryer at your disposal. You *can* make potato chips in a regular frying pan, but it's a somewhat dicey proposition. Here's a recipe we admire, along with three recipes for potato-chip dips that will make your eating-and-drinking pals shiver with ecstasy.

CHIPS OF GOLD

The potatoes called for in this recipe are the increasingly popular Yukon Golds. If you're familiar with them, you might think that they're an ancient "heirloom" variety, but they're actually a fairly recently created hybrid, developed by a Canadian potato-breeding program in 1980. Dense-fleshed and intensely flavorful, Yukon Golds lend themselves to virtually every sort of tater cookery, and they make for especially good potato chips.

Special equipment: deep fryer; mandoline (optional)

4 large or 6 medium Yukon Gold potatoes (about 2 pounds)
peanut oil, for frying
sea salt

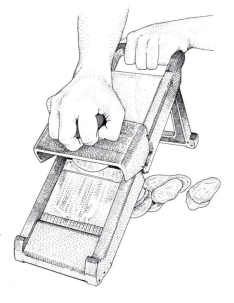

Wash and peel the potatoes. Using a very sharp knife or, much better, a mandoline-type vegetable slicer, slice the potatoes very evenly and very thin—⅛ inch thick or less, if possible. (The drawing here shows a mandoline in use; you should carefully follow the manufacturer's instructions for your particular model.)

Soak the potato slices in a bowl of ice water (put it in the fridge) for 1 to 2 hours. Remove the slices from the water and, using paper towels, pat them *as dry as possible.* (Heed this instruction: Excess water on the chips will cause the oil in the deep fryer to bubble up quite nastily.)

Prepare the deep fryer according to your model's specifications, filling it with oil to the maximum level and setting the control to the instruction manual's recommended temperature for frying potatoes.

Being careful not to overload the basket (again, follow the deep-fryer maker's recommendations), fry the chips in batches until they're a light golden brown. (You may want to start with one or several small test batches to make sure you achieve the desired level of doneness and crispness.) Drain on paper towels. Salt to taste. (In an airtight container, the chips will stay fresh for several days.)

VARIATION: SWEET POTATO CHIPS

Drinkology EATS likes sweet potato chips as much as chips made with regular potatoes. (*Sweet potato,* by the way, is rather a misnomer; despite the similarities in flesh and skin, this root vegetable is unrelated to the potato.) To make sweet potato chips, follow the recipe above, substituting medium-size sweet potatoes for the Yukon Golds and using corn oil rather than peanut oil for the deep frying. If sliced gossamer-thin, the sweet potato chips will quickly shrivel and darken when plunged into the oil—and that's quite OK.

DIPPITY DO DAHS

When it comes to chips, some people are just dippy. A chip without a dip to dunk it in is like an unfrosted cake, an unketchuped burger. *Drinkology EATS*'s dipsomania is of a different order, but to satisfy our dip-craving comrades' palates, we offer three of our favorite recipes.

STILTON—SOUR CREAM DIP

This and the dip recipe that follows are both made with the exceptional English blue cheese called Stilton. James prefers the first, which is lighter; Ramona likes the second, oilier and creamier, one better. The solution to this dispute is to mix up a batch of each.

2 ounces (about 2 fat tablespoons) crumbled Stilton
4 ounces (about 8 fat tablespoons) sour cream
½ teaspoon fresh lemon juice
¼ teaspoon salt
pinch freshly ground white pepper
finely chopped parsley

In a small mixing bowl, mash the cheese with a fork. Stir in the sour cream, lemon juice, salt, and white pepper and mix well. Transfer a serving bowl and sprinkle with the parsley.

STILTON-MAYONNAISE DIP

3 ounces (about 3 fat tablespoons) crumbled Stilton
1 cup mayonnaise
pinch freshly ground white pepper

In a small mixing bowl, mash the cheese with a fork. Stir in the mayonnaise and white pepper and mix well. Transfer to a serving bowl.

"CAVIAR" DIP

It's not beluga; it's not sevruga; it's not osetra. It's *lump*fish roe, for God's sake. But, hey, it's a potato-chip dip you're making, so there's no shame in settling for this supermarket standard. (Not to mention the fact that eating Caspian Sea caviar has, because of declining sturgeon stocks, become a crime against the environment.) Do feel free to substitute North American sturgeon or paddlefish roe, though these alternatives are pricier. Besides, this homely recipe is delicious as is.

8 ounces cream cheese, softened
1 cup sour cream
2 tablespoons lemon juice, or to taste
1 tablespoon finely chopped fresh chives
⅛ teaspoon freshly ground black pepper
1 4-ounce jar red lumpfish roe

Mix all the ingredients except the roe in a small bowl until smooth. Carefully fold in the roe. Cover and refrigerate until serving time. Taste and correct the seasonings if necessary.

Two Potato . . .

We hate to agree with the jingoists, but french fries are definitely *not* about freedom. Unlike the other foods presented in this chapter, home-made french fries cannot be fully prepared ahead of time (though, as you'll see, the basic prep work—including the first stage of frying—can be done several hours before serving). And making your own french fries involves a lot of time and effort, which is doubtless why so many of you resort to frozen "fries" or a quick trip to Mickie D's to satisfy that gnawing, primitive hunger that only french fries can staunch.

But here's the rub: Homemade french fries are well worth the trouble. As a bar food, they are nothing short of sublime—especially if served with mayonnaise or béarnaise sauce. (No ketchup, please!)

Drinkology EATS's deep fryer went on the fritz the very evening we'd decided to perfect our homemade french fries recipe. A call to the manufacturer's customer "service" number proved futile (though a friendly electronic voice did inform us that if we cared to leave a message, a representative would be sure to contact us within the next 24 to 48 hours). Did we despair? Well, yes, briefly, but then we dragged out the enameled cast iron Le Creuset Dutch oven that has helped us get through any number of culinary emergencies—resolved to deep fry our potatoes on top of the stove. It was scary (at least for James, who has a healthy fear of hot oil), but it worked like a charm. Do note that if you try the

stovetop method, you'll need a proper thermometer to gauge the temperature of the oil—and you *must* use a very heavy, very stable pot, to minimize the risk of accident. (The Le Creuset oval oven we used has a 5-quart capacity—the perfect size, as it turned out.)

FRENCH FRIES (POMMES FRITES)

The following recipe is a variation on the vaunted Belgian method for making French fries, or, as the Belgians call them, *pommes frites* (or just *frites,* for short). This time-honored technique requires that the fries be fried twice, with a rest period between the fryings. You don't really have to soak the cut potatoes in cold water before frying—some purists disparage the technique—but we think it makes for a *frite* that's crisper on the outside and more succulent within. Virtually any vegetable oil will do for frying, but we prefer corn oil or peanut oil. Note that different oils impart subtly (but definitely) different flavors to the fries. Note, too, that the suggestion of one large potato per person is a minimum; on the night of our testing, we easily—almost automatically—wolfed down two potatoes' worth of fries apiece.

1 large russet potato (about 6 inches long) per person, *at least*
vegetable oil
salt
mayonnaise or béarnaise sauce, for dipping

Cut and soak the fries: Wash and peel the potatoes and cut them into ⅜-inch slices. Cut each slice into fries that are ⅜ inch square, making sure that the fries are as even as possible. (Discard any pieces that are too small or too unevenly shaped.) Place the fries in a bowl, cover with cold water, and let soak in the refrigerator for at least 1 hour and up to 2 hours.

Precook the fries: Fill a deep fryer with oil to the maximum fill level and set the temperature at 320° F. (If you're doing the frying on the stovetop, use a heavy cast iron pot of at least 5 quarts capacity; fill it two-thirds full with oil and place a suitable thermometer in the pot. Over medium-high to high heat, heat the oil to 320° F.)

Drain the fries and pat them dry with paper towels. It is important that the fries be as dry as possible before being put in the hot oil, because excess water may cause the oil to bubble up frighteningly.

Working in small batches (of no more than 20 fries each), add the fries to the hot oil. (If you're using a deep fryer, you'll obviously be using the fryer's wire basket; if you're frying on the stovetop, gently lower the fries into the hot oil with a slotted spoon or, better, a Chinese bamboo skimmer.) The temperature of the oil will plummet when the fries are first added, then will gradually rise again. Stirring the fries gently and frequently to prevent them from sticking to one another, fry until just cooked through, about 6 minutes.

Remove the fries from the oil and drain on beds of paper towels. Repeat the precooking process until all the batches have been cooked, making sure that the oil returns to 320° F before adding each new batch. Let all the fries rest—or "sweat," as the experts say—for at least 30 minutes and up to 3 hours before frying them the second time. Turn off the deep fryer or stove during this period.

Complete the frying: Reheat the oil, bringing it up to a temperature of 360° F. Again working in small batches, add the precooked fries to the hot oil and fry, stirring gently, until medium brown and crispy, about 2 minutes. Briefly drain the finished fries on paper towels, salt to taste, and serve with room-temperature mayonnaise or warm béarnaise sauce (see recipe following) for dipping.

Note: The second frying takes very little time, so if you're only frying a few batches, wait until all the fries are done before serving. If you're frying four or more batches, however, serve them up batch by batch; otherwise they'll grow too cool and will lose some of their ineffable crispiness. *Drinkology EATS* likes serving them in the Belgian-restaurant manner: in stainless steel cups lined with brown craft paper.

BÉARNAISE SAUCE

Ramona and James debated offering you a recipe for homemade mayonnaise. We decided not to, figuring that you'd just ignore it. (We don't make our own mayonnaise, either.) But we thought we *would* provide a recipe for béarnaise sauce, which makes for a highly interesting french fry–dipping alternative—one we learned about at Arnaud's restaurant in New Orleans, which always serves its glorious *pommes soufflés* (french fries whose second frying, in super-hot oil, causes them to puff up) alongside a little dish of béarnaise.

This recipe calls for clarified butter—butter from which the milk solids have been removed. To make enough, start with 1 pound unsalted butter. Melt the butter in a saucepan over low heat. When completely melted, remove pan from heat and let stand for a few minutes until milk solids have risen to the top and settled to the bottom. Then skim the top and gently pour off the clarified butter, passing it through a fine-mesh sieve, and reserve until needed. (If there's a little left over, don't get annoyed. Refrigerated, clarified butter will keep for a long. long time, and it can be used for many of the purposes—scrambling eggs, for instance—ordinary butter is put to.)

½ cup tarragon vinegar
2 large shallots, minced
2 tablespoons fresh tarragon leaves, chopped
½ teaspoon freshly ground black pepper
5 large egg yolks
1¼ cups clarified butter
pinch cayenne pepper
salt to taste
fresh lemon juice (optional)

In a small saucepan, combine the vinegar, shallots, tarragon, and black pepper. Over high heat, bring to a boil and reduce by three-quarters. Remove from heat and set aside, letting cool until the reduction is just barely warm.

YOU SAY POTATO?

If you're under the impression that vodka is made from potatoes, you're (mostly) mistaken. By and large, good commercial vodkas are distilled from grains like wheat, barley, rye, and corn. Despite the popularity of your misconception, however, premium vodka—served neat—*does* make a faboo accompaniment to potatoes, especially those of the french fried persuasion.

The word *neat,* applied to booze, means "all by itself"—nothing added. That doesn't mean there's absolutely no preparation involved, however. Served neat, vodka should be extremely cold, so put the bottle in the freezer several hours before serving. *Drinkology EATS* loves the way neat vodka has been presented to us in Russian restaurants in Brighton Beach, Brooklyn: Fill a small silver bowl with crushed ice, pour the cold vodka into a hoddle (one of those single-drink glass carafes in which cocktails are sometimes delivered to the table in fancy restaurants), and set the hoddle in the bed of ice. From the hoddle, pour only an ounce or so of vodka into your glass, refilling it whenever you wish. (Cordial glasses work nicely.) It's elegant, and the vodka stays cold—enhancing the buttery mouthfeel that's one of this nearly flavorless spirit's prime attractions.

Fill the bottom pan of a double boiler half full with water, and bring to a very gentle simmer. Transfer the vinegar reduction to the double boiler's top pan, set above the simmering water, and add the egg yolks, whisking constantly as the mixture thickens and turns pale yellow. (Be very careful not to overheat; if the eggs begin to scramble, immediately remove the top pan from the double boiler, reduce the heat, and let the top pan cool slightly before recommencing.)

When the egg mixture has thickened so that each whisking reveals the bottom of the pan, remove from heat and add the clarified butter—at first drop by drop, and then in a thin stream—continuing to whisk constantly until all the butter has been used. (This takes a lot of elbow grease.) Add cayenne pepper and salt, to taste. If the sauce seems to lack piquancy, add fresh lemon juice in ¼-teaspoon increments until correct. The sauce can be prepared up to 1½ hours before serving; if necessary, re-warm by briefly setting above gently simmering water and whisking.

CHEESE IN CRACKERS

When it comes to fare for serving with drinks, nothing could be more standard (or more tedious, really) than cheese and crackers. Presumably, *Drinkology EATS*'s readers have spent enough time on earth to know how to open a box of crackers and slice up a chunk of cheese without our instruction. But what you may not realize is that it's a snap to make your own cheesy snacks—snacks, moreover, that don't require a cheese topping because they've already got a hefty dose of tangy cheese baked right in.

CHEDDAR-PARMESAN ICE-BOX CRACKERS

As a bar food, classic ice-box crackers are a near-perfect combo of carbs, fat, and protein. This truly scrumptious recipe is adapted from Laura Werlin's great *All American Cheese and Wine Book*. She recommends pairing the crackers with a Riesling or a rosé, though they do just as well (if not better) served alongside a frosty mug of beer or an icy cocktail.

4 ounces (about 1 cup) medium-sharp cheddar, coarsely grated
2 ounces (about ½ cup) Parmigiano-Reggiano, finely grated

¾ cup unbleached all-purpose flour
¼ teaspoon Coleman's dry mustard
¼ teaspoon sea salt
⅛ teaspoon ground cayenne pepper
4 tablespoons (½ stick) unsalted butter, cut into quarter-inch cubes
4 tablespoons cold water, plus more if needed

Place all the ingredients except the butter and water in a food processor, and pulse 5 or 6 times. Scatter the butter cubes evenly across the surface of the mixture, then pulse again until the pieces of butter are about the size of BBs. Add the water, 1 tablespoon at a time, and pulse until the dough just holds together when lightly pressed. If after 4 tablespoons of water the dough remains too crumbly, add more water (pulsing after each additional tablespoon) until the right consistency is achieved.

Turn the dough out onto a large piece of waxed paper or parchment paper. Using your hands, shape the dough into a log about 2 inches in diameter and 9 to 10 inches long. Square off the ends and wrap the log in plastic wrap. Refrigerate for at least 2 hours. (The dough can remain in the fridge for up to 2 days.)

Preheat to 375° F.

Remove the dough from the refrigerator and slice the log into ¼-inch rounds. Arrange the slices on a baking sheet about 1 inch apart. (If your oven holds only one baking sheet, you'll only be able to bake half the crackers at a time.) Bake on the center rack of the oven for 8 minutes, or until the crackers are a light golden color. Turn the crackers over and bake for an additional 5 minutes, until they're ever so slightly browned. Let the crackers cool on a wire rack.

The log of dough will keep in the freezer, tightly wrapped in plastic, for about 1 month. Let the dough thaw at room temperature for at least

1 hour—but no more than 2 hours—before slicing and baking. Makes 24 to 28 crackers

SPICY PARMESAN CHEESE CRISPS

This recipe is almost too simple to believe. (But believe us, it's sensational.) The basic version given here makes only eight crackers, but, obviously, you may double, triple, quadruple, or multiply it as many times as necessary to feed the famished hordes laying siege to your home bar.

½ cup Parmigiano-Reggiano, finely shredded
⅛ teaspoon dried basil
pinch freshly grated black pepper
pinch garlic powder
dash ground cayenne pepper

Preheat the oven to 400° F. Prepare a jelly-roll pan with a silicone liner, parchment paper, or cooking spray. In a bowl, toss the grated cheese and spices until well mixed. Form 8 compact mounds of the cheese mixture on the baking sheet, spacing an inch apart, and lightly pat down. Bake for 3 to 6 minutes, or until golden and crisp. Let cool before serving. (The crisps may be stored between paper towels in an airtight container for up to 3 days.)

IS THAT A MACHINE GUN I HEAR?

No, it's just the popcorn popping.

Popcorn, as the saying goes, is nothing but a medium for butter and salt—a sentiment that, for reasons already explained, makes a lot of sense when transforming plain-Jane popcorn into a suitable bar food. Always equitable, *Drinkology EATS* hasn't a thing against the buttered-and-salted version of this standard American snack (many a Hollywood blockbuster has been rendered vaguely tolerable by our ingesting a bucket of the stuff), but we're not against snazzing it up a bit, either. To that end, we've tailored a nice Italian suit to dress our popcorn in.

GARLIC ~~BREAD~~ POPCORN

This recipe's for those evenings you find yourself home alone and decide (as usual) to watch that DVD of *Goodfellas* or *The Godfather: Part II* for the umpteenth time. We suggest washing it down with a glass of vino or a cold *birra.* (In case a couple of gang members drop by, this recipe makes plenty to share.)

1 package microwaveable popcorn
1 tablespoon butter
1 tablespoon olive oil
3 cloves garlic, minced or pressed
½ teaspoon dried oregano
3 tablespoons Parmigiano-Reggiano, finely grated
salt (optional)

Pop the popcorn in a microwave oven.

Meanwhile, melt the butter together with the oil in a small pan over low heat. Add the garlic and oregano and sauté until the garlic is just softened, about 2 minutes. Transfer the popped corn to a large bowl, and pour the butter-oil mixture over it, tossing until well coated. Sprinkle with the cheese, and toss again.

AND HOWSABOUT
A LITTLE SOMETHING SWEET?

Most classic bar foods tend toward the savory end of the taste spectrum, which kind of leaves your sweet-toothed friends out in the cold. Since it's *Drinkology EATS*'s aim to extend a warm welcome to all comers, we decided we just couldn't end this chapter without dispensing a recipe for a little something sweet—as well as something that's just a *little* sweet, since foods that are too sugary overwhelm the palate and can interfere with the pleasure of drinking. To our mind, the twice-baked Italian cookies known as biscotti make a splendid fit with the bar-food bill of fare: They're about as far from cloying as cookies can get, they're easy to make in large batches, and, if properly stored, they stay fresh for a good long time.

Traditionally paired with dessert wines (think Moscato d'Alba) and with liqueur–and–hot coffee combos, biscotti are actually extremely versatile partners for mixed drinks, beer, and white wines (especially off-dry and semisweet still and sparkling wines). Our East-meets-West recipe combines mainstays of American baking (maple syrup, walnuts) with a zesty spice (star anise) more commonly encountered in Asian cooking.

Maple Biscotti with Walnuts and Star Anise

FOR THE BISCOTTI:

3¾ cups unbleached all-purpose flour
1 tablespoon baking powder
½ teaspoon salt
¾ teaspoon star anise seeds (plucked from the pod)
1 teaspoon aniseed
3 large eggs
1 cup maple syrup
10 tablespoons (1¼ sticks) unsalted butter, melted and cooled
2 teaspoons vanilla extract
1 cup walnuts, lightly toasted and coarsely chopped

FOR THE GLAZE:

1½ cups maple syrup
1 whole star anise pod

Make the biscotti: Preheat oven to 350° F.

Whisk together the flour, baking powder and salt in a large bowl. Using a mortar and pestle, grind the star anise seeds and aniseed together until powdered, then add them to the flour mixture.

In a separate large bowl, beat the eggs until light and foamy. Add the maple syrup, melted butter, and vanilla. Gradually add the flour mixture to the egg mixture and mix well. Stir in the walnuts.

Divide the dough into quarters. Flour a board and your hands. Shape each piece of dough into a flattish, loaf-shaped log, approximately 12 inches long by 2 inches wide. Transfer the logs to parchment paper–lined baking sheets, two per sheet, well separated.

Bake in the center of the oven until golden brown, about 30 minutes. Remove the logs from the oven, but leave the oven on. Let the logs cool for at least 10 minutes (and up to 30 minutes) on the baking sheets.

Transfer the logs to a cutting board, and discard the parchment paper. Using a serrated knife, cut the logs on the diagonal into ½-inch slices. Arrange the slices, cut side down, on the unlined baking sheets. Bake for 12 minutes. Turn the biscotti over and continue baking until just beginning to color, about 8 minutes. Transfer to a wire rack to cool.

Make the glaze: In a very large saucepan over medium-high heat, boil the maple syrup with the star anise pod for about 15 minutes, or until ¼ teaspoon of the syrup dropped into a glass of ice water forms a soft

BAR ASSOCIATIONS

FOR LICORICE LOVERS ONLY

The anise-flavored Italian liqueur called sambuca partners beautifully with coffee—or so we licorice lovers think. We also think it's hard to get enough of that inimitable licorice flavor, which leads us to pair this simple hot drink with the maple-and-anise biscotti.

CAFFÉ CON SAMBUCA

1 ounce Romana Black (or other *sambuca negra*)
about 5 ounces hot, strong brewed dark-roast coffee
sugar (optional)
whipped cream

Pour the sambuca into a warmed Irish coffee glass or ceramic mug. Add the coffee (almost to the brim) and sugar, if desired. Stir. Top with a dollop of whipped cream.

ball. Turn off the heat. Place a piece of parchment or waxed paper under the cooling rack. Before the syrup cools, dunk the top of each cookie into the hot syrup, coating it along its entire length. Return the biscotti to the rack and allow to cool completely, about 1 hour. Be careful as you coat the cookies—the syrup is very hot. (Keep that glass of ice water nearby in case you burn your fingers!) If the syrup starts to crystallize, reheat it until it melts again, turn off the heat, and continue as before. The glaze on the biscotti will crystallize as it cools. This is perfectly fine. (Stored in an airtight container at room temperature, the biscotti will keep for at least 1 week.)

Makes about 5 dozen biscotti

CHAPTER TWO

The Cooked and the Raw

MEAT AND SEAFOOD BAR SNACKS

W E KNOW, WE KNOW. IN CHAPTER 1, DRINKOLOGY EATS went on and on about the importance of bar food's being easy to prepare ahead of time and of its being relatively nonperishable, so that you can simply pop open a container whenever guests drop by (or you yourself come down with a case of intoxicant-induced munchies).

Well, we didn't tell you the whole story, and you'll just have to love us anyway.

Meat- and seafood-based bar foods are, of course, perishable, and for the most part they must be prepared in the hours before serving. Moreover, many of them aren't especially easy to make: kebab-style snacks and cocktail meatballs take time and attention, and shucking oysters is, as you'll see, akin to being sentenced to hard labor. The thing is, we can't bring ourselves to sacrifice the classic meat and seafood bar foods on the altar of convenience. They're just too damned good.

Neanderthal, Meet Brillat-Savarin

Kebab-style bar snacks satisfy urges both primitive and effete. On the one hand, these dishes bear a distant though distinct family resemblance to those served at cave-people get-togethers, where a spear was shoved through the haunch of a recently dispatched beast and the skewered meat positioned above the stone-ringed fire until nicely charred. On the other, these latter-day descendents of spit-roasted mastodon often demand meticulous seasoning, lengthy marination, and carefully timed cooking—not to mention that the beast in question must first be fastidiously carved into bite-size bits.

Serving note: When serving hors d'oeuvres that are held together with skewers, include a decoratively carved half-lemon (cut crosswise and trimmed on the end to make it stand up) on the tray, so that guests can stick their used picks into it.

Buffalo "Chips"

Having been brought back from the edge of extinction, American bison are now raised at ranches all over the United States, including many in *Drinkology EATS*'s neck o' the prairie, the Northeast. Relatively low in fat, buffalo meat is promoted as a low-cholesterol-diet-friendly alternative to beef. Buffalo's low fat content means, however, that it isn't as moist as beef. It therefore benefits greatly from marination, and you must be very careful not to overcook it.

The "chips" in this tastelessly-named-but-tasty dish are cipollini (chip-oh-LEE-nee). Interestingly, though they're usually identified as "cipollini onions" in specialty grocery stores, cipollini aren't onions at all: they're hyacinth bulbs.

1 buffalo (bison) strip steak, about 2 inches thick (about ¾ pound)

3or 4 large cipollini, about 2½ inches in diameter

1 cup dry red wine

2 tablespoons extra virgin olive oil

½ teaspoon freshly ground black pepper

1 teaspoon salt

2 sprigs fresh thyme

Soak 50 6-inch wooden skewers in water for 30 minutes. (Depending on the exact size of the steak, you may or may not need this many.) With a sharp knife, slice the steak into 1-inch cubes. Peel the cipollini, and cut each in half. Separate the outer 3 or 4 layers of each wedge, retaining only the larger pieces. Cut these into 1-inch squares; each bulb should yield 12 to 15 usable pieces (you will need as many cipollini pieces as cubes of steak). Retain the smaller pieces of cipollini for the marinade.

Place the bison and cipollini pieces in a large, resealable plastic bag or a nonreactive bowl. Add the wine, oil, pepper, salt, and thyme sprigs. Seal or cover, and let stand for at least 1 hour, gently turning the contents every 15 to 20 minutes so that the pieces marinate evenly. The cipollini pieces will become translucent and pliable.

When ready to prepare the skewers, drain the marinade from the meat and cipollini and discard. Spear each cipollini piece with a skewer, pushing the point through the convex side of the piece. Then push one cube of steak onto the skewer, nestling it inside the curve of the cipollini.

Preheat broiler. Arrange the skewers on broiler pan, making sure that the skewers are lying flat against the pan's surface. Broil for 3 to 4 minutes, until just done.

CHICKEN COCKTAIL KEBABS

This Turkish-style bar snack uses yogurt—the thick, extra-tangy Mediterranean kind—as the marinade's main ingredient. If you can't find Mediterranean-style yogurt (try Greek and Middle Eastern specialty shops), you can use drained American-style plain yogurt. (Begin with twice as much yogurt as the recipe calls for. Set a colander over a bowl and line the colander with doubled cheesecloth. Place the yogurt on the cheesecloth and let drain for 2 to 3 hours, until it has the consistency of sour cream.)

1 cup thick Mediterranean-style yogurt
¼ cup honey
3 tablespoons extra virgin olive oil
4 garlic cloves, minced
1 tablespoon ground cumin
2 teaspoons fresh thyme (leaves only)
1 teaspoon salt
¼ teaspoon ground cayenne pepper
¼ teaspoon sweet paprika
freshly ground black pepper, to taste
2 large skinless, boneless chicken breasts (about 1½ pounds)
3 additional tablespoons extra virgin olive oil, for frying
lemon wedges

Soak 36 6-inch wooden skewers in water for 30 minutes. In a bowl, mix the yogurt, honey, 3 tablespoons oil, garlic, cumin, salt, cayenne pepper, and paprika. Add black pepper to taste, and stir.

With a sharp knife, slice each breast into thirds lengthwise, then cut each third into 6 approximately equal chunks, making 36 chunks in all. Skewer each chunk. Place the skewers in a large, shallow bowl and pour the yogurt mixture over them, turning the skewers so that the meat is completely coated. Cover with plastic wrap and refrigerate for at least 2 hours. (Overnight is better.)

Preheat broiler. Remove skewers from marinade and arrange on broiler pan, making sure that the skewers are lying flat against the pan's surface. Broil for 6 to 8 minutes, turning once, until cooked through. Serve on a platter with lemon wedges.

Pork Saté

Ever internationalist, *Drinkology EATS* thinks nothing of hopping from the prairies of North America, to the bazaars of the Middle East, to the islands of the Indonesian archipelago—where the popular skewered snacks known as satés originated. This meat-on-a-stick dish is almost always served with a peanut dipping sauce, which, if possible, should be prepared a day ahead of time to allow the flavors to meld and heighten. Lemongrass, which can be found in many Asian groceries, isn't exactly an "optional" ingredient, but if it's out of season or otherwise unavailable, the saté is perfectly acceptable without. (If you do include the lemongrass, use only the bottom 6 inches of each stalk.)

FOR MARINATED PORK:
1 large pork tenderloin (about 1¼ pounds)
2 tablespoons soy sauce
2 teaspoons freshly squeezed lime juice
2 teaspoons fresh lemongrass, minced
2 teaspoons dark brown sugar
4 garlic cloves, minced

FOR DIPPING SAUCE:
1 cup chicken broth
½ cup creamy peanut butter

½ cup onion, finely chopped

⅓ cup fresh lemongrass, minced

½ jalapeño pepper, seeded and minced

2 tablespoons freshly squeezed lime juice

1 tablespoon dark brown sugar

1 teaspoon ground coriander

1 tablespoon chopped scallion (green tops only), for garnish

Prepare the marinated pork: Using a very sharp knife, trim fat from the tenderloin and it cut into strips approximately 3 inches long by 1 inch wide by ¼ inch thick. (The tenderloin should yield about two dozen pieces.) Note: It will be *much* easier to slice the tenderloin if it is very cold or has been frozen and partly thawed.

In a shallow bowl, mix the soy sauce, lime juice, lemongrass, sugar, and garlic. Add the pork and toss to coat. Cover and refrigerate for 1 hour. While the pork marinates, soak 24 8-inch wooden skewers in water for 30 minutes.

Make the dipping sauce: In a small saucepan, mix the chicken broth, peanut butter, onion, lemongrass, jalapeño, lime juice, sugar, and coriander. Bring to a boil, stirring frequently. Transfer to a blender and puree. Pass the puree through a strainer back into the saucepan, pressing on the solids with the back of a wooden spoon. On medium-low heat, simmer the sauce, reducing it until it thickens, 2 to 3 minutes. (If made a day ahead, the sauce should be covered and refrigerated. When reheating, add a small amount of chicken broth, if necessary, to thin.)

Complete the saté: Once the pork has marinated and the sauce has been prepared, preheat the broiler. Thread each pork strip onto a skewer, and arrange on broiling pan. Broil, turning once, until just cooked

(Continues on page 56)

RED, WHITE, AND GINGER

The untamed taste of our Buffalo "Chips" kebab needs to be matched by strong-flavored drink—and a red wine–based concoction like the Port Cobbler? (question mark intended), below, satisfies the handicapping requirement. The traditional Turkish-style chicken kebab merits pairing with raki, the drink that traditionally accompanies *mezeler* (appetizers) in the cafés of Istanbul. And the complexly flavored pork saté requires, we feel, a simple, subtle cocktail; our Gin Ginger does the trick.

PORT COBBLER?

Why the query mark following this drink's name? Well, frankly, we don't know how to classify it. It's a lot like a classic cobbler, in that it's a wine-based drink served over crushed ice. But it's sort of like an Old Fashioned or julep, too, in that the recipe's first step involves muddling sugar and fruit together at the bottom of a glass. Then again, the combination of wine and citrus makes it seem—and taste—sangria-like. Oh, well.

2 teaspoons superfine sugar
lemon slice
orange slice
maraschino cherry, stem removed
crushed ice
3 ounces good ruby Port
club soda or seltzer

Place the sugar in the bottom of a double old-fashioned glass. Add the citrus slices and cherry, and muddle until the fruit is thoroughly smashed. Fill the glass with crushed ice and add the Port. Top with club soda, and stir briefly.

RAKI AND WATER

Raki is *the* national drink of Turkey. If you've ever had ouzo, the anise-flavored liqueur that plays a similarly prominent role in the eating-and-drinking culture of Greece, you sort of know what raki tastes like—and how it behaves. Both of these clear, colorless liqueurs turn milky white when water is added. Though ouzo has a somewhat sharper flavor than raki, it's an acceptable substitute.

2 ice cubes
2 ounces raki (or ouzo)
water

Place the ice cubes in a collins glass and pour the raki over them. Top with water and stir very briefly.

GIN GINGER

A *Drinkology EATS* original, this drink is so simple and sensible we wonder why nobody thought of it before. For the ginger garnish, peel a sizable length of fresh ginger root (3 or 4 inches), and, with a sharp paring knife, cut away a long, very thin slice, about ¹⁄₁₆ inch thick.

🍸 very thin slice fresh ginger
2½ ounces gin

Rub the rim and entire inside of a chilled cocktail glass with the fresh ginger, and drop the ginger slice into the glass. Pour the gin into a mixing glass, with ice. Stir well, and strain into the prepared glass.

through (about 3 minutes on one side and 2 minutes on the other).

Pour sauce into serving bowl, sprinkle with chopped scallion, and set in the center of a platter. Surround with pork skewers.

SPHERICAL MASSES

The humble meatball, which Wikipedia somewhat bombastically defines as "a generally spherical mass of ground meat and other ingredients," is nearly ubiquitous in world cuisines. Each culture—Greek, Chinese, Albanian, you name it—seems to have its own version. Some meatballs, like those mounded in the spaghetti sauce at bad Italian restaurants, are tough, grainy, flavorless, and the size of billiard balls. If those are the only kind you've ever had, you're a real meatball yourself. But take heart: There's a whole world of generally spherical masses of ground meat awaiting you. Here are two recipes for small, tender, intensely flavorful meatballs that—served in their sauces and speared with cocktail picks—make exceptional bar snacks.

SWEDISH MEATBALLS

Swedish meatballs are definitely a cultural throwback—think sleek, teak Danish furniture and Marimekko fabrics stapled to canvas stretchers and hung on the walls—and this bothers *Drinkology EATS* not one whit. In fact, we prefer to imaginatively inhabit the late fifties and early sixties—before everything went to hell. But whether your sensibilities are retro or not, you'll love this dish.

FOR THE MEATBALLS:
¾ cup dry bread crumbs
¾ cup light cream or half and half

1 pound ground beef

¼ pound ground pork

¼ pound ground veal

1 egg

½ cup finely minced onion

2 tablespoons minced parsley

1 tablespoon caraway seeds

1 teaspoon salt

½ teaspoon freshly grated nutmeg

¼ teaspoon ground allspice

⅛ teaspoon freshly ground black pepper

¼ cup olive oil, for frying

FOR THE SAUCE:

2 tablespoons butter

2 tablespoons flour

1 cup beef broth

½ teaspoon salt

¼ teaspoon sweet paprika

½ teaspoon Worcestershire sauce

3 bay leaves

⅓ cup medium dry sherry, if desired

1 cup sour cream, room temperature

Make the meatballs: Soak the breadcrumbs in the cream for 10 to 20 minutes. Put the meats together in a food processor and pulse until well mixed. Transfer to a bowl, and add the soaked breadcrumbs, egg, onion, parsley, and seasonings. Mix until completely combined. (We use our—clean!—hands for this.) Cover the bowl and refrigerate for 1 to 2 hours. Form the mixture into very small meatballs, about ¾ inch to 1 inch in diameter. Heat the oil in a frying pan over medium heat and brown the meatballs thoroughly, turning them very gently as they cook. Remove from pan and set aside.

Make the sauce: Drain the oil from the pan and add the butter. Melt butter over medium heat, then add the flour, whisking until bubbly. Add

BAR ASSOCIATIONS

NORSE MIXOLOGY

If you're serving Swedish meatballs at your Danish teakwood bar set artfully beneath those (Finnish) Marimekko fabrics-on-stretchers, you may as well complete the picture by offering your guests *the* Scandinavian spirit: Aquavit—or, as the Danes spell it, Akvavit. *Aquavit* means "water of life" (but then so do the Celtic and Russian roots from which our words *whiskey* and *vodka,* respectively, are derived). In essence, aquavit is a lot like gin, in that it's a distilled neutral spirit that is then redistilled in the presence of "botanicals." (As the name implies, botanicals are flavoring agents—berries, seeds, and so on—that come from plants; the prime botanical in gin is juniper berries; in many aquavits, it's caraway or fennel seeds.)

In Scandinavia, aquavit is almost always served neat—and very, very cold—so get out those Iittala cordial glasses you bought on a whim at the Museum of Modern Art's gift shop five years ago. (You've been looking for an reason to use them.) As you would if you were serving vodka neat, put the bottle of aquavit in the freezer for at least a few hours before serving. American liquor stores generally stock only a single brand of aquavit: the "Taffel" akvavit made by the Danish distiller Aalborg. That's limiting but OK, since this caraway-flavored spirit is quite good.

the broth, salt, paprika, Worcestershire sauce, and bay leaves. Cook, stirring constantly, until the sauce has thickened. Reduce heat to low, add the sherry and sour cream, and stir. Add the meatballs, cover, and simmer for 20 minutes. Transfer to serving bowl. (Supply your guests with cocktail picks with which to spear the meatballs.)

Good, but idiosyncratic. In *Drinkology EATS*'s estimation, aquavit's taste is too unusual for it to serve as the basis for a wide range of cocktails. That said, a very dry Martini made from aquavit rather than gin or vodka is an interesting concoction. Not something you'd want to have every day, granted, but well worth a try. Here's a recipe:

AQUAVIT MARTINI

In its countries of origin, aquavit is often served with smoked, pickled, and salt-preserved fish, so putting an anchovy-stuffed olive in this drink squares—sort of—with Scandinavian culinary tradition.

2½ ounces aquavit
dash dry vermouth
🍸 anchovy-stuffed olive

Combine aquavit and vermouth in a mixing glass, with lots of ice. Stir well, and strain into a chilled cocktail glass. Garnish with the olive.

Meatballs Bourguignonne

This dish isn't really French; it's French*ish*. Though the recipe calls for red Burgundy wine (meaning *real* Burgundy, from over there in France), you may certainly substitute any decent Pinot Noir—from California, Oregon, New Zealand, or wherever. (And do have a glass while you cook.) Note: If you can't find very small mushrooms, use larger ones, but cut them into halves or quarters so that the mushroom pieces are about the same size as the meatballs.

FOR THE MEATBALLS:

1 pound ground beef (not too lean!)
½ cup oatmeal, uncooked
3 tablespoons red Burgundy wine
1 egg
1 teaspoon fresh thyme leaves
½ teaspoon salt
¼ teaspoon freshly grated nutmeg
¼ teaspoon freshly ground black pepper
2 tablespoons olive oil, for frying

FOR THE SAUCE:

2 tablespoons cognac
2 (14½-ounce) cans beef broth
½ cup red Burgundy wine
2 tablespoons cornstarch
2 tablespoons water
8 ounces small cremini or white button mushrooms, stems trimmed
salt and freshly ground black pepper to taste

Make the meatballs: Combine beef, oatmeal, 3 tablespoons wine, egg, and seasonings. Mix well. Shape into small meatballs, about 1 inch in diameter. Heat the oil in a large frying pan over medium heat and brown the meatballs thoroughly, turning them very gently as they cook. Remove from pan and set aside.

Make the sauce: Add the cognac to the frying pan. Heat briefly over high heat. When heated, ignite with a kitchen match. (Do this very carefully, keeping your head—and hair!—well away from the pan.) Swirl the pan to expose all the cognac to the flame. When the flame dies out, add the beef broth and wine. Bring to a boil, scraping up any bits left from the meatballs' browning. Combine cornstarch and water, mixing well. Add to the frying pan and stir until the sauce begins to thicken. Return the meatballs to the pan and add the mushrooms. Cover and simmer over medium heat about 10 minutes or until the meatballs reach the desired doneness. Add salt and pepper, to taste. Transfer to serving bowl. (Supply your guests with cocktail picks with which to spear the meatballs.)

BEYOND BUFFALO (WINGS, THAT IS)

In *Drinkology EATS* loves chicken wing–based bar snacks, whose origin dates to 1964, when Teressa Bellisimo, the mother of the barkeep at Buffalo, New York's Anchor Bar Restaurant, fried up the first-ever batch of Buffalo wings to serve to a group of her son's friends who'd showed up late at the bar, demanding to be fed. Old Lady Bellisimo's culinary ingenuity has, of course, inspired thousands. (A Google search for "chicken wings" in early 2006 drew more than 2 million hits, the vast majority for chicken-wing recipes—which nowadays might call for anything from peanut butter, to tequila, to that old standby of American cuisine, Lipton's soup mix.) We're inspired, too, and herewith offer you three variations.

SAN FRANCISCO WINGS

This recipe comes to us from Ramona's friend Chris March, who years ago did some hard time in a culinary academy. Now a New York City–based costume designer, Chris used to live in the City by the Bay, which is the only reason we've dubbed these San Francisco Wings.

4 pounds (about 20) large chicken wings
2 cups grated aged Asiago cheese
1 cup mayonnaise
1 teaspoon freshly ground black pepper
2 cloves garlic, minced

Preheat the oven to 400° F. Wash the wings and pat them dry. In a large, resealable plastic bag, mix together all the ingredients except the wings. Add the wings and mush them around until they are thoroughly coated. Arrange in a single layer on a jelly-roll pan and bake for 35 to 40 minutes. (Do *not* add salt to this recipe, as the cheese may be very salty.)

ATLANTA WINGS

Following Mrs. Bellisimo's lead, many creators of chicken-wing dishes name their recipes for cities. In that tradition, we've christened this sweet 'n' savory recipe Atlanta Wings. We'll let you guess why.

4 pounds (about 20) large chicken wings
1 (12–fluid ounce) can Coca-Cola
1 cup dark brown sugar, packed
2 tablespoons soy sauce
1 teaspoon onion powder
1 teaspoon salt
½ teaspoon garlic powder
¼ teaspoon freshly ground black pepper

Preheat the oven to 400° F. Wash the wings, pat them dry, and arrange in a single layer in a large, shallow-sided roasting pan. Mix the sauce ingredients well and pour the mixture over the wings. Bake uncovered, turning wings every 10 minutes, for 1 hour or until the sauce has become a thick, mahogany-colored glaze.

EAST MEETS WEST WINGS

We scratched our heads trying to come up with a city to name this wings dish after. Tokyo? Tijuana? Nothing worked—but the recipe, adapted from one passed on to us by our dear editor, Marisa Bulzone, works beautifully.

4 pounds (about 20) large chicken wings

½ cup soy sauce

½ cup white tequila

2 tablespoons sugar

½ teaspoon dry mustard

¼ teaspoon freshly ground black pepper

2 large garlic cloves, minced

½ teaspoon sesame oil

juice of ½ lime

Rinse the chicken wings and split at the joint. Cut off and discard the tips. Put the wings into a large, resealable plastic bag. Combine the remaining ingredients in a small bowl, stirring until the sugar has dissolved. Pour the mixture into the bag, seal it, and mush the wings around until they are thoroughly coated. Refrigerate, letting the wings marinate for at least 1 hour. (Overnight is better.)

Preheat the oven to 375° F. Arrange the wings in a single layer in a large, shallow-sided roasting pan. Pour the marinade over. Bake for 1½ hours, turning every 15 minutes, until the wings are dark brown and the marinade has largely evaporated or been absorbed.

HALF A SHELL IS BETTER THAN ONE

Though we didn't know one another till long after we'd moved to New York, Ramona and James both grew up in Maryland, in rough proximity to the Chesapeake Bay. Oysters were therefore staple components of our childhood diets—though it wasn't till either of us approached adulthood that we acquired a taste for *raw* oysters. Having conquered our squeamishness, we did as Saint Paul instructed and put away childish things—and oysters on the half shell remain, for both of us, a foretaste of heaven. (Which is not to say that we don't still see through a cocktail glass, darkly.)

Pairing oysters with hard liquor?

Freshly shucked oysters are a—perhaps *the*—classic bar food. There are plenty of people out there who think that raw oysters ought only to be paired with Champagne, or white wine, or—as our non-wine-drinking relatives did—with a glass of well-chilled beer. We're certainly not against any of these options, but we find them too limiting. Ain't a damned thing wrong with raw oysters and hard liquor, neither.

It took some nerve for James—a hard liquor drinker from the get-go—to cotton to this combo, however. Among the culinary doctrines inculcated in him was that raw oysters ought *never* to be consumed with spirits: he well remembers his grandmother telling him, in all serious-ness, that eating raw oysters while drinking hard liquor would cause the oysters to form "stones in your stomach"—her implication being that a grisly and painful death would soon ensue.

Rebel in more ways than one, James—soon after he'd reached drinking age—decided he'd put this bit of Old Wife's wisdom to a self-designed, self-administered test. He went out and bought himself a pint of shucked oysters and a half-pint of Southern Comfort, and proceeded to make himself a supper of sorts. Though that's not a repast he'd currently recommend—or ever try again—the experiment did work, in the sense that he has lived another three decades in which to tell the tale, and X-rays reveal no petrified oyster remains in his innards.

Note that James, for his little science project, bought oysters that somebody else had shucked. Although he was willing to risk grave bodily harm to see whether oysters could be washed down with whiskey, he wasn't about to shuck his own—too dangerous! And that's the problem—isn't it?—with serving oysters on the half shell at home. They've got to be fresh (still living, actually), so you have to shuck them yourself—a task that seems time-consuming, difficult, and physically perilous. (In truth, it is all of these things.) But, shuck it all, you'll just have to learn. The Technicalities sidebar on the next page tells you how.

When purchasing the oysters, make sure that each oyster's shell is closed up tighter than a clam. (Sorry.) Out of water, an open-shelled bivalve is a *dead* bivalve, and oysters are so extremely perishable that it's dangerous to eat one that has "passed over." If the oysters are fresh, they may last up to ten days in the fridge, *but* make sure you store them in a paper bag or even unwrapped in a bowl. Enclosed in a sealed plastic bag, the little buggers will suffocate and expire.

People who eat raw oysters tend to be very particular about how—and with what—they're to be eaten. Certain alpha males (and alpha

COMPLETELY SHUCKED

Every time we shuck oysters, we think of the poor souls who do this for a living and mutter a grateful, "There but for the grace of God . . . ." It's hardly impossible, but it's definitely *hard*. If you attempt it, make sure you use a real oyster knife—with a pointy tip and sturdy handle.

Note that oysters, being bivalves, have two half-shells held together by a ligamented hinge. No matter what the variety of oyster, one of these half-shells is relatively flat, while the other is convex, like a shallow bowl. Oyster shells sometimes shatter or crumble in the process of shuck-ing, and if it's the convex half-shell that breaks, you're more or less screwed. Though the oyster remains edible (once you pick out the bits of shell), you've ruined the half shell on which to serve it. To compensate for such (inevitable) losses, make sure you lay in a few extra oysters for every dozen you intend to serve. And after you've eaten the oysters, keep some of the empty, clean half-shells around to use in case you break a few shells the next time you do this.

Assuming there is a next time.

Before shucking, make sure to wash the oysters thoroughly in water, using a clean, stiff brush, if needed, to get rid of any grime.

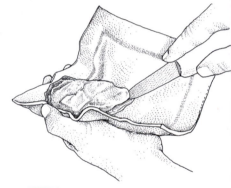

STEP 1
Place the oyster concave side down on a potholder or heavy, densely woven cloth. Do *not* hold the oyster in your bare hand during this step; you may, however, hold the potholder with the oyster nes-tled inside it, as the drawing shows. (*Drinkology EATS* uses a leather potholder, since the relatively impenetrable leather offers added protection should the knife slip.) Insert the point of the oys-ter knife at the "hinge" where the two half-shells are held together. Using as much force as you can muster, jam the knife into the shell. twisting the knife as you do so, until the shell pops open.

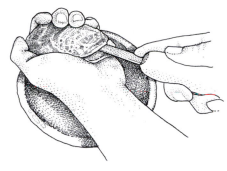

STEP 2

Phew! Compared to step 1, the rest is easy. You may now transfer the shell to you bare hand, but continue to proceed cautiously. Slide the knife inside the shell and work the blade around the top (flat) half-shell to sever the muscle that holds the half-shells together. Do this over a bowl, to catch any of the so-called liquor (the oyster's blood, actually) that may drip from the opened shell. (This liquor is quite tasty; strain whatever you catch in the bowl and use it to "refill" any half-shells from which too much liquor spills during shucking.)

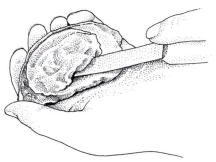

STEP 3

Once the interior muscle is severed, remove and discard the top half shell. Now, slide the knife's blade under the oyster to free it from the shell. Arrange the shucked oysters on an oyster plate or, better, in a shallow round metal pan filled with cracked ice. Garnish with lemon halves and little bowls or ramekins of cocktail sauce and mignonette sauce.

male wannabes of whichever gender) insist that raw oysters be utterly unadorned—not even a squirt of lemon juice is permissable—and that they be slurped down, from the tilted shell straight into the mouth. Whether or not one should chew the oyster—and, if so, how many times—are matters of teeth-baring, take-no-prisoners debate among such studly folk.

Drinkology EATS is really rather dandified on these scores. We like a little lemon juice; we like to use a cocktail fork to convey the oyster from shell to mouth; we give each oyster a weak-willed little half-chew as it slip-slides toward our gullet; and we've even been known to demurely bathe our raw oysters in mignonette sauce or cocktail sauce—oysters' traditional accompaniments—before consuming. On the off chance that your refined sensibilities might match our own, here are some sauce recipes we're partial to—two mignonettes and two cocktail sauces.

Red Mignonette

Mignonette comes from a French word meaning "dainty," and, indeed, mignonette sauces, served in little bowls or ramekins, do have a dainty appearance. These sour-peppery sauces pack a surprising wallop, however, so use them very sparingly, dunking the oyster in the sauce very briefly or spooning a tiny amount—no more than half a teaspoon—onto the oyster as it rests in the half shell.

½ cup red wine vinegar
2 large shallots, finely minced
1 tablespoon coarsely ground black pepper
1 to 3 teaspoons fresh lemon juice

Combine ingredients and chill until ready to serve.

CHAMPAGNE MIGNONETTE

½ cup champagne vinegar
1 large shallot, finely minced
1 tablespoon coarsely ground black pepper
1 tablespoon fresh lemon juice

Combine ingredients and chill until ready to serve.

COCKTAIL SAUCE NO. 1

There are many more than fifty-seven variations on this classic ketchup-based seafood sauce, but one must choose. This version is the milder of the two we offer.

½ cup ketchup
3 tablespoons fresh lemon juice
1 tablespoon Worcestershire sauce
2 teaspoons prepared horseradish
1 stalk celery, finely minced
2 tablespoons finely grated onion
¼ teaspoon salt

Combine ingredients and chill for at least 1 hour before serving.

COCKTAIL SAUCE NO. 2

And this variation is the spicier—*much* spicier.

¼ cup ketchup
¼ cup hot chili sauce, such as Asian chili garlic sauce
1 tablespoon fresh lemon juice
1 tablespoon prepared horseradish
½ teaspoon Worcestershire sauce

⅛ teaspoon cayenne pepper
⅛ teaspoon Tabasco sauce

Combine ingredients and chill for at least 1 hour before serving.

The Best?

We like all the bar snack recipes we've presented to you, but if we were to judge by own behavior, we'd have to say that we like good old-fashioned steamed shrimp best.

The afternoon we made steamed shrimp in *Drinkology EATS*'s "test kitchen" (i.e., the kitchen in James's Brooklyn digs) was a high point in Ramona's and James's research. Our pupils dilated as James unwrapped the shrimp, bought fresh that very morning. We argued animatedly and good-naturedly about the amounts of seasoning, about cooking time. Our salivary glands went into overdrive as the smell of Old Bay permeated the apartment. And our emotion when the shrimp were done? Pure animal anticipation. We could barely wait for the shrimp to cool before tearing into that glorious pile.

Steamed Shrimp

How many shrimp should you steam? Our mania for steamed shrimp leads us to the perhaps excessive estimate of 1 pound (9 or 10 large shrimp) per person. The recipe below calls for 4 pounds of shrimp (enough for four "normal" people); if you're steaming more, you'll have to increase the cooking time, but do check the pot—and test the shrimp on top for doneness—after each additional minute. The shrimp are done when they've turned pink and their flesh is white straight through.

It's essential not to cook them too long, since shrimp quickly become rubbery if overcooked.

If you have a pasta pentola—that's a "multipurpose" stockpot with a deep basket insert—use it for steaming the shrimp. If you haven't got a pentola, steam the shrimp in a large stockpot atop a collapsible vegetable steamer. (Place the steamer in the pot and fill with water or beer just to the level of the steamer, but do not add the shrimp or seasonings until the water or beer has begun to boil. Do this very carefully so as not to scald yourself.)

beer (optional)
4 pounds (about 40) large shrimp
about 2 tablespoons Old Bay seasoning
about 2 tablespoons kosher salt
about ½ teaspoon ground cayenne pepper

Insert the pasta basket in the pentola pot and fill with just enough water—or, if you prefer, beer—to reach the bottom of the basket.

BAR ASSOCIATIONS

FOR LICORICE LOVERS ONLY (CONTINUED)

The taste of shrimp partners exceedingly well with that of anise- or licorice-flavored liqueurs. Here are two cocktails that we think make fine companions to a mess o' steamed shrimp.

OBITUARY COCKTAIL

This anise-tinctured variation on the Martini is a New Orleans standard.

🍸 lemon twist
2 ounces gin
¼ ounce dry vermouth
¼ ounce Herbsaint or other anise-flavored liqueur

Rim a chilled cocktail glass with the twist. Combine the other ingredients in a mixing glass, with ice. Stir, and strain into the glass. Garnish with the twist.

Remove the basket from the pot and set it on paper towels or a large plate. Bring the water or beer to a boil over high heat.

Place a single layer of shrimp in the basket. Sprinkle with Old Bay and salt, and lightly dust with cayenne. Repeat until all the shrimp are in the pot.

When the water or beer comes to a boil, put the basket back in the pot and cover. Steam for 5 minutes, or until the shrimp are just done. Remove the basket and transfer shrimp to a serving platter. Allow guests to peel the shrimp themselves, providing them with empty bowls for the shells and finger bowls filled with lemon water for rinsing hands.

GOOD AND PLENTY

There are lots of versions of the Good and Plenty—a cocktail that simulates the taste of the licorice candy with the very similar name. James tried his hand at it, and arrived at this plenty-good combination. Amaro belongs to that class of dark, viscous, herbal liqueurs called *digestivo*s.

🍸 lemon twist
2 ounces vodka
½ ounce Kahlúa
¼ ounce Amaro
¼ ounce Herbsaint, Pernod, or other anise-flavored liqueur

Rim a chilled cocktail glass with the twist. Combine the other ingredients in a cocktail shaker, with ice. Shake well, and strain into the glass. Garnish with the twist.

SHRIMP COCKTAIL

This is the one alcohol-free cocktail we really like, and it's no less good for being absolutely predictable.

crushed ice
6 to 8 large steamed shrimp, peeled and deveined
cocktail sauce (recipes, page 69)
🍋 lemon wedge or slice

Fill an oversize cocktail glass two-thirds full with crushed ice. Hook the shrimp along the edge of the glass, tails dangling. Fill a small dish with cocktail sauce and set on the ice. Garnish with lemon wedge or slice.

CHAPTER THREE

Just Add Guests

AN "INSTANT" COCKTAIL PARTY

A SUCCESSFUL COCKTAIL PARTY CAN BE A BIG DEAL, DEMANDING LOTS of planning and (sometimes) days of preparation. In later chapters, *Drinkology EATS* offers ideas for several such meticulously planned and executed get-togethers, but to begin with, Ramona and James thought that we should offer you some guidance on putting together a cocktail party that requires only the most general sort of planning (assuming you've

We want you to wow 'em

got most of the ingredients for the food and drinks on hand) and that can be pulled together in no more than an hour.

If you're lucky (and we hope you are), you lead the kind of social life in which, at least once in a while, good friends drop by unexpectedly or with very little advance warning. The way to keep such a social life going, of course, is to make sure there's always enough around the house to satisfy surprise guests' hunger and thirst. And the way to keep yourself from going crazy is to make sure that you don't have to scurry to the supermarket and liquor store whenever unannounced visitors arrive.

But the pointers in this chapter aren't meant just for those times you find yourself having to entertain people you weren't expecting. These days, so many of us lead such busy lives that there are occasions when we *know* that friends are coming over for cocktails, but we just don't have adequate time—or *any* time, really—to get ready. If your pantry, fridge, and liquor cabinet contain all the makings for an "instant" cocktail party, however, you won't suffer even a twinge of anxiety. You can go through the day taking care of whatever other business needs doing, confident that your guests won't be disappointed—and even that they'll believe that you *did* spend lots of time and energy preparing for their arrival. (Granted, this illusion will be easier to sustain if you keep your house reasonably tidy.)

Take note: *Drinkology EATS* very much wants your instant cocktail party to be more than merely OK. In our book, a bag of tortilla chips, a tub of processed guac, and a bottle of Margarita mix just don't cut it. We want your guests—invited or uninvited—to *rave* about the food and drink, to express awe at your mixological wizardry and culinary genius. In other words, we want you to wow 'em, without having to go to any trouble whatsoever.

A Shopping List

To that end, here are the provisions you'll need to have on hand to make all of the simple-but-smashing food recipes in this chapter. We've divided the shopping list into two parts: The first consists of canned, bottled, and packaged ingredients that have long shelf lives and that, once you have them, don't need to be replaced with any great frequency. (Some will remain good virtually perpetually.) The second part consists of the more perishable ingredients—the ones you'll need to refrigerate and to use and replace at regular intervals.

IN THE CUPBOARD:

☐ pitted black olives, 16-ounce cans

☐ pimento-stuffed green olives, 10-ounce jars

☐ chickpeas, 16-ounce cans

☐ cannellini or other white beans,16-ounce cans

☐ tahini (sesame paste), small jar

☐ capers, 3.75-ounce jars

☐ anchovy fillets, packed in olive oil, 3-ounce jars

☐ sun-dried tomatoes, packed in olive oil, 7.5-ounce jars

☐ extra-virgin olive oil

☐ balsamic vinegar

☐ a selection of crackers and flatbreads, including rye crispbread

IN THE FRIDGE:

☐ prepared horseradish, 1 (6-ounce) jar (use and replace every month)

☐ fresh garlic (use and replace every few weeks)

☐ lemons (use and replace every few weeks)

☐ fresh cilantro and/or flat-leaf parsley (use and replace every week)

☐ fresh rosemary (use and replace every few weeks)

☐ unsalted butter (use and replace every few weeks)

☐ Macintosh apples (use and replace every few weeks)

☐ seedless green grapes, small bunch (use and replace every week)

☐ Brie, 6-ounce wedge (if bought ripe, use within a week; if unripe, may last two weeks or more)

☐ Camembert, small round (if bought ripe, use within a week; if unripe, may last two weeks or more)

☐ crème fraîche, 6-ounce tub (use and replace every two weeks)

☐ salmon roe (a.k.a. salmon caviar), 6-ounce jar (use and replace every two weeks)

BAR ASSOCIATIONS

FRENCH TWISTS

Drinkology EATS loves classic cocktails, especially spirits-and-vermouth combos like the Martini, Manhattan, and Rob Roy. (A complete list of the booze and condiments you need to make these and other well-known mixed drinks can be found in this book's companion volume, *Drinkology: The Art and Science of the Cocktail*; see "The Basic Bar," *Drinkology* pages 25–27.) But we also love to experiment, performing twists on the classic recipes just to see whether anything good might happen.

One of our most fruitful lines of scientific inquiry opened up when we decided to try substituting the French aromatized wines Lillet Blanc and Lillet Rouge for dry and sweet vermouth, respectively. After all, vermouths, whether French or Italian, are also aromatized wines—wines that have been slightly "fortified" with grape spirits and flavored with fruits, herbs, flowers, and other ingredients—so, we asked ourselves, how bad could the results be?

Answer: Not bad at all.

If you have all the components of *Drinkology*'s basic bar (and enough ice!), you'll always be able to offer drop-in guests a wide variety of mixed drinks. But by adding just a few more elements—a bottle each of Lillet Blanc and Lillet Rouge (keep both in the fridge), an orange-flavored vodka, and a little bottle of orange bitters—you'll also be able to make these "French twists" on three redoubtable cocktail classics.

Besides these ingredients, you'll need to steal a little cognac from your liquor cabinet, and you might also want to have ground cumin on your spice rack, though this last ingredient is optional.

At your impromptu cocktail party, you'll be serving your guests hummus or a white bean spread, a tapenade (we give you three different "colors" to choose from), a butter-based spread (two choices), and one of

LILLETINI

 Besides Lillet Blanc and orange-flavored vodka, this variation on the world's most beloved potable requires a dash of orange bitters. Once fashionable, orange bitters are now difficult to find in the U.S., but they are still manufactured by Fee Brothers, a nearly 150-year-old, family-owned firm in Rochester, New York. (To order, give Fee Brothers a call at 1-800-961-3337; as of this writing, you can't order directly from the company's website, feebrothers.com.)

♪ lemon twist
2½ ounces orange-flavored vodka
½ ounce Lillet Blanc
dash of orange bitters

Rim a chilled cocktail glass with the twist and drop it into the glass. Combine liquid ingredients in a mixing glass, with lots of ice. Stir well, and strain into the cocktail glass.

FRENCH TWISTS

PARIS-MANHATTAN

Lillet Rouge is more "wine-like" than sweet vermouth, so sub-stituting it for vermouth in the classic Manhattan recipe yields a cocktail that's redder than the traditional drink—and slightly drier, though the dryness is offset by the addition of a little syrup from the maraschino cherry jar.

2 ounces bourbon or Canadian blended whisky
¾ ounce Lillet Rouge
¼ teaspoon maraschino cherry syrup (from the jar)
2 dashes of Angostura bitters
♂ maraschino cherry

Combine liquid ingredients in a mixing glass, with ice. Stir, and strain into a chilled cocktail glass. Garnish with the cherry.

ROB ROI

Replacing dry vermouth with Lillet Blanc in this French twist on the dry Rob Roy makes more than an iota of difference. (And *Drinkology EATS* applauds your erudition if you get the joke in the previous sentence.)

♂ lemon twist
2½ ounces blended scotch
½ ounce Lillet Blanc
dash of Angostura bitters

Rim a chilled cocktail glass with the twist and drop it into the glass. Combine liquid ingredients in a mixing glass, with ice. Stir well, and strain into the cocktail glass.

two simple canapés that are as gorgeous as they are tasty. Suggestions for some special mixed drinks appear in the sidebar on pages 78–80.

On Your Mark, Get Set, . . .

Ramona's a whirlwind in the kitchen; James is rather a plodder. Still, we both believe that you can prepare at least four of the dishes in this chapter in an hour's time or less. We give you three tapenade choices, two choices of bean-based spreads, two butter-based spreads, and two ultra-quick canapés; limit yourself to one dish from each of these categories. Do the tapenade first (so that the flavors have a chance to meld), then the hummus or white bean spread, then the butter spread, and then the salmon-roe or apple wedge canapés. (You'll help yourself out by removing the butter and—if you choose the butter-Brie spread or the apple-Camembert wedges—the cheese from the fridge as soon as you start cooking, to allow them to soften a bit.) You will absolutely need a food processor to do the tapenade and bean spreads. If you follow these recipes, the tapenade, bean spread, butter spread, and canapés should easily satisfy the cocktail-hour peckishness of up to eight people. If they want dinner, too, give them a (friendly) dirty look and refer them to a local restaurant—and do tag along.

Green Tapenade

A tapenade (TAH-puh-nahd) is an olive-based dip or spread. Tapenades originated in Provence, in the south of France. True Provençal cooks would undoubtedly be horrified by the straight-out-of-the-can (or -jar) versions of these traditional dishes we offer here, but *nous ne regrettons rien.*

1½ cups (about one 12-ounce jar) pimiento-stuffed green olives, drained
12 anchovy filets
2 large cloves garlic, crushed
1 tablespoon capers, drained
⅜ cup extra-virgin olive oil
1 teaspoon fresh lemon juice
1 tablespoon chopped fresh cilantro or flat-leaf parsley
freshly ground black pepper to taste

Put the olives, anchovies, garlic, and capers in a food processor and pulse until smooth, scraping down the sides as necessary. Add the oil little by little, pulsing until the tapenade has a consistency similar to that of mayonnaise. Add the lemon juice, cilantro, and pepper and pulse to mix. Serve with a selection of crackers.

BLACK TAPENADE

Tapenade option number two uses black olives rather than green. It's sultrier and a little less racy than the recipe above.

1 (16-ounce) can pitted large black olives, drained
12 anchovy fillets
½ cup capers, drained
3 large cloves garlic, crushed
½ cup extra-virgin olive oil
1 ounce Amontillado sherry
1½ tablespoons fresh lemon juice
freshly ground black pepper to taste

Put the olives, anchovies, capers, and garlic in a food processor and pulse until smooth, scraping down the sides as necessary. Add the oil little by little, pulsing until the tapenade has a consistency similar to that of mayonnaise. Add the sherry, lemon juice, and pepper, and pulse to mix. Serve with a selection of crackers.

RED TAPENADE

You're bound to be getting the idea by now: Tapenades typically combine olives with a short list of other ingredients that usually include anchovies, capers, garlic, and oil. (If you don't like anchovies, save your distaste for the anchovy butter that's coming up; despite the largish number of fillets each tapenade recipe calls for, you really can't taste the anchovies—as a separate flavor, that is.)

1 (16-ounce) can pitted large black olives, drained
¾ cup oil-packed sun-dried tomatoes, drained
2 tablespoons capers, drained
7 anchovy filets
2 large cloves garlic, crushed
½ cup extra-virgin olive oil
1 teaspoon lemon zest
3 tablespoons fresh lemon juice
1 teaspoon balsamic vinegar
⅛ teaspoon freshly ground black pepper, or to taste

Put the olives, sun-dried tomatoes, capers, anchovies, and garlic in a food processor and pulse until smooth. Add the oil little by little, pulsing until the tapenade has a consistency similar to that of mayonnaise. Add the lemon zest, lemon juice, vinegar, and pepper, and pulse to mix. Serve with a selection of crackers.

Hummus bi Tahini

We admit it: Some of the brands of prepackaged hummus that you can find in the supermarket are pretty good. They cannot, however, compare with freshly made hummus (even when the "fresh" hummus contains *canned* chickpeas). Chickpeas, by the way, are a kind of bean—as their alternate name, *garbanzo beans,* reveals. *Hummus bi Tahini* is Arabic for "chickpeas with tahini"—tahini being the sesame-seed paste that's essential to so many Middle Eastern dishes.

1 (16-ounce) can chickpeas
¼ cup tahini
3 tablespoons fresh lemon juice
1 large clove garlic, crushed
½ teaspoon salt
¼ teaspoon freshly ground black pepper
¼ teaspoon ground cumin, or to taste (optional)

Drain the chickpeas and reserve the liquid. Put the chickpeas, tahini, lemon juice, and garlic in a food processor and pulse until smooth. If the hummus is too thick, add some of the reserved chickpea liquid. Add salt, pepper, and (if desired) cumin and pulse again. Serve with a selection of crackers. (*If* you have the time and inclination to do some additional shopping, buy a package of small pita loaves and quarter these to serve with the hummus.)

White Bean Spread

What could be more basic—or more satisfying, in a primal sort of way—than a simple white bean spread? This recipe is adapted from one sent us by *Drinkology EATS*'s friend Jane Cohn, who's been serving it at her cocktail parties for years. The Italian white kidney beans called cannellini work well in this recipe, though any canned white beans will do.

1 (16-ounce) can white beans
2 large cloves garlic, crushed
¼ cup plus 1 tablespoon extra-virgin olive oil
2 teaspoons fresh rosemary, finely minced
zest of two lemons
salt and freshly ground black pepper to taste

Drain the beans and discard the liquid. Put the beans and garlic into a food processor. Pulse until smooth. Add ¼ cup olive oil little by little, pulsing until the mixture has a consistency similar to that of mayonnaise. Transfer mixture to a bowl and stir in the rosemary, lemon zest, additional tablespoon of oil, and salt and pepper. Serve with a selection of crackers.

ANCHOVY BUTTER
James (who adores anchovies) introduced Ramona (who adores anchovies) to this utterly simple concoction. Ever since, it's starred at every impromptu cocktail party Ramona has hosted. (Make sure you use *un*salted butter; otherwise, the saltiness will be overwhelming.)

10 anchovy fillets
½ cup (1 stick) unsalted butter, softened

Mince the anchovy fillets very fine. Using a fork, thoroughly mix the anchovies and butter together in a small mixing bowl. (If you're taking the butter directly from the fridge, cut it into small pieces before adding it to the bowl.) Transfer the anchovy butter to a small serving bowl, and serve with a selection of crackers. (Suggest to your guests that they spread the butter *very* thinly; the anchovy flavor is intense.)

CANAPÉS 101

At fashionable cocktail parties, the canapés are sometimes so fastidiously crafted that you can find yourself wondering whether the caterer went to culinary school or took a degree from the Rhode Island School of Design. We admire (and occasionally aspire to) such workmanship, but we're here to tell you that, at bottom, the basic theory of canapé construction is actually very simple.

Most canapés are layered arrangements of three or, at the most, four different foods stacked one atop the other. In *Drinkology EATS*'s august opinion, a slice of Kraft cheddar on a saltine is *not* a canapé. Squeeze a tiny mound of French's mustard on that cheese slice, however, and voila!— *le canapé est arrivé.*

The original meaning of the French word *canapé* is "sofa," or "couch." And, in fact, making a canapé is akin to creating a piece of upholstered furniture. First, you need a frame, or platform, to support the production. This foundational layer is usually bread, toast, or a cracker (as in our rustic salmon-roe canapé) though slices of hard-fleshed vegetables (for example, cucumbers) or fruits (such as apples) can also provide an appropriate undergirding.

To continue with the furniture-making metaphor, a canapé's second layer is equivalent to a sofa or chair's *stuffing.*  The second layer is often a spreadable paste: butter, a soft cheese, sour cream or crème fraîche, or a spreadable salad (a finely chopped egg or shrimp salad, guacamole, or the like). Sometimes the second layer provides most of the canapé's flavor; sometimes its major purpose is to bind the layers together— as the crème fraîche does in our salmon-roe number.

THE "PLATFORM"

THE "STUFFING"

Straining the metaphor somewhat, we might say that putting the third layer on our edible settee is roughly equivalent to adding the fabric to an upholstered piece. A canapé's third layer provides its visual—and sometimes its gustatory—pizzazz. Color, pattern, and "fit" are essential to creating this third (often the topmost) layer, just as they are when selecting and installing fabric. On some, fancier canapés, the third layer is rigidly geometric and must be cut with precision. (Ramona loves using minuscule vegetable cutters to fashion wee—and twee—canapé decorations from carrot slices, bell-pepper skins, and the like.) The appeal of our salmon-roe canapé is, by contrast, decidedly shabby chic: You just pile on the roe and let the dramatic red-orange color and glistening texture suffice for artistry.

Things don't necessarily end with the third layer. Some canapés (including, for example, our smoked brook trout canapé; see page 341) have yet a fourth layer, which is usually an herb or spice garnish or sprinkle calculated to heighten the visual and gustatory effect. This is the culinary equivalent of adding tassels, fringe, and a few carefully placed throw pillows.

THE "FABRIC"

BRIE-BUTTER SPREAD

This traditional French butter-based spread is almost as simple as the one just given. It will work best if the Brie is very ripe and both the butter and the cheese are allowed to reach room temperature before mixing. Feel free to dress this up by throwing in some finely chopped fresh herbs (thyme? chives?), but only if you've a mind to. The cheese-and-butter duo is very tasty as is.

6 ounces Brie, ripe and soft
½ cup (1 stick) unsalted butter, softened

Scoop the Brie from the rind, and discard the rind. Using a fork, thoroughly mix the cheese and butter together in a small mixing bowl. Transfer the Brie-butter spread to a small serving bowl, and serve with a selection of crackers. (*If* you have the time and inclination to do some additional shopping, buy a baguette and slice it into very thin slices to serve with the Brie-butter spread.)

RUSTIC SALMON-ROE CANAPÉS

Canapés are often exquisitely engineered thingamabobs that take scads of time (and patience) to construct. (See the Technicalities sidebar on pages 86–87 for the basic procedure.) Not so with this "rustic" canapé or the one that follows: A whole slew of either can be dashed off in ten minutes. But they're no less attractive for being jerry-built.

8 pieces rye crispbread
6 ounces crème fraîche
6 ounces salmon roe (a.k.a. salmon caviar)

Break the crispbreads in half. Slather some crème fraîche on each piece, and top each with a generous dollop of salmon roe.

APPLE-CAMEMBERT WEDGES

Ramona and James first served these at a cocktail party that featured New York State agricultural products. (Upstate New York has long been famous for its orchards, of course, and artisanal cheesemakers in New York are now producing a variety of European-style cheeses.) The combo of tart, crisp apple and tangy, creamy Camembert is sensational. (The grape slice serves a merely decorative purpose; forgo it if you haven't the time.)

2 McIntosh apples
juice of 1 lemon
6 ounces Camembert, ripe and soft
8 seedless green grapes, thinly sliced lengthwise

Fill a bowl with water and add the lemon juice to it. Peel and core the apples, slicing each into 16 wedges. Immediately dunk the apple wedges into the lemon water (which will prevent them from oxidizing, at least for a little while). Remove the wedges from the water and drain on paper towels. Using a spreading knife, scoop small portions of Camembert from the rind and spread on the wedges. Dot each with a grape slice.

CHAPTER FOUR

Crumbs between the Sheets

CHAMPAGNE BREAKFASTS IN BED

AH, BREAKFAST IN BED. THE BREADCRUMBS LODGING BETWEEN THE sheets. The egg yolk dribbling on the pillowcases. The spilled coffee spattering the heirloom bedspread. The dog's (or toddler's) sudden and—literally—upsetting incursion into the china, glasses, and silverware.

How glam. And yet, accidents aside, breakfast in bed does seem the height of luxury, doesn't it? Or, better, the height of feeling *well taken care of.* Being served breakfast in bed is an extravagant and rare luxury.

Why so rare? Well, first, because life today is a little too hurried and fraught to accommodate breakfast in bed—or not, at least, very often. But second, there's also the fact that breakfast in bed involves a horrendously unequal division of labor between the person served, who has only to eat, drink, yawn, and lazily stretch his/her limbs, and the person cooking and serving, who has to do everything else. There's just no getting around it: For the cook, breakfast in bed entails an incredible amount of work.

But so does any true act of love, which is what presenting breakfast in bed to your spouse, partner, or paramour amounts to. (Like many true acts of love, it's also a great way of racking up points—to be cashed in at appropriate future moments.) *Drinkology EATS* can't make the cook's job any easier. And, besides, we want you to rack up a *lot* of points. Our Champagne breakfasts in bed—we give you two alternatives—do call for some planning and preparation.

With either of the breakfasts, serve a good but not-too-expensive brut Champagne or other dry sparkling wine *or* go the extra distance and treat your beloved to a sparkling wine cocktail. This book's companion volume, *Drinkology: The Art and Science of the Cocktail*, contains numerous recipes (see the chapter on Champagne); we offer three additional suggestions at the end of this chapter. Note that each of the egg-dish recipes—directly below and in the second menu—feeds two people. Cook's gotta to eat, too.

A SHIRRED EGGS BREAKFAST

This breakfast's centerpiece is shirred eggs—a method of cooking eggs (they're baked in cream) that used to be much more popular. It's high time for a revival.

Menu
SHIRRED EGGS
DATE BREAD
WHITE ASPARAGUS WITH HOLLANDAISE SAUCE
DRIED-FRUIT COMPOTE
SPARKLING WINE OR SPARKLING WINE COCKTAIL
COFFEE

First, some strategic pointers: Bake the date bread the day before; after it has cooled, it can be refrigerated, then sliced and rewarmed before serving. (In fact, chilling the bread makes it easier to cut it into elegantly thin slices.) The dessert—a warm dried-fruit compote—*must* be prepared ahead of time (which is fine; it keeps for days and can be reheated, and the recipe is large enough to supply you with dessert for several meals running).

Shirred Eggs

For this dish, use two ramekins or ovenproof bowls, each just large enough to accommodate two eggs.

4 tablespoons heavy cream
2 tablespoons thinly sliced scallions (about 1)
2 tablespoons thinly sliced grape tomatoes (about 4)
4 eggs
½ cup grated Gruyère
salt and freshly ground black pepper to taste
2 tablespoons butter, melted

Preheat the oven to 350° F. Place 2 tablespoons of cream, 1 tablespoon of scallions, and 1 tablespoon of tomatoes in each ramekin or ovenproof bowl. Add 2 eggs to each dish, and sprinkle with ¼ cup cheese and salt and pepper. Drizzle 1 tablespoon melted butter over each. Bake until egg whites are set but yolks are still runny, about 20 minutes. (For firm yolks, bake 5 minutes longer. Note that the eggs will continue to cook for several minutes after they are removed from the oven.) Handle the hot ramekins very carefully.

Date Bread

To repeat: Unless you're planning on rising hours before breakfast, bake this quickbread the day before.

1 cup finely chopped pitted dates, packed
1 teaspoon baking soda
2 tablespoons dark rum (optional)
1 cup boiling water
¼ cup (½ stick) butter, melted
1 cup brown sugar

1 egg
1 teaspoon vanilla
2 cups unbleached flour
1½ teaspoons baking powder
½ teaspoon salt
½ cup pecans, chopped

Place the dates in a medium-size bowl and sprinkle with the baking soda and rum (if desired). Add the boiling water and stir, separating the date pieces. (The mixture will bubble up.) Stirring occasionally, let cool to room temperature, about 30 minutes.

Preheat the oven to 325° F, and grease and flour a 9" x 5" x 3" loaf pan. Place the egg, sugar, butter, and vanilla in a large bowl and mix. In a separate bowl, whisk together the flour, salt, and baking powder. Add a small amount of the egg mixture to the flour mixture and stir; then add a small amount of the date mixture, alternating until all the mixtures are combined. Add the pecans and stir. Pour batter into loaf pan and bake for 40 to 60 minutes or until a knife inserted in the center comes out clean. Let cool thoroughly. Refrigerate to facilitate super-thin slicing. Serve plain or spread with butter.

WHITE ASPARAGUS WITH HOLLANDAISE SAUCE

This ritzy dish is down-home easy (because the hollandaise is whipped up in the blender). It doesn't matter whether the asparagus are served hot or at room temperature; they're good either way (but make sure the hollandaise is warm). Feel free to substitute the more familiar green asparagus if white asparagus are out of season or, as is usually the case in Ramona and James's uncouth neighborhoods, simply unavailable. This recipe serves two.

8 spears fresh white asparagus, trimmed
3 egg yolks
2 tablespoons fresh lemon juice
¼ teaspoon salt
dash of ground cayenne pepper
½ cup (1 stick) butter

Steam the asparagus until just tender, about 6 minutes. Remove from steamer and set aside. Melt butter in a small pan, heating until just bubbly. Meanwhile, place the egg yolks, lemon juice, salt, and cayenne pepper in a blender, cover, and blend at high speed for 2 or 3 seconds. Remove the clear plastic or glass knob from the center of the carafe's lid and, with blender on high speed, pour the hot butter through the hole in a thin, steady stream. Place 4 asparagus spears on each plate, and drizzle the hollandaise sauce over them.

DRIED-FRUIT COMPOTE

Now, granted, this recipe makes a whole heckuva lot more compote than you'll use for a two-person breakfast. But that's OK. In fact, it's just dandy, since leftover compote will keep well in the fridge. Not only does it make a great dessert, but (sans the whipped cream) it's a sensational accompaniment to roasted pork and lamb.

8 ounces (about 2 cups) dried apricots
8 ounces (about 2 cups) dried peaches
8 ounces (about 2 cups) dried pears
2 ounces (about ½ cup) dried cherries

2 ounces (about ½ cup) dried cranberries, preferably unsweetened
juice and zest of 1 lemon
juice and zest of 1 orange
¼ cup Grand Marnier or crème de cassis
3 to 4 cups orange juice
whipped cream (optional)

Preheat the oven to 325° F. Coarsely chop the dried fruits and combine them in a heavy ovenproof pot with lid (such as a Dutch oven). Add the fresh juices and zests, liqueur, and 2 cups of orange juice. Cover and bake for 2 to 2½ hours. Check every half hour, stirring and adding more orange juice as the fruit absorbs the liquid. (Do not add juice during the last hour; continue to check and stir, but let the liquid thicken into a sauce.) Serve in small portions with whipped cream, if desired.

If you prepare this a day or more ahead of time, let the compote cool thoroughly before refrigerating. Add a small amount of orange juice to the pot and stir before reheating.

AN EGGS RAREBIT BREAKFAST

The first breakfast menu is on the sweet 'n' creamy side; this one falls more toward the savory end of the flavor spectrum.

Menu
EGGS RAREBIT
TOMATOES VINAIGRETTE
LEMON CURD BARS
SPARKLING WINE OR SPARKLING WINE COCKTAIL
COFFEE

The main course is a variation (one of hundreds possible) on eggs Benedict. Because we are foolish foodies, we're recommending that you serve the eggs atop homemade crumpets, for which we include a recipe. You are no doubt more rational than we, and will therefore probably elect to use store-bought English muffins instead. (Be our guest.) The dessert we suggest—lemon curd bars—can be baked the afternoon or evening before your special breakfast; once they've cooled, place them in an airtight container until serving.

CRUMPETS

The English muffin's career has titanically thrived on this side of the Pond; the crumpet's appears to have sunk, mid-Atlantic. That's a shame. As yeast breads go, homemade crumpets are relatively easy to make. Inside, a crumpet's texture is appealingly moist and, like an English muffin's, slightly crumbly; outside, its architectural stolidity and precision makes the crumpet an impressive platform for eggs Benedict and similar poached-egg dishes.

Note, however, that crumpet-making requires a (small) investment in specialized equipment: to wit, crumpet rings—bangle-bracelet-size stainless steel hoops (4 inches in diameter, with sides about 1 inch high) that keep the crumpets intact as they "bake" on the stovetop. (Crumpet rings, which come in sets of four, are available from specialty housewares stores and Internet emporiums; the drawing on the following page shows them in use.) If you need to save time on the morning you're serving your sweetie breakfast in bed, prepare the crumpets ahead of time. Wrapped in plastic, they'll keep for a day or two.

Special equipment: crumpet rings (a.k.a. English muffin rings)

½ cup warm water

2 teaspoons sugar

1 tablespoon (1 envelope) active dry yeast

1½ cups milk, heated to skin temperature or just slightly above

2 tablespoons butter, melted (but not bubbling hot)

2 cups all-purpose flour

1 teaspoon salt

½ teaspoon baking soda dissolved in ¼ cup warm water

Pour the warm water into a large bowl, and stir in the sugar and yeast. Let stand until it bubbles, about 5 minutes. Stir in the milk, butter, flour, and salt and mix until the batter is slightly elastic. (Do not overmix.)

Cover with a towel and let rise in a warm place for 30 to 45 minutes. Stir in dissolved baking soda, cover again, and let rise for an additional 20 to 30 minutes.

Lightly grease a large frying pan and the insides of the crumpet rings. Place the rings on the cooking surface and preheat over medium heat. Fill each ring about half full with batter and reduce heat, cooking over medium-low heat until set, about 10 to 15 minutes. The tops will bubble (like cooking pancakes). The crumpets are set when their tops no longer look wet and are full of holes and their bottoms are golden brown. If you wish, you may remove the rings from the crumpets and flip them over to brown the other sides for 1 to 3 minutes. Re-grease the rings and repeat until all the batter is used. Toast before using in the eggs rarebit recipe, following.

Note: Obviously, this recipe produces many more crumpets—a total of 16—than are required for a two-person breakfast. Think of this as a good thing. The leftover crumpets can. like English muffins, be frozen and then toasted before use. Slathered with butter and jam, they make a fine breakfast on those days—*most* days—when you don't have time for a leisurely breakfast in bed.

EGGS RAREBIT

This recipe's an adaptation of the classic British teatime dish known as Welsh rarebit (which, basically, is a beery cheddar cheese sauce dumped on toast). Sometimes, Welsh rarebit is called Welsh rabbit. We briefly considered calling our creation "rabbit eggs," but found that the Easter Bunny holds the trademark. Like all eggs Benedict–type dishes, this one requires that the eggs be poached; for tips on making that sometimes-maddening procedure easier, see the "Technicalties" sidebar on page 101.

4 slices Canadian bacon

4 tablespoons (½ stick) unsalted butter

2 tablespoons finely chopped shallots

2 tablespoons cornstarch

1 cup milk

1½ cup grated sharp cheddar cheese

⅛ teaspoon freshly grated nutmeg

salt and freshly ground black pepper to taste

4 poached eggs

4 crumpets (see recipe above) or 2 English muffins

sweet paprika

Fry the Canadian bacon lightly and keep warm. Melt the butter in a small saucepan, then add the shallots and cook over medium heat until soft but not brown. Add ¾ cup milk and heat. (Do not allow to boil.) Mix the cornstarch with ¼ cup milk and stir into the heating milk. Cook over medium heat until the mixture thickens. Remove from the heat and immediately stir in the cheese and nutmeg. Season with salt and pepper. Cover and keep warm.

Poach the eggs. While the eggs are poaching, lightly toast the crumpets (or split and toast the English muffins, if you're using muffins instead).

Place 2 crumpets (or muffin halves) on each plate. Put a slice of bacon on each and top with a poached egg. Pour cheese sauce over each and sprinkle with paprika. Serve immediately, with tomatoes vinaigrette (see recipe following) on the side.

NOT EGG DROP SOUP

From nearly the time that he was hatched, James has preferred poached eggs to any other kind of eggs. His mother refused to make them, however, so he could only satisfy his craving on those rare occasions—usually during summer vacations—when he was taken to a restaurant for breakfast.

It wasn't till he had a kitchen of his own that James grasped the (sensible, not cruel) reason behind his mother's refusal. Poached eggs, it turns out, are damnably difficult to make well. James's first several attempts yielded what might kindly be described as egg drop soup—the egg whites exploding into a cobweb-like chaos of threads as soon as the eggs hit the water. It took years—and advice from friends whose culinary skills were more fully developed—for James to arrive at an acceptable technique, which involves adding a little vinegar to the poaching water, breaking each egg into a separate small cup (double espresso cups work well), and tipping the eggs into the boiling water with surpassing gentleness.

Note that we describe this technique as *acceptable.* Flawless, it isn't. Despite the exceeding care he took, James's poached eggs would still sometimes betray him, leading him to believe that eggs Benedict were named after Benedict *Arnold.* (They weren't, by the way.) It was not until James happened upon the marvelous little devices called *pocheuses* (that's French for "poachers") that his lifelong pursuit of the perfect home-made poached egg was consummated.

A *pocheuse* is a footed, perforated steel cup to which a long wire handle is attached. (Like the one pictured at right, *pocheuses* are sometimes egg shaped.) To poach eggs using *pocheuses,* fill a large, straight-sided frying pan with water to a depth of about 1½ inches, and add a little vinegar—about 2 tablespoons—to the water. Carefully set the pan on the stovetop, and turn the heat to its highest setting.

As the water is heating, lightly butter the cups of the *pocheuses* and break one egg into each. The egg white's viscosity and surface tension will prevent the egg from oozing through the little holes in the bottom of the *pocheuse*. (Oh, there may be a little seepage, but not enough to worry about.)

When the water reaches a full boil, set the *pocheuses* in the pan. The boiling water should just cover the surface of the eggs, as in the drawing below. Cook the eggs until the whites have just set, then immediately pluck the *pocheuses* from the pan. (Caution: The wire handles may get hot, so protect your hand with a potholder or kitchen towel.) The poached eggs should slide easily from the greased cups; if an egg sticks, gently run the point of a knife around the edge to free it.

One more note: It's best to allow eggs to warm to room temperature before poaching. If the eggs are cold, the water will stop boiling when they're lowered into the pan; not only will this lengthen the cooking time, but it increases the risk that the egg white will disperse.

TOMATOES VINAIGRETTE

Drinkology EATS likes its salads simple. This breakfast salad certainly fits the bill.

20 to 24 grape tomatoes, sliced lengthwise
1 scallion (white part only), diced
good balsamic vinegar
salt and freshly ground black pepper to taste

Combine tomatoes and scallions in small mixing bowl. Lightly drizzle with vinegar, add salt and pepper, and mix. Transfer half the salad to each serving plate.

LEMON CURD BARS

Do feel free to use store-bought lemon curd for this recipe. But because it's so easy to make your own (well, except for squeezing all those lemons!), we thought we'd offer you the whole megillah. Do note that this recipe produces many more cookies than you'll need for your *intime* breakfast. No matter: They'll keep for days in an airtight container.

FOR THE LEMON CURD:
4 eggs
1¼ cups sugar
¾ cup fresh lemon juice
¼ cup (½ stick) unsalted butter
1 tablespoon lemon zest

FOR THE BARS:
1 cup unsalted butter
2 cups all-purpose flour
1 cup sugar

½ teaspoon baking soda

10 ounces (1 ¼ cups) lemon curd

½ cup toasted, chopped almonds

Make the lemon curd: Beat the eggs for about 1 minute, until uniform in color and texture. In a double boiler over simmering water, combine the sugar, lemon juice, butter, and lemon zest and stir until the butter has melted, about 3 minutes. Add the beaten eggs to the lemon mixture, stirring constantly. Continue to cook until the mixture is thick enough to coat the back of a spoon, about 3 minutes more. If you see bits of egg white in the curd, pour the mixture through a chinois or other large, fine-mesh sieve immediately after removing from the heat. Let the curd cool to room temperature; it will continue to thicken as it cools.

Make the bars: Preheat the oven to 375° F. In a large mixing bowl, cream the butter and sugar together, then add the flour and baking soda, mixing until coarse crumbs are formed. Spread two-thirds of this mixture in a 9" × 13" × 2" baking pan, patting it down to form a crust. Bake for 10 minutes. Remove from oven and lower oven temperature to 350° F. Let the crust cool slightly before proceeding.

Spread the lemon curd over the baked crust. Add the almonds to the remaining one-third of the crumb mixture, mix, and sprinkle over the curd. Return the pan to the oven and bake for 25 minutes or until lightly browned. Let cool, then cut into 1" × 3" bars.

BAR ASSOCIATIONS

TOASTS FOR BREAKFAST

When asked what sort of toast she likes for breakfast, Ramona always answers, "Why, a Champagne toast, of course." In that spirit, we'd like to propose the three sparkling-wine cocktails following, all *Drinkology EATS* originals. (You'll find plenty more—including standards like the Mimosa and Kir Royale—in *Drinkology: The Art and Science of the Cocktail.*)

When making any sparkling wine cocktail, it's very important to put *all* the other ingredients into the flute before adding the sparkling wine—and to pour in the wine very gently, tilting the glass as you do so. (If you don't, the wine will froth up catastrophically.)

DELLA ROBBIA

This Italian take on the Champagne cocktail couples prosecco—the Italian sparkling wine made from the grape of the same name—and Cynar, an artichoke-based liqueur from Sicily.

♦ small wedge of orange or blood orange
½ ounce Cynar
about 5 ounces dry prosecco

Rim a Champagne flute with the orange wedge and drop it into the flute. Pour in the Cynar. Top with prosecco, pouring very slowly and tilting the flute as you do so.

MÛRE ROYAL

Always on the lookout for unusual spirits, Ramona's husband, Eric, discovered a bottle of crème de mûre in a New York City liquor store. This blackberry-based cordial—similar to the blackcurrant-based crème de cassis—makes for a superlative Champagne cocktail very much in the vein of the Kir Royale.

½ teaspoon crème de mûre
5 or 6 ounces brut Champagne
🍷 lemon twist (optional)

Pour the crème de mûre into a Champagne flute, and gently top with Champagne. (If using a twist, rim the flute beforehand and drop the twist into it before adding the crème de mûre.)

The Raspberries

Instead of giving your slugabed beloved an adoring peck on the cheek, you might consider giving him or her The Raspberries. By which we mean this cocktail made with raspberry-flavored Chambord liqueur and an unusual—though obtainable—*pétillant* rosé wine, Bugey Cerdon. Semisweet and not as fizzy as Champagne (that's what *pétillant* means), Bugey Cerdon has a flavor that's evocative of raspberries, as well.

🍷 lemon twist
½ teaspoon Chambord liqueur
about 5 ounces Bugey Cerdon demi-sec rosé

Rim a Champagne flute with the twist and drop the twist into the glass. Pour in the Chambord, and gently top with the wine.

CHAPTER FIVE

Warm Up, Pucker Up

A WINTERTIME TANGERINE BRUNCH

IT SNOWED A RECORD TWENTY-SEVEN INCHES IN NEW YORK CITY ON the Sunday Ramona and James hosted this tangerine brunch, so we greeted our dozen intrepid guests (the subways were running) with steaming hot cups of cocoa—which we'd spiked, of course.

Whether it snows or not, a citrus-themed brunch can brighten up a winter weekend afternoon considerably. Except, of course, for Valentine's Day, February's not good for much besides being the month in which citrus fruits reach the peak of their subtropical glory. We love them all: oranges, grapefruits, Cara Caras, blood oranges, mandarins,

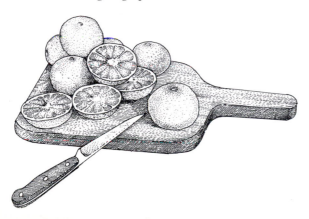

satsumas, and clementines. But honey tangerines might be our favorites. With a flavor that—if they're very ripe and fresh—reminds one of late-August honey dew melon, tangerines can seem the living reflection from a dream of summer. (And, yes, that was an allusion.) Plus, they're bursting with vitamin C—not a bad nutrient to load up on at a gathering where at least one person is likely to be coming down with a cold. Remember: Pucker up, but deliver air kisses only!

So as not to *over*load our guests with citrusy pleasure, we concentrated the fruit on the drinks side of our brunch menu. Except for the heavenly dessert—which couples tangerines and blood oranges with another wintertime gift from our planet's more southerly reaches (fresh pineapple)—the dishes we chose present a range of sweet and savory flavors that complement, and buffer, the citrus-laden drinks' tart punch.

There's nothing like trudging through snowdrifts to help one work up an appetite, so we were glad we'd decided to experiment by offering our brunch guests two different egg-based dishes: a quiche *and* a soufflé. Take careful note, here: Though eggs are traditional brunchtime fare, if you're having more than just a few people by you should restrict yourself to those kinds of egg dishes that can be largely prepped before the guests arrive and that don't require you to stay glued to the stove. (If you want to poach eggs for twelve people all at once, go get yourself a job as a short-order cook.)

Trudging through snowdrifts works up an appetite

Some notes on strategy: This brunch will take a whole day to prepare for, including shopping. The caramelized bacon can be made the day before the brunch. If you're worried about time, steam the haricots verts and grate the carrots for the quiche (and the cheeses for both egg dishes) the previous evening. And to make your morning's chores seem a little less monumental, you might even measure and mix the muffins' dry ingredients before going to bed that night. Schedule your guests' arrival for no earlier than 1:00 PM, so that you have time to accomplish nearly everything before they show up.

Except for the drinks, which you'll want to make individually, most of the recipes have been calibrated to serve twelve people. For a dozen guests, serve *two* quiches or *two* soufflés—or, if you're feeling specially adventurous, one of each.

Menu

EATS
MAPLE-PECAN MUFFINS
RED-LEAF LETTUCE SALAD
CARROT-FENNEL QUICHE *or* CHEESE SOUFFLÉ
CARAMELIZED BACON
HARICOTS VERTS WITH DIJON MUSTARD DRESSING
NOT-YOUR-GRANDMOTHER'S AMBROSIA

DRINKS
SPIKED COCOA
TANGERINE MIMOSA
LILLET MIDI
TANGERINE DROP

MAPLE-PECAN MUFFINS
These dense, extraordinarily nutty and spicy muffins *must* be served within an hour or two of baking. Plan on pulling them from the oven just before you put in the quiches or soufflés.

2 cups unbleached all-purpose flour
¼ cup firmly packed brown sugar
2 teaspoons baking powder
½ teaspoon salt
2 large eggs
½ cup maple syrup
½ cup milk
½ cup (1 stick) unsalted butter, melted
1 teaspoon vanilla extract
1 cup finely chopped pecans

FOR THE TOPPING:

1 tablespoon granulated sugar
¼ scant teaspoon ground cinnamon
⅓ cup finely chopped pecans
12 pecan halves
maple syrup

Make the muffins: Preheat the oven to 400° F and grease a 12-cup muffin pan. Whisk together the flour, brown sugar, baking powder, and salt in a large bowl. In a separate bowl, lightly beat the eggs and mix in the syrup, milk, butter, and vanilla. Add to the flour mixture, mixing until just moistened. Stir in the 1 cup chopped pecans. Spoon the batter into the muffin tin, filling each cup two-thirds full.

Make the topping: Mix the granulated sugar, cinnamon, and the ⅓ cup chopped pecans in a small bowl, and sprinkle 1 teaspoon of the mixture over each muffin. Dip the pecan halves in maple syrup and press one into the top of each muffin. Bake for 15 to 20 minutes or until golden brown.

WE'RE CUCKOO FOR . . .

. . . cocoa—and even more so when it's livened up with a shot of liquor. For our citrus-themed brunch, we laced the hot chocolate with Cointreau, a very sweet triple sec–like liqueur made from the peels of bitter oranges. Other liqueurs—we're thinking especially of coffee- and chocolate-flavored cordials and even of butterscotch schnapps—also perform admirably.

SPIKED COCOA

 This recipe, which calls for Scharffen Berger sweetened cocoa powder, will fill a largish mug. Multiply it by the number of guests you're serving.

3 level tablespoons Scharffen Berger sweetened cocoa powder
2 tablespoons water
8 ounces whole milk
1 ounce Cointreau
whipped cream (optional)

In a large coffee mug, mix the cocoa powder and water together, forming a smooth paste. Heat the milk and pour it into the mug. Stir briefly and add the Cointreau, stirring again. If you're feeling especially sybaritic, top with a dollop of whipped cream.

RED-LEAF LETTUCE SALAD

This salad could not be simpler. It's almost shocking just how good fresh, crisp lettuce can be if dressed only with good-quality olive oil and (lots of) salt. You may wash the lettuce early in the morning of the day of your brunch (putting the torn-up leaves in a plastic bag in the fridge), but do not dress until just before serving.

1 large head red-leaf lettuce
¼ cup extra virgin olive oil
1 teaspoon sea salt or to taste

Wash the lettuce leaves thoroughly, spin dry, and tear them into rough pieces. Place the lettuce in a large salad bowl, pour on the oil, and sprinkle with the salt. Toss by hand until all the lettuce pieces are coated with oil. (Taste a piece; if it's not salty enough for your craven taste, add more salt and toss again.)

CARROT-FENNEL QUICHE

"Should we include a pie crust recipe in this book?" asked James. "Nah," said Ramona. "We're asking them [our beloved readers] to do so much work as it is that they'll just kill us if we tell them they have to make their own pie crust, too." So with this quiche recipe we bow to the popular will and let you use one of those pre-made pie shells you'll find in your grocer's frozen foods section. (Full disclosure: We usually opt for this time- and trouble-saver ourselves.) Note that you should double this recipe (which serves six) for a twelve-person brunch.

1 9-inch frozen pie shell
¾ cup grated carrots
¼ cup grated fennel bulb
½ cup grated medium-sharp cheddar cheese

3 large eggs
1 cup light cream
¼ teaspoon dried basil
½ teaspoon salt
¼ teaspoon freshly ground black pepper
pinch of nutmeg

Preheat the oven to 375° F. Line the base of the pie shell with a circle of parchment paper and fill it with dried beans (navy beans will do just fine). Place on a cookie sheet and bake for 15 minutes. Carefully pour the beans from the pre-baked shell (reserving them for another such use in the future), remove the parchment, and return the pie shell to the oven for another 5 minutes. After again removing the shell from the oven, reduce the oven temperature to 325° F.

Mix together the carrots, fennel, and cheese and spread this filling in the pie shell. Whisk the eggs and stir in the cream and seasonings. Pour the mixture over the filling. Bake for 35 to 40 minutes, or until a knife inserted near the center comes out clean. Let stand for 5 to 10 minutes before cutting into wedges to serve.

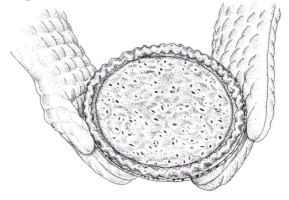

OUR HEARTS BELONG . . .

. . . to tangerines, especially in the dead of winter. Here are three twists on cocktail classics that are made even classier by their use of fresh-squeezed tangerine juice.

TANGERINE DROP

The famous cocktail known as the Lemon Drop—which, amazingly, tastes just like a lemon-drop hard candy—has long been a *Drinkology* favorite. For our citrus-drenched brunch, we tried our hand at creating a Tangerine Drop cocktail that has the same tongue-tingling mix of sweet and tart. This recipe does the trick.

small wedge of tangerine
superfine sugar
1 ounce orange-flavored vodka
1 ounce Mandarine Napoléon
1 ounce fresh-squeezed tangerine juice
½ ounce fresh lemon juice
½ ounce simple syrup
♦ half tangerine slice

Rim a chilled cocktail glass with the tangerine wedge and superfine sugar. (Discard the wedge.) Combine the liquid ingredients in a cocktail shaker, with ice. Shake well, and strain into the prepared glass. Garnish with the half-slice of tangerine. (Note: It's simple to make your own simple syrup. Mix together 2 cups granulated sugar and 1 cup water in a saucepan, and bring the mixture to a boil. Reduce the heat, and simmer—gently bubbling—for 10 minutes. Let the syrup cool, after which it may be bottled and stored in the refrigerator for up to 1 week.)

TANGERINE MIMOSA

More than any other drink besides, perhaps, the Bloody Mary, the Mimosa *means* brunch. Made with tangerine juice instead of orange juice and Mandarine Napoléon instead of triple sec, it's irresistible.

⚘ two or three mandarin orange sections
1 ounce fresh-squeezed tangerine juice
¼ ounce Mandarine Napoléon liqueur
about 5 ounces brut Champagne

Pour the tangerine juice and liqueur into a champagne flute, and drop in the mandarin sections. Now, very carefully (and tilting the flute as you do so), top with the Champagne.

LILLET MIDI

In chapter 3, we sang praises to the French aromatized wine Lillet. Here's a "midday" Lillet Blanc cocktail that snazzily complements our brunch menu. (To intensify the harmony, you might try substituting leftover juice from the ambrosia recipe for the plain tangerine juice in the recipe on page 121.)

2 ice cubes
2 tablespoons fresh-squeezed tangerine juice
3 ounces Lillet Blanc, chilled
tangerine slice

Place the ice cubes in a white wine glass. Pour in the tangerine juice and Lillet. Stir briefly, and garnish with the tangerine slice.

CHEESE SOUFFLÉ

James had always been too intimidated by soufflés to try to make one; Ramona demonstrated to him that it's not so tricky after all. This simple, flourless soufflé is (relatively speaking) a snap, though you'll have to restrain your guests from peeking in the oven as it rises. Note that you'll need to make two of these soufflés for a twelve-person brunch. (Don't just double the recipe; make the soufflés separately though simultaneously.)

softened butter
2 tablespoons grated Parmigiano Reggiano
1 cup milk
1 tablespoon cornstarch
½ teaspoon Coleman's dry mustard
½ teaspoon salt
2 large egg yolks
⅛ teaspoon freshly ground black pepper
pinch of ground cayenne pepper
pinch of freshly grated nutmeg
1 cup (4 ounces) grated Gruyère
3 large egg whites
⅛ teaspoon cream of tartar

Preheat the oven to 350° F. Butter a 6-cup soufflé dish and dust with the Parmigiano Reggiano. In a heavy, medium-size saucepan, bring ¼ cup of the milk just to a boil. Remove from the heat. In a small bowl, combine the remaining milk, the cornstarch, dry mustard, and salt; whisk into the hot milk, and cook over low heat, whisking constantly, until thickened. Remove from the heat and whisk in the egg yolks, black pepper, cayenne, and nutmeg. Mix in the Gruyère, reserving about 2 tablespoons to sprinkle on top of the soufflé about 5 minutes before it's done.

(Continues on page 119)

GIVING YOUR FOOD A BATH

Recipes for soufflés and some other eggy dishes (for example, custards, mousses, and some terrines) often require that they be baked in a water bath—or, to call it by the French term many chefs use, a *bain-marie*—to reduce the chance that the soufflé will curdle or break apart while cooking. Beginning cooks may be intimidated by the technique, though giving your food a hot bath of this sort is actually fairly easy. You must, however, be very careful not to scald yourself in the process.

To prepare a bain-marie, start by bringing several quarts of water to a boil on top of the stove.

For the "bathtub," choose a pan whose sides are 2 to 3 inches high—and one, obviously, that's wider than the dish that you'll be setting inside it. We find that a standard open roasting pan measuring about 13" x 15", with 2"-high sides, serves well in most cases. Fold a white (or color-fast) dish towel in quarters and place it on the bottom of this pan.

Once the water is boiling, the oven is preheated, and the soufflé has been prepared and is ready to bake, open the oven and pull the oven rack partway out, setting the "bathtub" pan on the rack.

Place the filled soufflé dish inside the "bathtub" (on top of the towel), and ladle or pour boiling water into the outer pan, being extremely careful not to let any hot water spill into the soufflé. Continue filling the "tub" until the water reaches a depth of 1½ to 2 inches— but not so close to the rim of the "tub" that you will have difficulty moving it without sloshing the water around. When enough water has been added, slowly push the rack back into the oven and close the door.

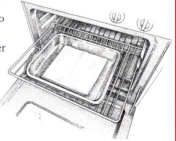

THE "BATHTUB" (WITH TOWEL) ON THE RACK

Giving Your Food a Bath

It's a good idea to keep some water gently boiling on top of the stove while the soufflé is in the oven, in case the bain-marie needs to be replenished during the later stages of baking. (Do remember that the oven door should *not* be opened during the first 20 minutes!)

The last part—removing the soufflé and the bain-marie from

THE SOUFFLÉ AWAITING ITS BATH

the oven—is the hardest and potentially most dangerous. Once you've determined that the soufflé is done, gently pull the oven rack partway out, and, taking great care to avoid scalding yourself, lift the soufflé dish from the water bath. We recommend using silicon oven mitts, which are waterproof as well as heatproof, for this procedure. If you don't need to bake something else, turn the oven off and allow the water in the bain-marie to cool before removing the larger pan from the oven.

If you *do* need to use the oven immediately, be *extremely* careful when removing the bain-marie. Make sure your sink is empty, so that you can immediately transfer the hot water–filled pan to it. Rather than pouring the hot water from the bain-marie, set the full pan on the bottom of the sink and run cold water into it, allowing it to overflow until the pan and the water inside it are cool.

ADDING THE HOT WATER

In a mixing bowl, beat the egg whites and cream of tartar until stiff but not dry. Pour the cheese mixture over the whites and gently fold together until the cheese mixture is well incorporated. Very carefully pour the batter into the prepared soufflé dish. Bake in a bain-marie filled with boiling water to a depth of about 2 inches (see the sidebar on the previous pages) for about 1 hour, or until the soufflé is very puffy and golden brown. Serve immediately. *Important: Do not disturb or open the oven for the first 20 minutes.*

CARAMELIZED BACON

As if plain bacon weren't scary enough, we're upping the ante by transforming it into what can only be described as spicy bacon *candy*. (Yum!) Note that this recipe, designed to serve twelve people, requires two jelly-roll pans; if your oven isn't big enough to accommodate both at once, bake one batch at a time. Since the caramelized bacon should not be served piping hot, it doesn't matter if the first batch cools as the second cooks.

24 slices (2 pounds) thick-sliced bacon, preferably double-smoked
1 cup packed brown sugar
4 tablespoons water *or* bourbon or sour mash whiskey
1 teaspoon ground cayenne pepper *or* Coleman's dry mustard

Preheat the oven to 375° F. Line two 10" × 15" jelly roll pans with heavy-duty aluminum foil. Spray two wire racks with nonstick cooking spray and place the racks on beds of paper towels. Cut the bacon slices in half crosswise, and arrange the pieces in a single layer on each of the wire racks. Combine the brown sugar, water (or whiskey) and cayenne (or dry mustard) in a small bowl and mix well. Brush the mixture generously over all the pieces of bacon, letting the excess drip onto the paper towels. When the dripping has more or less stopped, transfer the racks to the jelly roll pans. Bake for 20 to 25 minutes or until the bacon is very brown but not burned. Transfer to a platter and let stand for a while before serving; the bacon should be served slightly warm or at room temperature.

(Caramelized bacon can be prepared the previous day. After the bacon has been baked and allowed to cool, lay the pieces between sheets of wax paper, put them in a resealable plastic bag, and refrigerate. Before serving, let the bacon stand at room temperature for 30 to 45 minutes.)

HARICOTS VERTS WITH DIJON MUSTARD DRESSING

Haricots verts (AH-ree-koh VAIR) means "green beans" in French, but these French-style beans are leaner, greener, and more intensely flavored than garden-variety American string beans. They're also a lot pricier, but your brunch guests are worth the expense—aren't they? Clean the beans by washing them and snapping (or cutting) off their ends. The dressing accompanying this cold bean salad is quite versatile; you might also try it with, for example, cold asparagus or a mixed green salad.

1 pound haricots verts, cleaned
½ red bell pepper, sliced into strips
2 tablespoons olive oil

FOR THE DRESSING:
2 egg yolks
2 cloves garlic, pressed
¼ cup grated Parmigiano-Reggiano

1 tablespoons Dijon mustard
5 teaspoons balsamic or red wine vinegar
½ teaspoon salt
⅛ teaspoon freshly ground black pepper
⅓ to ½ cup extra-virgin olive oil

Steam the beans for 5 minutes, or until bright green and slightly tender, then plunge them immediately into an ice-water bath. Drain the beans, let them dry, and arrange on a serving platter.

Heat the 2 tablespoons of oil in a frying pan. Add the bell pepper and sauté over medium heat until softened, about 10 minutes. Remove the pepper strips from the pan, drain on a paper towel, and arrange them on top of the beans.

Make the dressing: In a large bowl, whisk together all the dressing ingredients except the oil. Add the oil in a thin stream, whisking constantly, until emulsified. Drizzle the dressing over the beans and serve.

Not-Your-Grandmother's Ambrosia

At their soirées on Olympus, the Greek gods feasted on ambrosia. No one knows just what the ancient Greeks thought ambrosia *was*, but sometime during the past fifty-odd years, some enterprising American cook presumed to solve the riddle, concocting a brightly colored amalgam—half-salad, half-dessert—that was soon showing up on church-supper sideboards everywhere. (You know the ambrosia we're talking about: canned fruit cocktail, miniature marshmallows, Cool Whip, and orange Jell-O are its primary constituents.) Now, granted, there will ever be a soft spot in our hearts (or heads?) for our grandmothers' ambrosia, but we think that *Drinkology EATS*'s tangerine brunch merits something a little more, well, divine.

FOR THE SALAD:

1½ cups shredded unsweetened coconut

½ cup blanched, sliced almonds

1 ripe pineapple

5 tangerines

2 blood oranges

2 tablespoons Cointreau, Mandarine Napoléon, or other orange or tangerine liqueur

¼ cup confectioners' sugar, sifted

½ pint fresh raspberries

 fresh mint sprigs

FOR THE DRESSING:

3 ounces cream cheese, softened

½ cup confectioners' sugar

1 cup sour cream

⅓ cup frozen tangerine or orange juice concentrate, thawed

2 tablespoons orange or tangerine liqueur

1 teaspoon tangerine zest

1 teaspoon blood-orange zest

1 teaspoon lemon zest

1 cup whipping cream

Make the salad: Preheat the oven to 325° F. Spread the coconut in a thin and even layer on a nonstick cookie sheet. Bake for 5 minutes, stir the coconut, and continue to toast for 5 to 10 more minutes or until lightly browned. Remove the cookie sheet from the oven, transfer the toasted coconut to a bowl, and set aside. Spread the almonds on the same cookie sheet and bake for 5 to 10 minutes, until lightly browned and fragrant. Remove the cookie sheet from the oven, transfer the toasted almonds to a separate bowl, and set aside. *(Continues on page 124)*

CORE CURRICULUM

Peeling and coring a pineapple with a knife can be a difficult and sloppy process—often with unsatisfactory results. Modern gadgetry has, in its mercy, supplied us with a fix: the pineapple corer. This ingenious device peels and cores a pineapple and slices it into rings, all in one corkscrew-like motion. Make sure your pineapple is ripe.

STEP 2
Set the pineapple in a shallow bowl to catch the juice. Position the corer's blade atop one of the pineapple's cut ends, and begin "screwing" it into the flesh, exerting pressure as you do so.

STEP 1
With a butcher knife, slice the top *and* bottom off the pineapple. Make sure your cuts are even and straight—and that the diameter of the circle of exposed flesh is slightly larger than that of the corer's circular plastic blade.

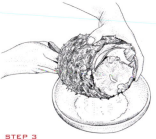

STEP 3
As the blade approaches the other end of the pineapple, lift the fruit from the bowl so that the slicing action can be fully completed. (Do hold the fruit above the bowl, to catch the remaining juice.)

STEP 4
Detach the pineapple corer's handle, which will free the blade and center post (now containing the core). Remove the blade and post and lift the pineapple shell off the flesh, which has now been sliced into a stack of perfect rings. Depending on the use, cut the rings into wedge-shaped chunks or keep whole.

Peel and core the pineapple, cutting the flesh into bite-size chunks and reserving the juice. (We prefer performing this operation using a pineapple corer; see the Technicalities sidebar on the previous page.)

Working with 1 tangerine at a time, cut a thin slice off the top and the bottom, exposing the flesh. Stand the tangerine upright and, with a sharp knife, thickly cut off the peel, following the contour of the fruit and removing all the white pith and membrane. Holding the peeled tangerine over a bowl, carefully cut along both sides of each section to free it from the membrane. As you work, discard any seeds and let the sections and juice fall into the bowl. Repeat with the remaining tangerines and the blood oranges. Pour off and reserve the juice; if necessary, add juice from the pineapple to make ½ cup. In a large bowl, combine the pineapple chunks and citrus slices. Add the almonds and 1 cup of the coconut (reserving the remainder for the garnish). Toss gently to mix well.

Combine the fruit juice, the 2 tablespoons liqueur, and the ¼ cup confectioners' sugar, stirring until sugar dissolves; pour over the fruit. Cover and chill until serving time. Garnish with additional coconut, fresh raspberries, and sprigs of mint.

Make the dressing: Beat together the cream cheese and the ½ cup confectioners' sugar. Gradually beat in the sour cream and tangerine juice concentrate. Stir in the 2 tablespoons liqueur and the citrus zests. Whip the cream and fold it into the cream cheese mixture. Serve the ambrosia with the dressing on the side.

CHAPTER SIX

Alice through the Cocktail Glass

A FOUR-MARTINI TEA

POOR ALICE. AMONG THE MANY CONSTERNATING EXCHANGES SHE suffers her way through during her visit to Wonderland is the following, which occurs during the Mad Hatter's tea party:

> "Have some wine," the March Hare said in an encouraging tone.
>
> Alice looked all round the table, but there was nothing on it but tea. "I don't see any wine," she remarked.
>
> "There isn't any," said the March Hare.
>
> "Then it wasn't very civil of you to offer it," said Alice angrily.

Don't get us wrong. We're not suggesting, even dimly, that little girls be served alcohol with their afternoon tea. Nevertheless, Alice's experience is telling. Most *adult* tea parties, nowadays, don't include alcoholic beverages among their offerings. But teatime *isn't* teetotaling-time, or needn't be, for those of drinking age. "Why, there are some young women out there who don't even *know* you can drink during tea," Ramona remarked—the outrage in her voice barely suppressed—when we were first planning this chapter. *Drinkology EATS* intends to repair that strand of cultural amnesia by offering you ideas for a "four-Martini" tea. Civility demands it.

Of course, we're also not suggesting that anyone consume as many as four Martinis in the middle of the afternoon, but simply that you present your guests with some interesting beverage options besides, or in addition to, the star attraction—which is the pot o' tea itself, dearie.

READING TEA LEAVES

Having brought it up, let's talk a little more about that pot of tea. For the tea aficionado, tea is every bit as complicated a subject as wine is for the wine connoisseur. (And it can seem just as forbidding a subject to the uninitiated.) Obviously, there isn't space in a little book like this to delve too deeply into tea leaves' arcane mysteries, but there are just a few things of an elementary sort that you might like to know.

The first is that, properly speaking, *tea* is a beverage made by infusing the leaves of the tea plant *(Thea sinensis)* in hot water. Under this definition, tea does not include any of the so-called herb teas—chamomile, peppermint, rose hips, and all the rest. Now, *Drinkology EATS* has nothing against these herbal infusions; in fact, we often resort to a cup of chamomile to calm our agitated nerves at the end of a stressful day. But herb "teas" are *not* tea, and, in our rigid and uncompromising view, they shouldn't be served at an afternoon tea party.

Second: There are, on the most basic level, four different kinds of tea, which differ according to how the tea leaves are processed. These are *white tea, green tea, oolong tea,* and *black tea.* White and green teas are unfermented, which means that the leaves (or, in the case of white tea, the leaf buds) are dried soon after picking and before they begin to oxidize. In recent years, white and green teas have become fashionable among the health-conscious set because both contain high levels of various antioxidant compounds and are thus touted as good preventive medicine against heart disease, cancer, and the depredations of age. That may well be, but white and green teas make unsuitable beverages for an afternoon tea party, because their taste is simply too subtle and mild to stand up to the food. (That said, we do offer a recipe for a Martini incorporating green tea—our possibly disingenuous nod to healthy living. See the Bar Associations sidebar on page 150.)

Oolong tea is semi-fermented

The leaves used in oolong and black teas *are* allowed to ferment before being dried, though because oolong's fermentation is interrupted after just a few hours it is often referred to as "semi-fermented." Fermentation, whether briefer (for oolong) or longer (for black tea), darkens the tea leaves' color and emboldens their flavor. Moreover, both oolong and black teas are forcibly dried through a baking process called *firing*, which usually involves subjecting the partly or fully fermented leaves to a stream of hot air.

Because they are fermented and fired, oolong and black teas are much more powerful and complex than white and green teas, so you should choose either an oolong or a black tea—or, better, a selection of several oolongs and/or black teas—to serve at your tea party. Note, however, that the concentration of caffeine—a natural constituent of tea— is higher in oolong and *much* higher in black tea than it is in white or green tea. If any of your guests are averse to caffeine, you might consider including a decaffeinated black tea among your offerings.

And, now, a confession: Having advised you to choose oolong or black teas for your party, we must add that we've told you almost *nothing*.

Remember how we were saying that tea is a complicated subject? Boy, howdy. Besides being distinguished by processing method, teas are also classified by *leaf grades* (a topic too intricate to deal with here) and—of great importance—by where the tea is grown. The tea bush is as sensitive as the grapevine to what wine snobs call *terroir*—which embraces all those variables of soil, climate, weather, altitude, and so on that make every agricultural estate (of whatever kind) unique. Teas are therefore sometimes named for the places they come from: A Kenya tea (from that East African nation) tastes different from a Darjeeling tea (from northeastern India), which tastes different from an Assam tea (from India's far-northeastern Assam province), which, in turn, tastes different from a Ceylon tea (from the island of Sri Lanka, formerly Ceylon). These are all black teas, but the principle also extends to oolongs: A Formosa oolong—from Taiwan, formerly known as Formosa—is in many respects unlike an oolong from the Chinese mainland, though here the differences result from specific processing techniques as well as growing conditions.

That different subspecies of the *Thea sinensis* plant are grown in different regions also affects teas' flavors. And (as if all this weren't enough to contend with) there's also the fact that many teas are *blends*—of various grades of leaf, of teas from various places, and sometimes of tea(s) and other ingredients. Familiar tea monikers such as English Breakfast, Earl Grey, Irish Breakfast, and Russian Caravan all indicate traditional kinds of blends: Earl Grey, for example, is usually a blend of China tea, Darjeeling tea, and the peel of an orange-like citrus fruit called the bergamot. And need we mention that different tea merchants style their blends differently—that the Earl Grey tea made by Twinings of London tastes subtly different from the Earl Grey tea made by Taylors of Harrogate? (We thought not.)

"Stop! Enough! I just want a bloody pot of tea!" We hear (and acknowledge) your irate yet pitiful cry, and we *will,* we promise, bring this lecture to a close—in just a sec. But we need to mention just one thing more: that, these days, there's a growing interest among the tea cognoscenti in what are called *single-estate teas.* These premium teas—you might pay fifteen to twenty dollars for a couple of ounces—are the polar opposite of blends. Because tea is a natural product, the flavor of the tea from a particular plantation will naturally vary from harvest to harvest; in blending teas, a tea merchant's goal is to achieve consistency of taste over the long haul. But the rage for single-estate teas celebrates—and makes a virtue of—the horticultural variability.

Single-estate teas are all the rage

So, is tea yet another field of gustatory knowledge designed to humiliate you and make you feel inadequate? Well, you could look at it that way, and stick to the Lipton's. But—assuming you like tea—you might do as *Drinkology EATS* does, and happily experiment. For the tea party we put together when researching this book, James chatted up the proprietor of a local coffee and tea shop. At his urging, James chose a couple of those vaunted single-estate teas (a Darjeeling and an Assam), as well as the shop's own Russian Caravan blend. Knowledgeable tea merchants are a godsend to the tea neophyte; if you're lucky enough to live in a city with good tea shops, take advantage of their staffs' expertise. A little bit of reading will also help you gear up for your tea adventures; Jane Pettigrew's *The Tea Companion* (Running Press, 2004) provides basic background and contains an extremely enlightening tea "atlas," with photos illustrating how various teas look in leaf form and showing their colors when brewed.

BRITANNIA RULES

The Brits, who invented the meal known as afternoon tea, adhere to a strict set of rules regarding how tea is to be prepared, and *Drinkology EATS* is not about to question the received wisdom. (Well, mostly not.)

First off, you *must* use loose tea—not teabags! (The paper boxes in which teabags are sold don't preserve tea's freshness very well, and the smaller tea leaves generally used in teabags infuse almost immediately, depriving the tea of the richness that results when a tea is steeped for several minutes.)

Second, make sure you empty your kettle and refill it with fresh, cold water from the tap. (The oxygen dissolved in tap water is a plus, so don't use bottled water.) Set the kettle on high heat, and just before it reaches a boil, pour some of the hot water into your teapot. Slosh it around to warm the entire inside of the pot, then pour it out. True tea lovers insist on this step, pointing out that pre-warming the pot will prevent the temperature from dropping too precipitously (thus retarding infusion) when the boiling water is added to the pot a moment later.

Setting the kettle back on the stove, bring the water to a galloping (as they say) boil. As the water heats, put the loose tea directly into the teapot, measuring out 1 heaping teaspoon of tea for each cup your teapot holds, plus one extra "for the pot." Note that *cup,* here, doesn't mean a standard cup measure but rather the amount held by a typical teacup or mug—usually about ¾ cup. Filled, *Drinkology EATS*'s beloved,

THE BELOVED FRANKOMA POT

HOW LONG TO STEEP?

appealingly homely Frankoma teapot holds about 5 standard cups, which equals 6-plus teacups' worth of brewed tea. We therefore add 7 teaspoons of loose tea to the pot. You'll be wise to measure your own teapot's volume beforehand, then calculate the amount of loose tea required.

An aside: We know that the water's just about to boil, and we'll get right back to it, but we can hear you asking, "I should put the tea directly into the pot? Shouldn't I use a tea ball?" Quick answer: No, you shouldn't. If your teapot includes an insertable infuser, do use it, by all means. But don't put the tea in a wire-mesh ball, which will compact the moistened leaves as they swell, interfering with infusion. Sure, the loose leaves make for a bit of a mess, but you can strain the tea as you pour it, and it's not all that big a deal to empty the pot of the wet leaves once all the tea's been poured. Now, back to the program:

As soon as it reaches that galloping boil, pour the water into the teapot. Don't let it continue to boil for more than a few seconds. The tea experts claim that allowing the water to keep on boiling rids it of oxygen, and that de-oxygenated water "results in a bitter muddy brew." (The quote comes from *The London Ritz Book of Afternoon Tea,* and we can't imagine a more authoritative authority.)

The water's in the pot, the teapot's lid is back in place, and now the tea must steep. But for how long? Well, the proper steeping time differs from tea to tea, depending on the size of the leaves. Commercial tea tins' labels usually include recommended steeping times, but if your tea tin doesn't say—or you're using tea sold loose by the tea shop—take a stab at 5 minutes. (If the tea leaves seem very small, test the strength of the tea after 3 minutes.) Once the tea's steeped—and assuming your pot doesn't have an infuser—pour it through a tea strainer into the cups. (The drawings opposite and below show strainers of two types: the ornate, old-fashioned sort and a modern, plainly functional sieve.)

Apparently, tea is never served with lemon in Great Britain—milk or light cream only. And some authorities insist that the milk or cream be poured into the cup *before* the tea. Some Brits also look askance at those who take sugar in their tea. ("Sugar is not fashionable any more," declares the haughty Gwendolen to the bumpkinesque Cicely in Oscar Wilde's *Importance of Being Earnest*.) But on these matters of what seem to us purely personal taste, *Drinkology EATS* must finally issue a declaration of independence. If your guests want lemon, give them lemon. If they want sugar, sugar they shall have.

Tea for Two + Two + Two

As traditionally structured, tea is a three-course mini-meal served at around four o'clock in the afternoon. Note, by the way, that afternoon tea is not at all the same thing as *high tea,* which is a more substantial, early-evening meal. Tea—*afternoon* tea—was created and popularized by nineteenth-century upper-class British women who felt the need for just a little something to stave off the hunger pangs that descended upon them between lunch and dinner. (Though how those tightly corseted Victorian dames managed to eat four meals a day is beyond us.) High tea, by contrast (and despite its elevated-sounding name), is an earthy, working-class supper. That *high,* in this case, equals *low* on the social totem pole is something that Americans find impossibly difficult to understand (just as we're stymied by the fact that "public schools," in Great Britain, aren't public at all). But do try to get the upside-down-seeming terminology right side up.

A traditional tea could be viewed, uncharitably, as an exercise in carb-loading. The three courses consist of (1) mostly starch, in the form of savory sandwiches; (2) more starch, in the form of tea breads and tea cakes; and (3) yet more starch, in the form of sweet desserts. Now, tea is definitely among our favorite meals (we're also very fond of breakfast, lunch, dinner, and assorted snacks), but we've got to admit that a traditional tea party is not the sort of gathering to which you'd want to invite a friend who's struggling to stick with the South Beach diet.

A tea party is also a rather intimate affair: a time for a few good friends to get together and chew the fat (or, rather, the starch), gossiping uproariously about everyone who wasn't invited. (Mad Hatters ourselves, we don't much like tea parties at which everyone speaks demurely, in polite, hushed tones.) We thus advise you to limit your tea party to no more than six people.

We're going to give you *lots* of suggestions about what you might serve—especially for the first (and, we think, most interesting) course. But don't forget that tea is supposed to be a *small* meal: a small guest-list and a small number of dishes served in small portions. We recommend that, in planning your tea, you choose two or, at the most, three dishes for the first course (perhaps tea eggs, one vegetable-filled sandwich, and one salad-filled sandwich), one or two breads/cakes for the second, and a single dessert for the third. If you're feeling lazy, you might substitute a plain, good bread and an herbed butter or cream cheese for one of the savory sandwiches. If you're feeling especially energetic, you might want to wow your guests with a fresh marmalade (we provide two recipes—one savory, one sweet).

And please don't forget the Martinis: The tea will stimulate your guests' minds; the Martinis will lubricate their wicked tongues.

THE FIRST COURSE: SAVORY SANDWICHES (MOSTLY)

Ask most people what they'd expect to be served at a British-style tea, and they'll doubtless answer: cucumber and watercress sandwiches. These are, in fact, standards, but they hardly exhaust the possibilities when it comes to what you might offer your guests for the tea's first course. In the pages that follow, you'll find recipes for the requisite vegetable-filled sandwiches; for numerous other sandwich fillings, including vegetable- , meat- , and seafood-based salads; and for butter and cream cheese spreads. (We're also including a recipe for one non-sandwich-related delicacy—tea eggs.)

When making salads to fill tea sandwiches, it's crucial that all the ingredients be chopped fine so that the salads can be spread across the bread in a thin, even layer. (We might also mention that any of the salad recipes presented in this chapter would perform well as an ingredient in a cocktail-party canapé.)

Tea sandwiches—often referred to as *finger sandwiches*—are of an entirely different sandwich genus from the grilled pastrami-and-cole slaw monstrosities served by the Carnegie Deli and similar establishments. They're delicate, crustless, and usually Lilliputian in dimension. The Technicalities sidebar on the next page illustrates a classic method for preparing finger sandwiches that begins with a whole, uncut loaf of bread. But you can certainly use pre-sliced bread—thin-sliced white bread works especially well. No matter which kind of bread you're using, fill the sandwich first, then cut off the crusts. Then, aiming at the highest level of geometrical perfection your delirium tremens–ravaged hands can attain, slice the crustless sandwich into smaller, rectangle- or triangle-shaped sandwiches. Finger sandwiches can, with the aid of a biscuit cutter, even be cut into circle shapes; if you attempt this, freeze the (thin-)sliced bread first, spread the filling on the frozen slices, and then apply the biscuit cutter. The stiffness of the frozen bread will prevent crumbling—and the thin-sliced bread will, of course, thaw within a few minutes.

Cucumber Sandwiches

This is the sine qua non of tea sandwiches. James well remembers the first time he had cucumber sandwiches: at a tea party celebrating the Queen's birthday, thrown by an Anglican clergyman who was, himself, a British queen. What follows is Ramona's recipe, which calls for an English hothouse cucumber—one of those long and very dark green

(Continues on page 139)

SLICING YOUR FINGER (SANDWICHES, THAT IS)

Sandwich chefs at British tea establishments (like the Palm Court at London's Ritz Hotel) employ a method similar to that described below in fashioning their tea sandwiches, though they work with specially baked extra-long loaves of bread. For your tea sandwiches, try to find what are called *Pullman* loaves. (Buy them unsliced, of course.) Pullman loaves are doubly advantageous: Baked in rectangular tins, they have square corners and flat sides, and because the tins are covered during baking, the crusts of Pullman loaves are softer than those of most other breads, which makes the job of slicing easier. White Pullman loaves are carried by many bakeries; it's also possible to find whole wheat Pullman loaves and some-times other varieties, such as the raisin Pullman loaf shown in the draw-ings. The finger sandwiches we're making here have the nutted cheese filling whose recipe you'll find on page 160, but the sandwich-making method is the same for any finger sandwich, savory or sweet.

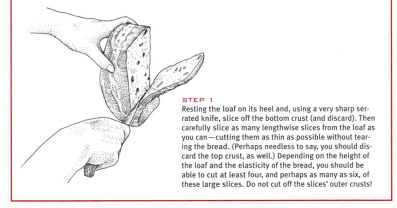

STEP 1
Resting the loaf on its heel and, using a very sharp ser-rated knife, slice off the bottom crust (and discard). Then carefully slice as many lengthwise slices from the loaf as you can—cutting them as thin as possible without tear-ing the bread. (Perhaps needless to say, you should dis-card the top crust, as well.) Depending on the height of the loaf and the elasticity of the bread, you should be able to cut at least four, and perhaps as many as six, of these large slices. Do not cut off the slices' outer crusts!

Slicing Your Finger (Sandwiches)

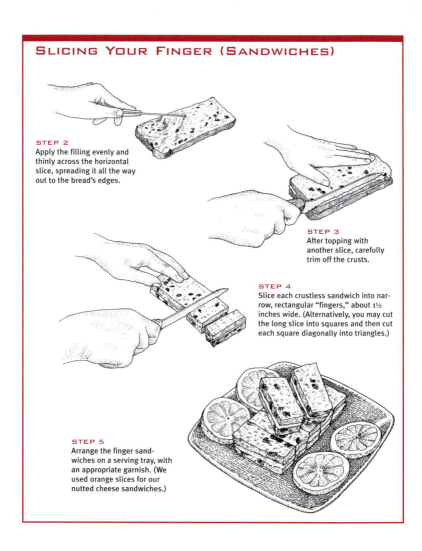

STEP 2
Apply the filling evenly and thinly across the horizontal slice, spreading it all the way out to the bread's edges.

STEP 3
After topping with another slice, carefully trim off the crusts.

STEP 4
Slice each crustless sandwich into narrow, rectangular "fingers," about 1½ inches wide. (Alternatively, you may cut the long slice into squares and then cut each square diagonally into triangles.)

STEP 5
Arrange the finger sandwiches on a serving tray, with an appropriate garnish. (We used orange slices for our nutted cheese sandwiches.)

cukes that come shrink-wrapped in plastic and that, being thin-skinned and nearly seedless, are just right for this purpose. Ramona also likes to marinate the cucumber slices in rice wine vinegar, whose bite is less stinging than other vinegars', though you may use white vinegar instead.

1 hothouse cucumber
3 tablespoons rice wine vinegar
½ teaspoon fine sea salt
whole wheat bread
unsalted butter, softened
fresh parsley sprigs

Peel the cucumber. Using a very sharp knife or a vegetable peeler (see drawing), slice it into paper-thin slices. (You should end up with about 1½ cups.) Place the cucumber slices in a medium-size glass or ceramic bowl and sprinkle with the vinegar and salt. Let stand for 20 to 30 minutes, until the slices are soft.

Drain the cucumbers. Butter a slice of bread and cover it with two layers of cucumber slices. Top with another buttered slice (buttered side down!). Using the palm of your hand, press down on the sandwich gently but firmly to flatten it slightly. Using a very sharp serrated knife, trim the crusts and cut the sandwich into bars or triangles. Repeat with additional slices of bread. Arrange finger sandwiches on a serving plate and garnish each with a sprig of parsley.

VARIATION: RADISH SANDWICHES

Radishes—sliced ultra-thin and marinated in vinegar and salt—make for an unexpected and interesting variation. Because the marinated radishes are, surprisingly, milder in flavor than cucumbers, use white bread rather than whole wheat for these sandwiches.

2 bunches medium-size radishes (12 to 14)
3 tablespoons rice wine vinegar
½ teaspoon fine sea salt
white bread
unsalted butter, softened
fresh parsley sprigs

Cut off the radishes' tops and roots and wash the radishes thoroughly. Using a very sharp knife, slice them into paper-thin slices. (You should end up with about 1½ cups.) Place the radish slices in a medium-size glass or ceramic bowl and sprinkle with the vinegar and salt. Let stand for 20 to 30 minutes, until the slices are soft.

Drain the radishes. Butter a slice of bread and cover it with two layers of radish slices. Top with another buttered slice (buttered side down!). Using the palm of your hand, press down on the sandwich gently but firmly to flatten it slightly. Using a very sharp serrated knife, trim the crusts and cut the sandwich into bars or triangles. Repeat with additional slices of bread. Arrange finger sandwiches on a serving plate, and garnish each with a sprig of parsley.

WATERCRESS SANDWICHES

Prepared properly, watercress sandwiches are—as tea sandwiches go—almost barbarous. You don't need to trim the breadcrusts, and it's perfectly OK if the watercress leaves stick out beyond the sandwiches' edges. Make special note of the fact that you should use *salted* butter on these.

1 bunch watercress
6 slices dark rye or pumpernickel bread
salted butter, softened

Wash the watercress thoroughly and spin it dry in a salad spinner. Remove the larger stems. Butter the bread slices. Distribute the watercress on three of the slices, and top these with the other three slices. Using the palm of your hand, press down on each sandwich gently but firmly to flatten it slightly. Slice each sandwich in half and arrange the halves on a serving plate.

ROASTED BEET SANDWICH SPREAD

Its toothy flavor and luscious, wine-dark color makes this spread an especially inviting filling for finger sandwiches made with dark breads—whole wheat or pumpernickel.

1 small beet (about 2 inches in diameter), peeled
1 teaspoon extra-virgin olive oil
6 ounces goat cheese, softened
2 ounces cream cheese, softened
½ teaspoon freshly ground black pepper
salt to taste

Place the beet in a microwaveable bowl with the oil. Roll the beet to coat it with oil. Cover with plastic wrap and microwave on high power for 3 to 5 minutes or until tender. Let the beet cool, then finely mince it, reserving any liquid given off during cooking. (You should end up with about ½ cup minced beets.)

In a small bowl, mix the beets and cooking liquid with the rest of the ingredients. Let stand, covered, until ready to use. (Color and flavor will improve if the spread stands for at least 1 hour.) The spread can be made a day ahead and stored in the refrigerator. If you chill it, let it soften at room temperature and stir well before using.

ALICE B. TOKLAS'S
MUSHROOM SANDWICH SPREAD

In the years following her companion Gertrude Stein's death, Alice B. Toklas found herself running out of money. She couldn't bear to part with any of the Picassos Stein had bequeathed to her (really, who could?), so she wrote a cookbook. Published in 1954, and most famous for the hashish fudge scandalously included among its recipes, *The Alice B. Toklas Cookbook* is a literary and culinary masterpiece, though of a decidedly peculiar sort. (The recipes, for example, are sometimes sketchy when it comes to specific ingredients and the amounts and cooking times required.) Adapting Miss Toklas's instructions, James created the following sandwich spread. Note that the mushrooms are of the cremini, not the psilocybin, variety.

3 large cremini mushrooms, cleaned, stemmed, and finely chopped
3 tablespoons butter
1 tablespoon fresh lemon juice
1 scrambled egg
1 tablespoon grated Parmigiano-Reggiano
¼ teaspoon salt
pinch of ground cayenne pepper

In a small saucepan over medium-low heat, sauté the mushrooms in 1 tablespoon of the butter and the lemon juice until most of the liquid has evaporated, 6 to 8 minutes. Remove from the heat and let cool. Place the sautéed mushrooms, remaining 2 tablespoons butter, the scrambled egg, cheese, salt, and cayenne pepper in a blender and pulse until smooth. Use on sandwiches made with white bread.

Carrot-Ginger Sandwich Spread

It seems fitting to offer you a tea sandwich filling that incorporates fresh ginger, since ginger's such a favored ingredient in British cookery.

2 medium-size carrots, finely grated
2 tablespoons cream cheese, softened
2 tablespoons mayonnaise
¼ teaspoon grated fresh ginger
salt and freshly ground black pepper to taste

In a small bowl, combine all the ingredients and mix well. Use on sandwiches made with white or whole wheat bread.

Ham Salad

Ham salad is so good, we wonder why we encounter it so seldom. Any strong-flavored cooked ham will work well in this recipe.

1 cup cooked ham, coarsely chopped
½ cup mayonnaise
1 tablespoon hot brown mustard
2 teaspoons chopped sweet pickle or drained sweet relish
½ teaspoon freshly grated horseradish
pinch of freshly ground black pepper

Place the ham in a food processor and pulse until finely chopped. Transfer to a medium-size bowl, add the rest of the ingredients, and mix well. Use on sandwiches made with white, whole wheat, or rye bread.

Tarragon Chicken Salad

We believe that the Deity created tarragon knowing, in gracious omnis-cience, that the progeny of Adam and Eve would someday get around to inventing chicken salad. There's simply no herb that suits chicken better.

1½ cups cooked chicken breast, finely chopped
¼ cup mayonnaise
¼ cup sour cream
1½ teaspoons Dijon mustard
1½ teaspoons fresh lemon juice
1 tablespoon minced celery
1 tablespoon finely chopped fresh tarragon
1 tablespoon minced onion
1 tablespoon finely chopped water chestnuts
salt and freshly ground white pepper to taste

Combine all the ingredients in a medium-size bowl and mix well. Cover and refrigerate for at least 1 hour before serving. (Overnight is better.) Use on sandwiches made with white or whole wheat bread.

Salmon Salad

Among the biggest hits at *Drinkology EATS*'s tea party was the salmon salad. Made with fresh (not canned) salmon, it's delectable.

1 pound salmon fillet

FOR THE POACHING LIQUID:

2 cups water
½ cup dry white wine
1 tablespoon fresh lemon juice
1 carrot
1 celery stalk

½ small onion
1 small clove garlic, crushed
1 bay leaf
1 teaspoon salt
¼ teaspoon whole black peppercorns

FOR THE DRESSING:
½ cup sour cream
¼ cup mayonnaise
2 tablespoons minced celery
2 tablespoons minced fresh dill
2 teaspoons fresh lemon juice
1 teaspoon freshly grated horseradish
⅛ teaspoon sweet paprika
salt and freshly ground white pepper to taste

fresh dill sprigs

Poach the salmon: Put the water, wine, lemon juice, and the rest of the poaching-liquid ingredients in a medium-size saucepan and bring to a boil over medium-high heat. Reduce the heat to medium low, cover, and simmer for 5 minutes. Add the salmon fillet, cover, and poach for 5 minutes. Remove the pan from the heat and let the salmon cool completely in the poaching liquid, at least 1 hour. (You may do this up to 2 days ahead; if you do so, store the cooled, covered pan in the refrigerator; do not remove the salmon from the liquid during this time.)

Make the salad: Remove the salmon from the poaching liquid. Remove any skin and the dark, oily meat from the skin side of the fillet and discard. Flake the fish into a medium-size bowl, being careful to remove any bones. Add all of the dressing ingredients and mix well. Use on sandwiches made with white bread, garnishing with dill sprigs.

Shrimp Salad with Fennel

Because Ramona's and James's enthusiasm for shrimp knows no bounds (see page 70), we propose three shrimp salad variations. As we've said elsewhere, licorice and anise flavors marry exceedingly well with shrimp, and so this first shrimp salad incorporates ground fennel seeds as well as the New Orleans anise-flavored liqueur called Herbsaint. (You may substitute Pernod or anisette.)

½ pound medium to large shrimp, cooked, peeled, deveined, and coarsely chopped
4 generous tablespoons mayonnaise
1 teaspoon Herbsaint or other anise-flavored liqueur
½ teaspoon ground fennel seeds
salt to taste
fresh dill sprigs

Place the shrimp in a food processor and pulse until finely chopped. Transfer to a medium-size mixing bowl; add the mayonnaise, Herbsaint, and fennel and mix well. Taste before adding salt. Use on sandwiches made with white bread, garnishing the serving plate with dill sprigs.

Curried Shrimp Salad

Shrimp is so promiscuous. It marries well with anise, but can also carry on a splendidly passionate affair with curry.

½ pound medium to large shrimp, cooked, peeled, deveined, and coarsely chopped
4 generous tablespoons mayonnaise
2 generous teaspoons sweet pickle relish
1 teaspoon hot Madras curry powder
salt to taste
gherkins

Place the shrimp in a food processor and pulse until finely chopped. Transfer to a medium-size mixing bowl; add the mayonnaise, relish, and curry powder and mix well. Taste before adding salt. Use on sandwiches made with white bread, garnishing the serving plate with gherkins.

SUMMER SHRIMP SALAD

In the shrimp romance department, this salad's the high-school sweetheart. Not at all exotic—just wholesome, fresh, and good.

½ pound medium to large shrimp, cooked, peeled, deveined, and coarsely chopped
4 generous tablespoons mayonnaise
2 tablespoons finely minced celery
½ teaspoon Dijon mustard
¼ teaspoon celery seed
salt to taste
fresh parsley sprigs

Place the shrimp in a food processor and pulse until finely chopped. Transfer to a medium-size mixing bowl; add the mayonnaise, celery, mustard, and celery seed and mix well. Taste before adding salt. Use on sandwiches made with white bread, garnishing the serving plate with parsley sprigs.

MARBLED TEA EGGS

At last—a teatime recipe that doesn't involve making sandwiches. With an appearance that can fairly be described as bizarre, marbled tea eggs will add a visually interesting touch to your first-course spread. The subtle smoky-savory flavor is also quite appealing. Do note that the eggs must be cooked a day ahead of time.

12 eggs

¼ cup soy sauce

3 tablespoons loose black tea, such as Russian Caravan

1 tablespoon orange or tangerine zest

2 teaspoons salt

1 teaspoon five-spice powder

2 whole star anise pods

Cook the eggs according to the instructions for our all-but-foolproof hard-boiled eggs (see page 26). When the eggs have finished cooking, transfer the pot to the sink and run cold water into it, letting it overflow until the water in the pot is cold. Let the eggs cool in the water for several minutes, then drain.

Using the back of a spoon, gently and finely crack each egg's shell all over. (This is called "crazing" the eggs.) Place the crazed eggs back in the pot and add water to cover by 1 inch. Add the rest of the ingredients to the pot and bring to a boil over high heat. Reduce the heat to low, cover, and simmer for 1½ to 2 hours. (Check the pot frequently. If the water level drops so that the eggs are exposed, add boiling water to cover them.)

Remove the pot from the heat and let stand overnight. Before serving, remove the eggs from the liquid and gently peel them. They may be served whole or sliced into halves or wedges. Serve with small bowls of salt, for dipping.

Sweet Mint Butter

Several scenes of Oscar Wilde's eternally hilarious play *The Importance of Being Earnest* are enacted over afternoon tea. One scene includes the following exchange between Jack Worthing's ward, Cecily Cardew, and his fiancée, Gwendolen Fairfax:

Cecily. [Severely.] Cake or bread and butter?
Gwendolen. [In a bored manner.] Bread and butter, please. Cake is rarely seen at the best houses nowadays.

If you're feeling indolent—*aristocratically* indolent—do take Gwendolen's cue and serve your guests bread and butter as one of the first-course (or, for that matter, second-course) offerings. But serve it with something more engaging than plain butter—perhaps, for instance, this sweetened herb butter:

½ cup (1 stick) salted butter, softened
¼ cup finely chopped fresh mint (black peppermint, if available)
1 tablespoon confectioners' sugar

In a small bowl, mix all the ingredients well. Let the minted butter stand at room temperature for 1 hour before serving. Serve with sliced white bread.

HERBED CREAM CHEESE
Or if not an herbed butter, then an herbed cream cheese.

1 (8-ounce) package cream cheese, softened
2 tablespoons finely chopped fresh parsley
1 tablespoon finely chopped fresh chives
1 tablespoon finely chopped fresh dill *or* mint
1 tablespoon finely chopped fresh tarragon leaves *or* chervil
½ teaspoon finely grated lemon zest
pinch of freshly ground white pepper
pinch of sweet paprika
salt to taste

In a small bowl, mix all the ingredients except the salt. Taste before salting. Let the herbed cheese stand at room temperature for 1 hour before serving.

MarTEAnis

So what does the word *Martini* even mean, these days? Well, for good or ill, depending on your perspective, pretty much anything. Back when he was writing this series' first volume, *Drinkology: The Art and Science of the Cocktail,* James adhered to a conservative, fairly hard-line view regarding the Martini: A Martini had to be a drink composed of gin or vodka—preferably gin—and a small amount of dry vermouth. (The amount could be very small, but the vermouth had to *be there.*) It had to be a stirred—not a shaken—drink. It had, of course, to be served "up," in a cocktail glass (a.k.a. Martini glass). And it had to be garnished with an olive (or olives) or a lemon twist. Advancing age, which has brought with it either wisdom or addlepatededness (or maybe a touch of both), has weakened James's convictions.

To a certain extent. He's still of the mind that a Martini should include gin or vodka and be served in a cocktail glass. But the foundations of his formerly stalwart philosophy are crumbling fast. (Witness the Aquavit Martini on page 59.) Where shall it all end? Will the day come when James walks into a tavern, sidles up to the bar, and orders an *amaretto* Martini? A *Galliano* Martini? Hopefully, Ramona will be there to blockade the barroom door, but stay tuned.

In the meantime, here are four "Martinis" (or Martini-like cocktails) that James thinks just might complement your afternoon tea.

ORANGE GIN

This cocktail is a variation on the classic British drink called Pink Gin. Pink Gin uses angostura bitters; our Orange Gin calls for orange bitters instead. (The orangeness, by the way, resides more in the subtle flavor than in the color: At this proportion, the bitters barely color the drink.)

about 1 teaspoon orange bitters
3 ounces gin
🍷 ½ orange slice

Chill the gin in the freezer for several hours before serving. Pour the bitters into a chilled cocktail glass, then slowly and carefully tilt and swirl the glass until the entire interior is coated. Discard any excess bitters. Pour in the gin. Garnish with the orange slice.

THE SAKE-TINI

There are many tea-drinking nations (Turkey, Russia, and so on), but only two that have elevated the serving of tea to an art form—Britain and, of course, Japan. This pristine, almost ascetic cocktail combines these tea-loving countries' *alcoholic* contributions to world culture.

🍷 lemon twist
2½ ounces London dry gin
¼ ounce very dry sake

Rim a chilled cocktail glass with the twist and drop the twist into the glass. Fill a mixing glass with ice, pour in the gin and sake, and stir. Strain into the cocktail glass.

MarTEAnis

The Reverse Martini

This cocktail will doubtless drive dry-Martini lovers to drink. But if you can conquer your prejudices, you might just enjoy it. (It was, by the way, one of Julia Child's favorite aperitifs.) Do make sure that the vermouth is *very* fresh (preferably from a just-opened bottle).

2 ounces dry vermouth
½ ounce gin
♣ 2 or 3 olives

Fill a mixing glass with ice, pour in the vermouth and gin, and stir. Strain into a chilled cocktail glass. Garnish with the olives.

The Green-tea-ni

Drinkology EATS's taste testers loudly expressed a derisive and hurtful skepticism when James announced he would create a Martini employing green tea in place of the vermouth. Yeah, well, they all laughed at Hershey and his chocolate bar, too. The drink is spectacular.

♣ lemon twist
2½ ounces gin
½ ounce brewed, chilled green tea

Rim a chilled cocktail glass with the twist and drop the twist into the glass. Fill a mixing glass with ice, pour in the gin and tea, and stir. Strain into the glass.

Note that all these (so-called?) Martini recipes are calibrated for standard-size cocktail glasses, which hold about four ounces if filled to the absolute brim. Frankly, we don't think that most cocktails ought to be larger than that—and especially not ones served in the afternoon, at tea. In fact, Ramona suggests that you might consider serving your tea-time cocktails in even smaller glasses. "Standard" cocktail glasses used to be substantially smaller than they are today—holding only two or three ounces. You can occasionally find sets of these teeny-Martini glasses at antiques shops and flea markets, and they're perfect for tea-time portions. If you use smaller glasses, measure their volume and adjust the recipes accordingly.

You might also want to prepare batches of Martinis in advance of the tea party. You can't do that with the Orange Gin, of course—that drink must be made individually—but the other cocktails in this sidebar can, except for the rimming and garnishing of the glasses, be mixed up an hour or two before the event. Multiply the ingredients by the number of cocktails you want to serve, mix them in a glass pitcher, and refrigerate. Just before serving, add a tray's worth of ice cubes to the pitcher and stir well before straining into the glasses. The small amount of water that the ice cubes release is an essential component—increasing the cocktail's volume slightly and slightly weakening its strength—so don't forgo this crucial step.

THE SECOND COURSE:
TEA BREADS AND CAKES (MOSTLY)

As we've said, an afternoon tea's second course generally consists of tea breads and (not-too-sweet) tea cakes. The best-known of the traditional tea breads are English muffins, crumpets, and scones. To tell you the truth, we've tried our hand at several, and we just *cannot* find a recipe that produces English muffins that are anywhere near as good as the ones you can buy in the bread section of your supermarket. Our crumpet recipe, in chapter 4 (see page 97), is just dandy for afternoon tea, however. (Remember that the crumpets can be prepared ahead of time—can even be frozen—and then toasted just before serving.) And the scones recipe we provide in this section is, frankly, to die for. English muffins, crumpets, and scones should all be served with butter and/or clotted cream (available at British groceries and other specialty shops)—*and*, of course, with marmalade. Our recipes for the second course include a sweet-but-savory onion marmalade (suitable for spreading on muffins or crumpets) and a liqueur-laden orange marmalade (suitable for spreading on any of the tea breads).

The tea cake we offer is of a very traditional kind—Madeira cake, it's called. And then we offer one more recipe—for nutted-cheese sandwiches. Although these are, indeed, sandwiches, they're delicately sweet, and seem to us therefore to belong to the second rather than the first course.

Again, we advise you to be chary with the number of dishes. For the second course, serve your guests one kind of tea bread and one other offering—either the tea cake or the nutted-cheese sandwiches. Both the marmalades require a lot of work; undertake making a marmalade *only* if you have time to spare during the days preceding your party.

ONION MARMALADE

Don't faint dead away. We're not about to try to teach you how to "put up" marmalade. (Though Ramona, good country girl that she once was, did recently instruct James in the rudiments of canning—but where in his tiny apartment he'll put all the jams, jellies, and pickles he wants to make remains an open question.) The truth is, if you're making a relatively small amount, there's no need to go to the trouble of processing the marmalade in Mason jars. Simply put the finished, cooled marmalade in a covered container, stick it in the fridge, and try to consume all of it within a few weeks— same as you would an opened jar of store-bought marmalade. (When mold forests its surface, it's no good.) This savory onion marmalade makes a sensational spread for English muffins or crumpets. (It is also a superb accompaniment to roasted meats—lamb and pork, especially.)

10 black peppercorns, cracked
½ cinnamon stick
3 whole cloves
3 whole star anise pods
2 bay leaves
2 small dried chile peppers
1 cardamom pod
3 large onions, finely chopped
1½ cups red wine vinegar
1½ cups sugar
½ teaspoon salt
zest and juice of 1 orange

Place the first seven ingredients in a large tea ball or tie them in a cheesecloth bag. Place this sachet along with all the other ingredients in a nonreactive, heavy-bottomed pot. Bring to a boil over high heat, then reduce the heat to low and simmer until almost all the liquid has evaporated, about 2 hours. Stir occasionally during the first hour of cooking, but watch the pot closely and stir more frequently during the final hour, especially during the last 15 minutes. During the last 5 minutes of cooking, when the liquid has become a syrup, stir constantly. As soon as the mixture has thickened to marmalade consistency, remove the pot from the heat. Discard the spice sachet. Let the marmalade cool to room temperature before spooning it into a container and refrigerating.

ORANGE MARMALADE WITH COINTREAU

Snipping the tiny little slices of orange rind that this recipe requires is the most tedious kitchen duty that James has ever performed (which is saying a lot: he once spent an afternoon making about a thousand gnocchi). He intended never to forgive Ramona for assigning him the task—until, that is, he tasted the marmalade. All rancor and resentment (well, most, anyway) immediately fled from his soul. Despite all the work, this is a superlative recipe. The marmalade—suitable for spreading on any tea bread—may be prepared several days in advance; note that the citrus rinds must be sliced a day before the marmalade is cooked. The blood orange gives this marmalade a marvelously rich color, but feel free to use three juice oranges (altogether) instead, if blood oranges are not in season.

Special equipment: candy thermometer

2 juice oranges
1 blood orange
1 lemon
2¼ cups sugar
½ cup Cointreau

Slice the rinds off the oranges and lemon, being very careful to remove as little of the white pith as possible. (The pith will add an unpleasant bitterness to the finished marmalade.) Using a very sharp paring knife or kitchen shears, cut the rind slices crosswise into small, extremely thin strips, and place the strips in a glass or ceramic bowl. Barely cover the strips with water, cover the bowl, and let stand in a cool place overnight. Retain the peeled fruits, sealing them in a plastic bag and refrigerating until the next day.

The following day, remove the pith from the peeled fruits and chop the flesh as finely as possible, removing and retaining the seeds, if any. Put the seeds into a tea ball or tie in a cheesecloth bag. If you wish, you may grind the de-seeded flesh in a food processor.

Put the rinds, the water used to cover them, the chopped citrus flesh, and the tea ball or bag containing the seeds into a large saucepan (whose capacity is at least four times the volume of the liquid). Over high heat, bring the liquid to a boil, then immediately reduce the heat to low and simmer for 1 hour, or until most, but not all, of the liquid has evaporated. Discard the seeds. Add the sugar and liqueur, place a candy thermometer in the pan, and bring back to a simmer. (The mixture will bubble up as it cooks.) Cook, stirring frequently, for about 30 minutes or until the marmalade reaches a temperature of 220° F and has begun to gel. Immediately remove the pan from the heat. Let the marmalade cool to room temperature before spooning it into a container and refrigerating.

CREAM SCONES WITH CURRANTS

Sure, you've had scones. But you've never had *these* scones, which are miraculous. They're best when freshly baked, so try to make them just before your guests arrive, keeping them warm during the first course.

¼ cup heavy cream, plus more for brushing the scones

1 extra-large egg

½ teaspoon vanilla extract

2 tablespoons sugar, plus more for sprinkling the scones

1 cup plus 1 tablespoon unbleached all-purpose flour, plus more for the baking sheet

1½ teaspoons baking powder

½ teaspoon baking soda

¼ teaspoon salt

3 tablespoons unsalted butter, softened

¼ cup dried currants

Preheat the oven to 400° F. In a small mixing bowl, mix the ¼ cup cream, the egg, and the vanilla until well combined. In a large bowl, whisk together the 1 cup plus 1 tablespoon flour, the 2 tablespoons sugar, and the baking powder, baking soda, and salt until well blended. Using a pastry blender, cut the butter into the flour mixture until the mixture resembles coarse meal. Add the cream mixture and the currants and stir with a fork until all the flour mixture is barely moistened.

Sprinkle a baking sheet lightly with flour. With a spatula, scrape the dough into a ball, handling it as little as possible, and push it onto the floured surface. Flip the dough over so that it forms a disc, floured on both sides. Pat it out to create a circle 8 to 9 inches in diameter. With the tines of a fork, deeply prick the surface of the dough to mark six equal wedges.

Brush the scones with the additional cream and lightly sprinkle with the additional sugar. Bake for 15 to 20 minutes or until the scones are just golden. Let cool for 10 minutes, then break along the perforation lines and serve warm.

MADEIRA CAKE

The name of this classic British cake may seem a misnomer. As traditionally made, it contains no Madeira; rather, it's meant to be *served with* a glass of Madeira. Well, we think that if a cake's going to be named after a kind of booze, it should contain some booze. And so our Madeira cake does. (Feel free, please, to substitute amontillado sherry if you can't find Madeira). The plainness of this cake, its beautifully rigid architecture when baked in a square pan, and its density (it can be sliced very thin without crumbling) make it, we believe, a perfect tea cake.

¾ cup (1½ sticks) unsalted butter, softened
¾ cup sugar
1 teaspoon Malmsey Madeira or amontillado sherry
1 tablespoon blanched almonds, very finely chopped
3 large eggs, lightly beaten
1½ cups self-rising flour
zest of 1½ lemons

Preheat the oven to 325° F. Grease a square, high-sided cake pan (5" x 5" x 2½"). Cut a 4¾-inch square of parchment paper, lay it on the bottom of the greased pan, and lightly grease the parchment paper.

In a large mixing bowl, cream the butter and sugar until fluffy. Add the Madeira and almonds and stir. Add the eggs little by little, beating constantly until thoroughly combined. Add the flour a little at a time, folding it into the mixture with a spatula. Add the lemon zest and stir.

Transfer the batter to the prepared pan and bake for 1 hour, or until a toothpick inserted into the center of the cake comes out clean. Remove the pan from the oven and place on a wire rack. Let the cake cool for at least 20 minutes before turning it out of the pan.

NUTTED-CHEESE SANDWICHES

These are the finger sandwiches shown being made in the Technicalities sidebar on page 137. In creating the recipe, Ramona and James have tried to recapture the flavor of the nutted-cheese sandwiches that James used to so enjoy at Chock Full O' Nuts coffee shops. (Once thick on the ground in Manhattan, the Chock Full O' Nuts shops closed years ago. The chain's failure was a low point in James's life; he's still trying to recover.) Nutted-cheese sandwiches must be made with raisin bread. If you can't find a Pullman raisin loaf, use sliced raisin bread instead.

¼ finely chopped walnuts
¼ cup orange juice
¼ cup finely chopped pitted dates
½ cup (4 ounces) cream cheese, softened
pinch of cinnamon
2 horizontal slices Pullman-style raisin bread, or 6 slices regular raisin bread

Preheat the oven to 350° F. Spread the walnuts on a baking sheet and bake for 7 to 8 minutes, until well toasted but not burned. In a small saucepan, heat the orange juice over medium-high heat until it boils. Remove the pan from the stove, add the dates, and stir. Let stand for at least 5 but no longer than 30 minutes. Drain the dates. In a small bowl, mix together the nuts, dates, cream cheese, and cinnamon until well combined.

If using a Pullman loaf, prepare the sandwiches as illustrated on pages 137–138. (This recipe provides enough spread for one long sandwich, which can be cut into six or seven 1½-inch bars.) If using regular, sliced raisin bread, spread the nutted cheese on three slices, cover with the other three slices, trim the crusts, and cut the sandwiches into bars or triangles.

The Third Course: Desserts (Solely)

By the time the third course of your tea rolls around, your guests won't want (or need) much more—just a little something sweet to bring the meal to a close. Our dessert suggestions are therefore exceedingly simple. Choose just one to round off a tea party's menu.

Ginger-Oat Snaps

These wheatless cookies are a standard in Ramona's baking repertoire. (The one somewhat unusual ingredient—powdered guar gum—is available in most health foods stores.)

1 cup (2 sticks) unsalted butter, softened
1 cup packed brown sugar
1 large egg yolk
1 teaspoon vanilla extract
½ cup minced crystallized ginger
1½ cups oat flour
1½ teaspoons baking powder
1 teaspoon powdered guar gum
½ teaspoon salt
¼ teaspoon ground ginger

Preheat the oven to 350° F. Line a baking sheet with parchment paper. In a large mixing bowl, cream the butter and brown sugar. Add the egg yolk and vanilla and mix well. Stir in the crystallized ginger. In a separate, medium-size bowl, whisk together the oat flour, baking powder, guar gum, salt, and ginger. Add the dry mixture to the batter and mix well. Drop by the teaspoonful onto the parchment-lined baking sheet. Bake for 12 to 15 minutes or until set and golden.

TEA COZIES

Here's a curious fact: Hot alcoholic beverages based on coffee abound, as do hot drinks in which the heat's supplied by plain old boiling water. But aside from some hot tea toddies, there are very few traditional hot alcoholic beverages based on tea. Could it be, we wondered, that tea just doesn't lend itself to being spiked? We just couldn't accept that possibility, and our skepticism led us to the tea shelf in our cupboard and, of course, to our liquor cabinet. We brewed up a couple of pots of tea, poured out some cups, and began adding 1 ounce of this or that liquor or liqueur to each—and, if it seemed promising, some light cream, as well. Some of the experiments did not work out (to our surprise, tea and cognac is a truly dispiriting combination), but some of the results were splendid. Here are three—any of which might help you relax and get cozy after your teatime guests have departed.

DEAD GRANDMOTHER

 This very successful combination was suggested by Ramona's hubby, Eric Mueller—as was the objectionable name. We're appalled, naturally, but we can't think of anything better, so we're letting the name stand. Address all complaints to the publisher, please.

1 ounce amaretto
hot Ceylon tea

Pour the amaretto into a warmed ceramic mug. Add the tea and stir.

SCOTCH TEA

The moniker we've supplied for this drink isn't exactly accurate. It's made not with scotch whisky but with Drambuie—the Scottish liqueur based on scotch. The light cream rounds out the flavor nicely.

1 ounce Drambuie
hot Darjeeling tea
light cream or half-and-half

Pour the Drambuie into a warmed ceramic mug. Pour in the tea, leaving room for some cream. Add cream to taste, and stir.

CC&C

Of the combos tried, this proved James's favorite. The tea we used is the well-known Constant Comment, produced by the Connecticut tea merchant R. C. Bigelow, Inc. The Constant Comment blend, which includes orange peels, partners terrifically with Cointreau, an orange peel–based liqueur.

1 ounce Cointreau
hot Constant Comment tea
♂ orange slice

Pour the Cointreau into a warmed ceramic mug. Add the tea and stir. Garnish with the orange slice.

Peanut Butter Bars

Granted, peanut butter bars aren't very British. That doesn't bother James, whose Anglophilia, though pronounced, is not uncontaminated. It occurred to him that this standard, easier-than-pie American dessert might go very well with tea. It does.

2 cups unbleached all-purpose flour
½ teaspoon salt
¾ cup (1½ sticks) unsalted butter, softened
1 cup sugar
1 cup creamy peanut butter
2 large eggs
1 teaspoon vanilla extract

Preheat the oven to 350° F. Lightly butter a jelly-roll pan. In a medium-size bowl, whisk together the flour and salt. In a separate, large mixing bowl, cream the butter and sugar. Add the peanut butter and mix well. Add the eggs and vanilla and beat with an electric hand mixer until well combined. Add the flour and salt mixture, continuing to beat until just combined. Turn the batter out onto the jelly roll pan and pat it into a rectangle about 9" × 12". Bake for 20 to 25 minutes, or until a toothpick inserted in the center comes out clean. Let cool completely, then slice into small bars, about 1½" × 4½" each.

Meringues with Chocolate

Made of nothing more than egg white and sugar (the cream of tartar doesn't really count), hard meringues are the simplest of confections. Good all by themselves, they're even better drizzled with bittersweet chocolate.

1 large egg white
⅛ teaspoon cream of tartar
¼ cup superfine sugar
2 ounces very good bittersweet chocolate

Preheat the oven to 200° F. Line a baking sheet with parchment paper. Beat the egg white together with the cream of tartar until soft peaks form. Add the superfine sugar little by little, continuing to beat until stiff peaks form. Immediately spoon the meringue into a resealable plastic bag. Cut off one corner and pipe the meringue in 3-inch-long strips onto the prepared baking sheet. Bake for at least 2 hours, or until golden brown and firm to the touch. Turn off the heat but leave the meringues in the oven until they are cool. (They should be crisp and dry.) Melt the chocolate in a small pan over simmering water and drizzle it over the meringues. Refrigerate until set.

CHAPTER SEVEN

No Chugging Allowed

A BEER PARTY FOR GROWNUPS

A DINNER BUFFET ORGANIZED ENTIRELY AROUND BEER? IT'S AN IDEA that seems as if it must've been spawned in the muddy channels of some former fraternity boy's brain. But neither James nor Ramona has ever been a frat boy. Honest. Nor do we rue the fact.

Which doesn't mean that either of us is free of a biographical disposition toward beer—or, rather, toward enjoying the kind of food that goes well with beer. We're both, you see, part German, and we both grew up in households where beer was often and gustily drunk and where many of the meals laid upon the family table were *echt Deutsch* in origin.

As French food lends itself to wine and American food lends itself to Diet Dr Pepper, so does German food (or northern and central European food more generally) lend itself to beer. Although beer was (probably) first brewed in ancient Egypt, and although beers and ales are now made virtually everywhere in the world, it was the brewers of northern and central Europe—including those offshore outcroppings, the British Isles—who raised the craft of brewing to an art. Northern and central European culinary traditions developed right alongside beermaking, and it's from them that the dishes in this chapter draw their inspiration.

Notice that we say "inspiration." Not everything here is authentically European in origin. The cut of meat—perhaps we should say "meat product"—that flavors our buffet's soup and that then goes on nervously to star as the main course's main attraction is the Porkette. The process for brining and smoking this boneless pork shoulder

Cut of meat or "meat product"?

butt (what a phrase!) was invented in the 1920s by one Julian Freirich of Long Island City, Queens, New York. Still made by the J. Freirich Company (now relocated to North Carolina) and immediately recognizable by the bright-red plastic wrapper it's sold in, the poor Porkette

is burdened by a risible brand name and saddled with an unfairly cheap-date sort of reputation, roughly equivalent to that of Spam. If you're familiar with the Porkette at all, you probably disdain it as something worthy of a school-cafeteria collation, at best. Well, climb down off your gastronomic high horse and join us peasants in a scrumptious feast. Tender, buttery, and sweet, the Porkette is infinitely better than most of the packaged hams you'll find nestling up next to it in your grocer's meat case.

About the beer: Although we make suggestions regarding the kind of beers or ales that might be served with each of our buffet's courses, these are hardly dictates meant to be religiously followed. We don't pretend to be beer experts, and we encourage you to experiment with your own selections—to make your beer buffet a beer-tasting party. (Which, note, does not mean a beer-*guzzling* party. Pour small portions, and have plenty of glasses on hand so that you can give your guests fresh, clean glasses for the beers accompanying each successive course.) Chances are that if you choose lighter-colored, lighter-bodied beers (lagers, pilsners, Bavarian wheat beers) for the first two courses—the fondue and the soup—and darker, fuller-bodied beers and ales for the main course and dessert, you'll do just fine. We do, however, particularly recommend that you serve one of the remarkable ales known as barley wines with the cheese course that ends the meal. Here's the menu:

Menu

APPETIZER
BEER AND CHEESE FONDUE
served with a lager or pilsner

SOUP COURSE
YELLOW SPLIT PEA SOUP
PUMPERNICKEL BREAD
served with a wheat beer

MAIN COURSE
PORKETTE (SMOKED PORK SHOULDER BUTT)
HOMEMADE APPLESAUCE
GERMAN POTATO SALAD

RED CABBAGE WITH APPLES
TWICE-COOKED BRUSSELS SPROUTS
served with a lambic or lambic-style beer

DESSERT
AUNT BABE'S CAKE
served with a porter

CHEESE COURSE
SELECTION OF BLUE CHEESES
served with a barley wine

The recipes in this chapter have been designed for a buffet for eight to ten people. Strategy notes: Plan your beer buffet for early evening. Begin the day by making the cake (and its glaze) and the pumpernickel loaves. Make the potato salad, the red cabbage dish, and the soup (with the Porkette)—which can be reheated just before serving—in the middle of the day. In the late afternoon, prepare the applesauce (it takes surprisingly little time) and the brussels sprouts. Wait to prepare the fondue until just before the guests arrive.

BEER AND CHEESE FONDUE

Fondues hail from Switzerland, and this beer and cheese fondue, which incorporates two famous hard Swiss cheeses, Emmenthaler and Gruyère, is a classic. There was a time, several decades back, when fondue parties were all the rage among middle-class Americans; a suburban home without a fondue pot was as unthinkable as one without a lawn. *Drinkology EATS* loves retro activities, and so we join with all the others who've so tirelessly been trying to revive fondue's popularity. Note that fondue pots are typically equipped with only six forks; if you're serving more than six, equip your guests with long wooden or bamboo skewers for spearing the bread cubes and dipping them into the fondue. (Or invest in an extra set of fondue forks, which are commonly offered for sale on eBay.)

Beer: We suggest serving a light, crisp, pale lager or pilsner with this appetizer. For our beer buffet, we actually chose a *non*-European lager, the Indian beer called Kingfisher, whose slight bitterness played nicely against the fondue's creamy sweetness.

Special equipment: Fondue pot

3 cups (two 12-ounce bottles or cans) beer (pilsner or pale lager)
4 teaspoons Worcestershire sauce

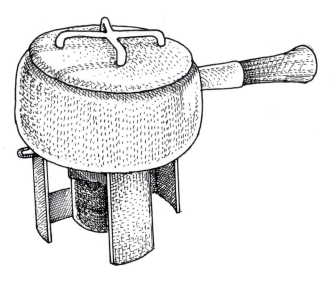

1 large clove garlic, minced
1 teaspoon dry mustard
½ teaspoon paprika
4 cups (about 1 pound) grated Emmenthaler
4 cups (about 1 pound) grated Gruyère
1 tablespoon cornstarch
1 long baguette, cut into 1-inch cubes

In a large, heavy pot, combine the beer, Worcestershire sauce, garlic, mustard, and paprika. Bring to a simmer over medium heat, then gradually add the cheeses and stir gently until melted. Stir the cornstarch into 2 tablespoons water. When smooth, add to the fondue and stir vigorously until smooth. Do not boil. Transfer to a fondue pot set over a flame, with the bread cubes on the side. If the fondue starts to separate or the cheese begins to clump, reheat and stir well until smooth again.

YELLOW SPLIT PEA SOUP

In preparing this soup, you'll also be cooking the meat for the main course. When the soup's done, set the Porkette aside until it's time to bring the dishes for the main course to the table. There is, by the way, no need to presoak the peas for this soup: They'll soften and begin to disintegrate during the hour and a half of cooking.

Beer: For this course, we recommend that you choose a Bavarian wheat beer (called *Weissbier* or *Hefe-Weizen* in German). Most beers are made primarily from fermented barley malt; wheat beers' distinctive taste results from their being brewed from both barley and wheat malts. Bavarian *Weissbier*s are pale in color but possess a fuller body and a richer, sweeter flavor than most other light-colored beers.

1 whole Porkette (smoked pork shoulder butt), about 3 pounds
3 cups (1½ pounds) dried yellow split peas
1 pound medium-size carrots, peeled and sliced into ⅜-inch coins
1 tablespoon dried marjoram
salt to taste
lemon wedges

Remove the Porkette's cheesecloth netting and place the butt in a large stockpot. Add the split peas and carrots to the pot, along with 2½ quarts (10 cups) water. (It's OK if the water does not quite cover the butt, but make sure that all the peas and carrots are covered with water.) Sprinkle in the marjoram. Bring the soup to a boil over high heat, then immediately reduce the heat to medium low and, stirring occasionally, simmer for 1½ hours, or until the peas are very tender. Stir more often during the last 30 minutes, to prevent the Porkette from sticking to the bottom of the pot or the soup from burning. Add more water if it appears that the thickened soup may burn.

Remove the Porkette from the pot and set aside. Working in batches if necessary, transfer about three-quarters of the soup to a blender and puree, returning the pureed soup to the pot and mixing it thoroughly with the portion not pureed. (The soup should be ever so slightly chunky.) Taste before serving, and add salt if necessary. Serve with lemon wedges—and with sliced pumpernickel bread and unsalted butter.

PUMPERNICKEL BREAD

Once again, *Drinkology EATS* errs on the side of inauthenticity, and you'll be glad we do. As traditionally made, real German pumpernickel requires an enormously lengthy baking time (sixteen to twenty-four hours) in a low-temp oven; the chemical reactions that occur during this long, slow bake are what produce pumpernickel's distinctive caramel and chocolate flavors. Our faux pumpernickel recipe amounts to a shortcut: The caramel and chocolate flavors are induced through the addition of molasses and cocoa powder to the dough. Note that the recipe makes two loaves; serve one with the soup and the other with the buffet's main course. Make sure there's plenty of unsalted butter on hand, for spreading.

2 cups boiling (or very hot) water
¼ cup molasses
¼ cup (½ stick) unsalted butter, plus ¼ cup melted butter
2 packages (2 tablespoons) active dry yeast
¼ cup brown sugar
¼ cup unsweetened cocoa powder
1 tablespoon caraway seeds
1½ teaspoons salt
3 cups rye flour
about 3 cups unbleached all-purpose flour
1 egg white, lightly beaten
1 teaspoon coarse salt

In a large bowl, combine the hot water, molasses, and ¼ cup solid butter until the butter is melted and the molasses is well incorporated. Let stand until just warm to the touch. Stir in the yeast and brown sugar and let stand until the yeast is foamy. In a separate bowl, whisk together the cocoa powder, caraway seeds, salt, and rye flour, then add this mixture to the liquid and mix well. Starting with 2 to 2½ cups, add enough all-purpose flour to make a soft dough. (Add more all-purpose flour, up to 3 cups total, if necessary.) Knead until the dough is smooth and elastic, about 5 minutes. Place the dough in a lightly greased bowl and brush with melted butter. Cover with a towel and let rise in a warm place until doubled in volume, 45 to 60 minutes.

Punch down the dough and divide it in half. Shape each half into a round or oblong loaf. Place each on a buttered baking sheet. Again, butter each loaf with melted butter. Cover the loaves, set them in a warm place, and let them rise until doubled in size, 1½ to 2 hours. (The loaves will not expand further during baking, so let them rise as much as possible before putting them in the oven.)

Preheat the oven to 375°F. Brush the top of each loaf with egg white and sprinkle with coarse salt. Bake for 30 to 40 minutes, until the loaves sound hollow when tapped. Let cool for 5 minutes, then transfer to a wire rack to finish cooling.

PORKETTE, REDUX

Removed from the pea soup, the Porkette has been waiting in the wings for its star turn. When it's time for the main course, carve the Porkette into ⅜-inch slices, arrange them on a platter, and serve with bowls of Dijon mustard and homemade applesauce (recipe follows) close at hand. Don't forget to slice up the other loaf of pumpernickel—some guests may want to make Porkette sandwiches. (Note: As the Porkette cools, the soup adhering to its skin will become crusty. This doesn't bother us, but if it disgusts you, wipe the Porkette clean with a moistened paper towel before carving.)

Beer: With the main course, you might try serving a Belgian lambic beer or a lambic-style beer from elsewhere. True lambic beers, which come only from Belgium, are unusual in several respects: They're fermented with natural (as opposed to cultured) yeasts; they're aged (sometimes lengthily) in casks previously used for aging Port or other wines; and they're sometimes sweetened with the addition of fruits or fruit syrups. With our beer buffet's main course, we served an American lambic-style beer—the Three Philosophers ale made by the Ommegang Brewery of Cooperstown, New York (to which some real, cherry-flavored Belgian lambic is added). The beer's fruitiness, which we heightened by adding a tiny amount of the raspberry-flavored liqueur Chambord to each glass, nicely complemented all the main course's dishes.

HOMEMADE APPLESAUCE

We know you. You'll think, "Gee, I guess it'd be nice to make home-made applesauce, but I think I'll just buy a jar instead." Well, you gotta do what you gotta do, but homemade applesauce is really terrifically easy—and *so* much better than the commercial kind.

10 to 12 small, hard, tart or sweet-tart apples, such as Northern Spy,
    McIntosh, or Cortland
fresh lemon juice or sugar, if needed

Wash the apples carefully. Cut them into quarters and remove the cores, immediately placing the quartered apples in a large, heavy-bottomed, nonreactive pot and adding water to a depth of about 1 inch. (Do not let the apples sit after they have been cut, as they will discolor and acquire a metallic flavor.) Cover the pot and quickly bring to a boil over high heat. As soon as the water boils, reduce the heat to low and simmer gently until the apples are soft and have begun to disintegrate, about 10 minutes. Immediately remove from the heat and let stand for 10 minutes. Using a fork, mash the apple skins into the apple pulp until all the skins are covered. Let stand for several hours (or as much time as you can spare). The apples will absorb some or all of the cooking liquid, as well as some of the color from the apple skins, if red-skinned apples are used.

Drain the apples if necessary, and retain any cooking liquid. Pass the apples through a food mill and discard the skins. Add any leftover cooking liquid until the sauce gains the proper consistency.

Taste the applesauce. If it seems a little bland, add lemon juice, ¼ teaspoon at a time, until the sauce is sprightly. If it is too sour, add sugar, a teaspoonful at a time, to taste. (Note, however, that adding lemon juice or sugar is rarely necessary.)

GERMAN POTATO SALAD

German potato salad is a far cry from the mayo-laden American version. This recipe closely approximates the German potato salad Ramona remembers from childhood.

½ pound bacon
3 pounds white-fleshed potatoes
4 hard-boiled eggs, peeled
2 stalks celery, chopped
1 medium-size onion, diced
2 tablespoons cider vinegar
¼ cup extra-virgin olive oil
1 teaspoon celery seed
½ teaspoon salt
⅛ teaspoon freshly ground black pepper
⅛ teaspoon sweet paprika

Chop the bacon into small pieces and fry until crisp. Drain, reserving the bacon fat. Scrub the potatoes but do not peel them. Boil until tender. Drain and let stand until just cool enough to handle, then remove the skins (which should come away easily) and chop the potatoes into bite-size pieces, placing them in a large mixing bowl. Chop the eggs coarsely, and add the eggs, bacon pieces, celery, and onions to the potatoes. Mix gently. In a small saucepan, combine the vinegar, oil, ¼ cup of the reserved bacon fat, and the seasonings. Heat over high heat until the mixture boils, then reduce the heat and simmer for 5 minutes. Pour over the potato mixture and stir gently to coat. Serve at room temperature. (Note: If the amount of bacon this book is suggesting you consume is beginning to bother you, you can make a vegetarian version of this salad by omitting the bacon and increasing the oil to ½ cup.)

RED CABBAGE WITH APPLES

We debated whether we should really include two cruciferous vegetable dishes in the same meal. (Cruciferous vegetables are members of the cabbage family, and, besides cabbage, include brussels sprouts, broccoli, and cauliflower.) Wouldn't it be redundant? Well, no, as it turns out. The appearance and flavor of this dish and those of the brussels sprouts recipe that follows are as different as could be.

1 medium-size sweet onion
2 tablespoons extra-virgin olive oil
1 small head red cabbage (about 1 pound)
2 to 3 cups apple juice
1 teaspoon celery seed
1 teaspoon salt
¼ teaspoon freshly ground black pepper
¼ teaspoon ground cloves
2 bay leaves
2 sweet apples, such as Golden Delicious or Macoun

Cut the onion in half and slice it thinly. Pour the oil into a large, heavy-bottomed pot, add the onions, and sauté until the onions are translucent, 5 to 7 minutes. Cut the cabbage into quarters, cut out the core, and thinly slice the cabbage. Add to the pot, along with 1 cup of the apple juice. Add the seasonings, cover, and simmer for 30 minutes. Peel and core the apples, slice them into very thin wedges, and add them to the cabbage along with 1 more cup of the apple juice. Cover and continue to simmer, adding more apple juice as the liquid evaporates, until the cabbage is soft and the apples have disappeared, about 1 hour more. Serve hot or at room temperature.

TWICE-COOKED BRUSSELS SPROUTS

We love brussels sprouts, though we understand that they're not everyone's favorite vegetable. If you think you detest brussels sprouts but have only had them steamed or boiled, this recipe's medley of flavors may cause you to reconsider.

2 pounds brussels sprouts, cleaned and trimmed but left whole
½ cup (1 stick) unsalted butter
2 medium-size sweet onions, thinly sliced
2 teaspoons fresh thyme leaves
1 cup heavy cream
½ cup freshly grated horseradish
⅛ teaspoon ground allspice
salt and freshly ground black pepper to taste

Boil the brussels sprouts until tender, 5 to 7 minutes. Drain and let stand until cool enough to handle. Cut in half lengthwise and set aside. Melt the butter in a large, heavy frying pan. Add the onions and cook over medium heat until translucent, 5 to 7 minutes. Add the thyme, stir, and cook until fragrant, about 30 seconds. Add the brussels sprouts, cream, horseradish, and allspice and continue to cook over medium heat until the brussels sprouts are heated through and well coated. Season with salt and pepper. Serve hot.

AUNT BABE'S CAKE

Now for the dessert course. The recipe for this traditional hot milk cake came to James from his Aunt Babe (whose given name is Amelia but who has never been called anything but Babe). James has been baking it for years, usually for holiday parties, but we decided to include it in our beer buffet as a nod to Aunt Babe's own preference for washing down a slice of cake with a glass of cold beer. This simple, dense, moist cake need not be drizzled with the chocolate glaze that we suggest; it's just as good served plain or lightly dusted with a mixture of ground cinnamon and confectioners' sugar.

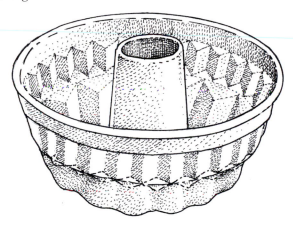

Beer: Back in her beer-drinking days, Aunt Babe would undoubtedly have "paired" her slice of cake with a light American lager. But we recommend that the cake be served with a toothier, altogether more interesting kind of beer—an English porter. Porters—named for the railway porters who first served these beers to thirsty passengers—acquire their dark color and tangy flavor from the roasted barley malt used in their making. (We especially like the deservedly well-known Taddy Porter produced by the Yorkshire, England, brewer Samuel Smith.)

1 cup milk
½ cup (1 stick) salted butter
2 cups unbleached all-purpose flour
3 teaspoons baking powder
pinch of salt
4 large eggs
3 teaspoons vanilla extract
3 teaspoons fresh lemon juice, strained
2 cups sugar
chocolate butter cream glaze (recipe follows)

Preheat the oven to 350° F. Grease and flour a bundt pan. (Make sure you do this extremely thoroughly; every nook and cranny of the pan must be greased and dusted with flour.) In a small saucepan, heat the milk and butter together until the butter melts and the milk begins to bubble at the edge of the pan. Do not boil; if the milk approaches boiling before you're ready to use it, turn off the heat. (It will remain hot enough.)

In a medium-size mixing bowl, sift together the flour, baking powder, and salt. In a separate, large mixing bowl, beat the eggs together with the vanilla and lemon juice. Add the sugar to the eggs and beat for 2 minutes. Gradually add the hot milk and butter to the egg-sugar mixture, continuing to beat as you do so. Little by little—and continuing to beat the mixture—add the flour mixture. When all the flour has been added, beat on medium speed for 2 minutes. Pour the batter into the prepared pan and bake for 50 to 75 minutes. Begin testing for doneness at 50 minutes by sticking a toothpick into the cake. Retest every 5 minutes. When the toothpick comes out clean and the surface of the cake is a golden brown color, it is done.

Remove the cake from the oven and let it stand on a wire rack for 5 to 10 minutes, then turn it out onto a cake plate. (Wear oven mitts or heat-resistant rubber gloves while handling the pan, which will still be very hot.) Drizzle the still-warm cake with chocolate butter cream glaze.

CHOCOLATE BUTTER CREAM GLAZE

As we've said, there's no absolute need to frost Aunt Babe's Cake. If you do, do so sparingly—by drizzling this chocolate glaze artfully over the cake. The glaze will harden slightly as it dries.

3 tablespoons unsalted butter, softened
2 cups confectioners' sugar
¼ cup unsweetened cocoa powder
½ teaspoon vanilla extract
about ¼ cup whole milk

In a medium-size mixing bowl, cream the butter with 1 cup of the confectioners' sugar. In a separate bowl, combine the remaining sugar with the cocoa powder. Add the vanilla to the creamed butter and mix well. Add the sugar-cocoa mixture and mix as well as possible. Add the milk 1 teaspoonful at a time, stirring constantly, until the glaze is of a thin enough consistency to drizzle.

THE CHEESE COURSE

As our beer buffet begins with beer and cheese (in the form of fondue), so does it end—with a cheese course that brings together a selection of blue cheeses with a highly unusual kind of beer known as *barley wine*. (No, it's not really wine. But more about that in just a second.)

Like the Port wines whose flavor they evoke, barley wines pair magnificently with the English blue cheese called Stilton. But, hey, we've already trumpeted Stilton's goodness elsewhere in this book (see page 33). So let's try something different—though in the same moldy vein— for this cheese course: a sampling of three other British blue cheeses. We recommend a Shropshire blue, a Cheshire blue, and a brand-name blue cheese from Lancashire, Butler's Blacksticks Blue. Cut the cheeses into small wedges or pieces (large portions are neither necessary nor desirable at the end of this redoubtable meal!) and give each guest a small plate on which you've placed a sampling of all three. Encourage your guests to pick up the cheese wedges with their fingers. (Crackers or additional bread likewise seems *de trop* at this point.)

Beer: Barley wines are strange beers, indeed. (Technically, barley wines belong to the category of beer called ale, since the yeast used in their fermentation rises to the top of the fermentation vessel. The yeast used for beer sinks to the vessel's bottom, and this divergence between *top fermentation* and *bottom fermentation* is what distinguishes ale from other beers.) The experience of sipping a barley wine—barley wines are often served in brandy snifters, in portions measuring just a few ounces—is so fundamentally different from knocking back a cold Bud that it's hard to believe that these beverages belong to the same general class of potables. Unlike most other beers and ales, barley wines benefit from bottle aging. (Most beers just go stale if not drunk within a few months of brewing.) Dark, complex, viscous, and higher in alcohol—sometimes substantially so—than other beers, barley wines confer a contemplative kind of pleasure more usually associated with fortified wines such as Port and Madeira. And that's exactly what makes a barley wine the best choice for closing our beer buffet. Though they originated in Britain, barley wines are now produced by upwards of fifty American microbreweries. (A brand called Old Foghorn, made by San Francisco's Anchor Brewery was the first, and is highly regarded by "beer geeks.") Note that barley wines are sold in bottles that range from the very small (seven ounces) to the very large (twenty-five-plus ounces—the same size as a standard wine bottle). They're not as expensive as you might guess (ten dollars is about the most you'll pay—and that for one of the larger bottles), so you might consider presenting your guests with a selection to sample along with the cheeses.

BAR ASSOCIATIONS

BEERTAILS?

Beer, it seems, is the new vodka. We keep reading about the purportedly ever more popular fad for beer cocktails, or "beertails" as they're sometimes—and rather unfortunately—called. (Granted, the term "beertinis," which we've also encountered, is even worse.) Apparently, there are few ingredients that the world's trendiest bartenders won't try mixing with beer. Beer and orange juice. Beer and Jägermeister. Beer and soy sauce. What's next? The Beer Colada?

Do pardon us for being skeptical—not to mention a tad repelled. Oh, we're hardly beer purists. We very much approve of squeezing a wedge of lime into a light, crisp Mexican lager like Corona or Tecate. And we're not constitutionally opposed to any and all beer-based mixed drinks. We love the northern European tradition of enhancing a glass of beer with a shot of a sweet, fruity liqueur (Chambord, cherry Heering, crème de cassis) or a berry-based eau-de-vie such as framboise. (See *Drinkology: The Art and Science of the Cocktail* for recipes for some other well-known, time-honored beer-based concoctions.) But there are certain places we just don't want to go. Beer and orange juice? Um . . . no thanks.

In other words, we've learned to respect our gag reflex. Interestingly, however, a few of the newer beer-and-other-stuff combos we'd read about didn't *automatically* set our stomachs to churning. And so, in good *Drinkology EATS* fashion, we decided to experiment. Here are two recipes that, somewhat to our surprise, we find pleasing.

WEST END

Various Internet cocktail sites informed us that a beer-and-cola drink called the Broadway is popular in Japan. We thought about it, and (perhaps weirdly) it kind of seemed OK. We've no idea what kind of beer (or brand of cola, for that matter) Japanese Broadway fans prefer, but it occurred to us that the Young's Double Chocolate Stout—a dark and toothsome British beer whose ingredients include chocolate and chocolate malt—might work if combined with Coca-Cola. And guess what? The Coke's sweetness softens the stout's sharper edges without fundamentally changing its taste. We tremble to say it, but this drink—which we've dubbed the West End in honor of its British heritage—is delicious.

about 7 ounces cold Young's Double Chocolate Stout
about 7 ounces cold Coca-Cola

Carefully pour the stout and cola into a chilled beer mug or 16-ounce glass. (When mixed, the beer and cola form quite a head, so pour this one especially slowly.)

MOJITO FIDEL

If Internet-disseminated legend's to be believed (always an extremely iffy proposition), Cuban strongman Fidel Castro prefers his Mojitos topped with cerveza rather than the more usual club soda. (Hence this drink's name.) Whatever one thinks of Fidel's brand of communism, his mixological instincts aren't half bad. Ideally, this drink would be prepared with Cuban beer. Since the American embargo on trade with Cuba makes that impossible in the United States, use a pale Mexican lager instead. Note, please, that this is not a drink to serve with our beer buffet! It's best served as a hot-weather refresher.

8 or more large fresh mint leaves
¾ ounce simple syrup
½ lime
crushed ice
2 ounces light rum
beer (a pale lager is best)
🍸 sprig of fresh mint

In the bottom of a highball glass, muddle the mint leaves and simple syrup, thoroughly crushing the leaves. Squeeze the half lime into the glass and stir briefly. Fill the glass with crushed ice, pour in the rum, and carefully top with the beer. Garnish with the mint sprig.

CHAPTER 8

Mason-Dixon

WINTER AND SUMMER SEAFOOD BUFFETS

As we've mentioned, Ramona and James were both raised in Maryland, so when it came time to decide what sort of seafood-centered eating and drinking party we should offer *Drinkology EATS*'s readers, our thoughts naturally drifted back to the oyster and crab dishes we'd known and loved so well while growing up. (We've found it astonishing how much we share in this regard, despite Ramona's having been raised in the country and James in the city.)

Historically, Maryland was a border state: The famous Mason-Dixon line that forms the state's northern boundary marked the geographical and cultural division between North and South. What people who have seldom experienced Maryland-style cooking may not realize, however, is that the state's in-between-ness applies to its culinary traditions, as well—especially where seafood is concerned. Maryland-style seafood cookery hasn't the austerity of New England's white chowders and plain lobster-and-drawn-butter dishes, but neither is it as spicy and complex as, say, the Gulf Coast's seafood gumbos. Though many Maryland seafood dishes are seasoned, they're usually seasoned lightly, even cautiously, so as not to obscure or overwhelm the flavor of the fish or shellfish itself. (The one big exception to this rule is Maryland-style steamed hard crabs, which are often encrusted in red pepper and fiery hot.)

Back when Ramona and James were children, Marylanders' relationship with their two favored kinds of seafood—oysters and crabs—was strictly seasonal. Culinary rhythms were in synch with the rhythms of life on (and in) the Chesapeake Bay. Autumn, winter, and early spring were oyster season: Our parents' and grandparents' generations adhered to the old rule that oysters should be harvested and eaten only during months whose names contain the letter *R*—that is, September through April. (Oysters are stationary creatures; they don't move someplace else for the summer. But they spawn during the warmer months, and they aren't as good to eat during this time.) The eating of Maryland's prized blue crabs, by contrast, was solely a summertime entertainment—with the peak crab season arriving in August and September.

Neither austere nor too spicy

Much has changed since our childhoods. For one thing, the Chesapeake's oyster population has sadly dwindled to nearly nothing—the result of overharvesting, habitat loss, and several mysterious bouts of parasitic disease. (The outcome of recent efforts to revive Maryland's oyster fishery through the introduction of parasite-resistant non-native oysters remains very uncertain.) Oh, Marylanders still relish oysters—but almost all the oysters they eat hail from elsewhere.

Blue crab catches have also suffered declines in recent years—though the total harvest can vary from season to season. But beyond the shrinking harvests, there's been another significant alteration in Marylanders' relationship with the shellfish their bay once provided in such abundance. In case you hadn't noticed, America's food supply has, over the past several decades, become thoroughly globalized. Crabbers do still work the Chesapeake, and at least some of the live blue crabs that Marylanders use for steaming still come from the local waters. (Scarcity has, unsurprisingly, driven up their price astronomically.) But the processing plants that were once major employers in Maryland's bayside towns have mostly shut their doors, and the processed (meaning nothing more than pre-steamed and picked) blue-crab meat that Marylanders prefer for their crab cakes and crab imperial is more likely to have come from elsewhere—even from as far away as Asia.

And, of course, globalization has also meant that both oysters and blue-crab meat, despite their depletion locally, are now available in Maryland, as everywhere else, year round—for a premium price. The local, seasonal cycle has been broken.

Looked at one way, the disruption of that intimate, local, seasonal relationship with one's food does have its positive aspects. (Whether you live in Louisville, Tucson, or Des Moines, you can enjoy oysters and crab.) But we can't help also experiencing it as a loss. Nationwide, year-round availability of foods insulates us from the calendar's natural progression, plays a role in divesting us of a sense of our particular place, and robs us of the wonderful anticipation that accompanied the strictly seasonal arrival of oysters, crabs—and asparagus, for that matter. We're not romantics (or not totally so). We don't exactly want to return to the "good old days," which were better only in certain respects. But we do indulge our nostalgia.

And it's that nostalgia for an era of wintertime oyster "roasts" (as Marylanders called oyster-eating parties) and summertime crab "feasts" that's guided us as we've put this chapter together. We've divided the chapter into two parts: the first a wintertime oyster buffet, the second a

We indulge our nostalgia

late-summer buffet that, besides the requisite crab dishes, also celebrates late summer's bounty of farm-fresh produce: tomatoes, sweet corn, and peaches. Nostalgia also informs some of our cocktail choices; see the sidebar on page 202.

THE WINTERTIME (OYSTER) BUFFET

This and the buffet that follows have each been designed to feed twelve people. Each includes an appetizer, a soup course, a main course (with sides), and a dessert. Because oyster dishes—especially oyster stew—are traditional holiday fare in Maryland, this buffet provides a suitable way to entertain a not-too-sizable group of friends and family during the Christmas–New Year's season. Here's the complete bill of fare:

Oyster Buffet

EATS
ANGELS ON HORSEBACK
OYSTER STEW
PAN-FRIED OYSTERS WITH SPICY TARTAR SAUCE
STEWED TOMATOES
WINTER SUCCOTASH
MARYLAND-STYLE CORNBREAD
LADY BALTIMORE CAKE

DRINKS
CLASSIC HIGHBALL
7 AND 7
BOURBON AND BRANCH

Some pointers on strategy: The tactical worry presented by this meal is that oysters don't take well to being cooked ahead of time. Frankly, though, that doesn't amount to too much of a problem, since it's also true that oysters take very little time to cook. Plan your buffet for early evening. If possible, make the Spicy Tartar Sauce the day before and refrigerate it till serving time; the flavors will meld, and the pepperiness of the sauce will heighten. On the day of the buffet, begin the morning by making the Lady Baltimore Cake—admittedly one of the more difficult and time-consuming recipes in all of *Drinkology Eats* (but worth every ounce of energy you expend). The cornbread, too, can be baked early in the day and rewarmed before serving. In the middle of the day, assemble the angels on horseback and refrigerate them, and bread the oysters that will be pan-fried later. (The breaded oysters will actually benefit from a several-hour-long nap in the fridge.) In the afternoon, make the stewed tomatoes, which, once cooked, can simply sit there in the pot to be quickly reheated when the time comes. The only dishes that must be fully prepared just before serving are the oyster stew and, for the main course, the succotash side—but they're both quickly made.

One other note: When you drain the oysters for the angels and fried oysters, be sure to reserve their "liquor" (the viscous liquid in which the oysters live inside their shells, and in which shucked oysters are packed). Adding this extra liquor to the oyster stew will deepen its flavor.

And, by the way, we should mention that if you want to augment the buffet's appetizer with several platters of freshly shucked raw oysters on the half shell (see pages 64–70), we won't stand in your way. In fact, invite us over!

ANGELS ON HORSEBACK

Utterly simple and utterly delectable, angels on horseback are popular cocktail-party fare. They make a stunning hors d'oeuvre for this meal. Note that shucked oysters are generally sold in half-pint (eight-ounce) plastic containers, and that it can be difficult to judge how large the oysters are and, therefore, how many each container holds. To be safe, buy four eight-ounce containers. If there are extra oysters, make additional angels or add the leftover oysters to the oyster stew.

4 tablespoons minced fresh flat-leaf parsley
1 teaspoon freshly ground black pepper
1 teaspoon sweet paprika
48 medium-size shucked oysters, drained (reserve liquor for oyster stew)
24 slices bacon, cut in half crosswise

In a small bowl, combine the parsley, pepper, and paprika. Place an oyster on each half-slice of bacon. Sprinkle with the parsley mixture. Wrap the bacon around the oyster and secure with a toothpick. Arrange the angels on a broiler tray, making sure that the toothpicks are lying flat against the tray, and broil for 8 to 10 minutes, or until the bacon is crisp on one side. Turn carefully and broil for 4 to 5 minutes more, until the bacon is crisp and the oysters have begun to curl at the edges. Allow to cool for a moment before serving. (Note that the angels can be assembled ahead of time and refrigerated until it's time to broil them.)

OYSTER STEW

When James discussed this recipe with his mother, she said, "Make sure you tell them [meaning you, *Drinkology EATS*'s readers] that oyster stew is *hard* to make." Well, OK, Mom. What she really means is that the stew—which isn't a stew at all, but rather an unthickened, milky soup—must be carefully watched to make sure that it does not boil (which may cause it to curdle). Small oysters (no longer than two inches) work best for oyster stew. Note that the butter will not combine with the milk but will rise in small, golden globules to the stew's surface. That's the way it's s'posed to be.

1½ quarts whole milk
1½ quarts half-and-half
3 (8-ounce) containers shucked fresh oysters
½ cup (1 stick) salted butter
reserved oyster liquor from other oyster dishes in this menu
1 tablespoon Worcestershire sauce
½ teaspoon Tabasco sauce
⅛ teaspoon ground mace or ground celery seed
salt to taste
oyster crackers

If possible, take the milk and half-and-half out of the refrigerator and let stand at room temperature for 30 minutes before starting the stew. (The butter, however, should be cold when you begin.)

Drain the oysters, reserving the liquor, and set aside. Place the butter and the oyster liquor (including any reserved from the oysters for the other dishes) in a 5-quart pot and heat over medium-low heat until the butter has just melted. Add the oysters and heat for about 1 minute more, until they begin to plump and the edges begin to curl. Add the milk, half-and-half, Worcestershire sauce, Tabasco sauce, and mace (or celery seed). Stir. Continue to heat over medium-low to medium heat, stirring occasionally, until the stew is thoroughly heated through and has begun to steam. Do not allow it to boil. Add salt to taste and serve immediately in mugs or small, deep bowls (rice bowls work beautifully for a buffet), about 1 cup per person. When ladling out the stew, make sure that each serving includes several oysters. Place bowls of oyster crackers on the buffet table so that guests may add them to the stew themselves.

Pan-Fried Oysters

Now for the main course—and the winter buffet's pièce de résistance. There are two tricks to making tender, juicy, succulent fried oysters: (1) They should be pan-fried in butter, *not* deep-fried; (2) they must *not* be overcooked. Allowing the breaded oysters to rest in the fridge for several hours before frying firms them up slightly, making them easier to handle when frying.

2 cups cornmeal
2 cups cracker meal
4 eggs
48 medium to large shucked oysters (about four 8-ounce containers)
½ cup (1 stick) salted butter
pimiento strips
lemon wedges
Spicy Tartar Sauce (recipe follows)

In a medium-size bowl, whisk together the cornmeal and cracker meal until well combined. In a separate bowl, lightly beat the eggs. Dip each oyster in the egg, then dredge in the cornmeal mixture. Place the coated oysters on a large platter and cover them with whatever cornmeal mixture remains after dredging. Lightly cover with plastic wrap and refrigerate for at least 1 and up to 4 hours.

Remove the oysters from the refrigerator and let stand at room temperature for 15 minutes. Melt the butter in a large frying pan over medium heat. (Do not allow it to brown.) Pluck the oysters from the meal and place them in the pan, raising heat to medium-high. Fry them, turning once, until just done, about 2 minutes per side for large oysters. Arrange on individual plates (4 oysters per plate), garnish with pimiento strips, and serve immediately with lemon wedges and a dollop of Spicy Tartar Sauce.

SPICY TARTAR SAUCE

It didn't take too much ingenuity, but James is nevertheless very proud of having invented this colorful, flavorful variation on ordinary tartar sauce. If possible, make the sauce up to a day ahead of time, which will meld the flavors and intensify the peppery hotness. Note that when seeding and mincing jalapeños, it's wise to wear rubber gloves or to sheathe your hands in plastic bags and to take the additional precaution of washing your hands thoroughly in warm, soapy water afterwards. You *really* don't want any of the capsaicin—that's the chemical compound that makes hot peppers hot—to remain on your fingers, lest you inadvertently touch your eye.

1 cup mayonnaise
2 small jalapeño chiles, seeded and finely minced
½ small red onion, finely minced
2 tablespoons sweet pickle relish

Combine all the ingredients in a small mixing bowl. Refrigerate until ready to serve.

STEWED TOMATOES

With this dish, James has taken certain liberties with traditional Maryland cooking—especially with the addition of the sweet, almost caramel-like sherry called Pedro Xímenez (named for the Spanish grape used in its making). Canned tomatoes are typically very salty, so do not add salt to this dish.

4 tablespoons extra-virgin olive oil
1 medium-size onion, chopped
3 thick slices stale white bread, crusts removed and cubed

3 ounces Pedro Ximenez sherry
3 (14½-ounce) cans diced tomatoes, with juice (do not drain)
2 teaspoons brown sugar
¾ teaspoon hot red pepper flakes
½ teaspoon dried oregano

Heat the oil in a large saucepan over medium-high heat. Add the onion, reduce heat to medium, and sauté, stirring frequently, until the onion begins to soften, about 4 minutes. Add the bread cubes and stir until all the oil has been absorbed. Add the sherry and stir, continuing to cook until most of the liquid has evaporated or been absorbed. Add the tomatoes and their juice as well as the brown sugar, red pepper flakes, and oregano. When the mixture begins to gently boil, reduce the heat to low and simmer, uncovered, for 45 minutes, stirring occasionally. If the stew becomes too thick, add up to ½ cup water and stir. If you stew the tomatoes in the afternoon, just turn off the heat when they're done and let them sit in the pot, covered, to be quickly reheated before serving that evening.

WINTER SUCCOTASH

Winter succotash means succotash made from frozen and canned vegetables. The inclusion of baby peas makes for an interesting variation on this simple dish.

2 (10-ounce) packages frozen Fordhook lima beans
½ (10-ounce) package frozen baby peas
2 (11-ounce) cans whole-kernel sweet corn, drained
½ cup (1 stick) salted butter
8 to 10 fresh mint leaves, chopped
salt and freshly ground black pepper to taste

Place a steamer basket in a large pot, fill the pot with water to the level of the basket's bottom, and bring the water to a boil. Add the lima beans and peas, cover, and steam for 5 minutes, or until just tender. Add the corn and steam for 1 minute more.

In a large mixing bowl, cut the butter into chunks. Add the steamed vegetables and sprinkle with the mint. Mix until the butter has melted. Add salt and pepper to taste, then mix again. Transfer to a serving bowl and serve immediately.

MARYLAND-STYLE CORNBREAD

The sugar's presence marks this as a "Northern" sort of cornbread; the bacon fat (preferred to butter or corn oil, though either of these may be used as an alternative) signals that the cornbread is "Southern." See what we mean about Maryland being in-between? Please note that this is a *double* recipe, meant for a party of twelve. If you're making only a single cornbread, cut all the amounts in half.

2 cups unbleached all-purpose flour
2 cups yellow cornmeal
⅔ cup sugar
2 tablespoons baking powder
1 teaspoon salt
4 large eggs
2 cups milk
½ cup melted bacon fat (or melted butter, or corn oil)

Preheat the oven to 400° F. Grease two 9-inch round cake pans (or two 8-by-8-inch square pans). In a large mixing bowl, whisk together the dry ingredients. In a medium-size bowl, lightly beat the eggs, then pour in the milk and melted fat and mix. Make a well in the center of the dry ingredients and pour the liquid ingredients into it. With a wooden spoon or a spatula, mix until all the flour is just moistened. Do not over-mix. Pour half the batter into each pan. Bake for 20 to 25 minutes, until the center springs back when you press gently with your finger and a knife inserted into the center comes out clean.

LADY BALTIMORE CAKE

With this extraordinary cake, we're cheating a little. Despite its name, it's not really a Maryland dessert, or wasn't originally. It has, in fact, a highly unusual origin. In 1906, a romance writer by the name of Owen Wister (fine name, that, for a writer of bodice-rippers) published a novel set in Charleston, South Carolina. One of the characters was a Lady Baltimore, who in the book created a white cake, with nuts, and named it for herself. It took two sisters who ran a Charleston tea room—and who were fans of Wister's—to bring this fictional confection into real-ity. Many versions of the cake now exist, though all share the ultra-fluffy "boiled" frosting and the nougat-like filling. Here's Ramona's recipe. Because the cake, filling, and frosting are (of course) made separately, we present the ingredients and instructions as separate steps.

FOR THE CAKE:
¾ cup (1½ sticks) unsalted butter
2 cups sugar
½ cup milk
½ cup water
2 teaspoons vanilla extract
3 cups cake flour

3 teaspoons baking powder
½ teaspoon salt
6 large egg whites

Make the cake: Preheat the oven to 350° F. Grease and flour two round 9-inch cake pans. In a large mixing bowl, cream the butter and sugar until fluffy. In a small bowl, combine the milk, water, and vanilla. In another small bowl, sift together the flour, baking powder, and salt. In small amounts, add the dry ingredients and the liquid ingredients alternately to the creamed butter, beating well. In another bowl, beat the egg whites until stiff, then fold them gently into the batter. Pour the batter into the prepared pans. Bake for 25 minutes or until a toothpick inserted in the center of each layer comes out clean. Transfer the pans to wire racks and let the cake layers cool before turning them out of the pans.

FOR THE FILLING:

Special equipment: candy thermometer

1½ cups sugar
⅛ teaspoon cream of tartar
6 tablespoons water
2 large egg whites, at room temperature
1 teaspoon vanilla extract
1 tablespoon finely grated lemon zest
1 cup chopped dried figs
1 cup chopped raisins
¾ cup chopped pecans
¾ cup chopped walnuts

Make the filling: Combine the sugar, cream of tartar, and water in a heavy saucepan. Insert a candy thermometer in the pan and cook the mixture over medium heat, stirring frequently, until the mixture—now a syrup—reaches the soft-ball stage (235° to 240° F).

In a medium-size mixing bowl, beat the egg whites until soft peaks form. Continuing to beat, slowly pour the hot syrup in a thin stream

into the egg whites and beat until stiff peaks form. Add the vanilla and lemon zest and beat until just blended. Stir in the fruits and nuts.

Assemble the cake: Place one layer top side down on a serving plate. Spread with the filling. Trim the top of the other layer so that it is flat, and place this layer, also top side down, atop the first layer. Let stand until the frosting is ready.

FOR THE FROSTING:

1 cup sugar
4 large egg whites, at room temperature
1 tablespoon light corn syrup
⅛ teaspoon salt
3 tablespoons cold water
1 teaspoon vanilla extract
walnut halves and finely grated lemon zest

Make the frosting: Fill the bottom of a large double boiler two-thirds full with water and bring the water to a boil. In the double boiler's top (off the heat), combine the sugar, egg whites, corn syrup, and salt. Add the cold water and beat at low speed with an electric mixer until just blended, about 30 seconds. Now place over the boiling water and beat at high speed until stiff peaks form, about 7 minutes. Remove from the heat and place over a bowl of cold water. Let stand for 5 minutes, then stir in the vanilla.

Spoon the still-warm frosting on top of the filled cake. Smooth the sides. Garnish the top and sides with walnut halves. Immediately before serving, sprinkle the center of the top with freshly grated lemon zest.

BAR ASSOCIATIONS

ORCHESTRAS AND SETUPS

The wintertime oyster roasts of not-so-many-decades-ago Maryland were relatively formal, evening affairs. Men and women dressed up for these social occasions. Bands played—James's relatives called them "orchestras," even if they were smallish combos—and people danced. Roasts sponsored by organizations such as political groups and charities typically offered, along with the food, "beer and setups." Setups, in case you can't guess, were mixers for mixed drinks—sodas, mostly. If you were intending to have cocktails, you were expected to bring your own hard liquor. (Wine, of course, was virtually unknown among the working- and middle-class Marylanders of the day.)

And because the roasts were held during the colder months, the liquor that you'd bring along would be "brown" liquor—that is, whiskey. This was hardly just a Maryland tradition, this cultural dictate that brown liquor was to be drunk in winter, white liquor in summer. A gin and tonic in January? Unthinkable. Just not done. (The gin Martini alone managed to escape such seasonal censure; think of it as the rule-proving exception.)

And what kinds of mixed drinks would be concocted with that brown liquor and those setups? Well, you'd probably be pouring your own, and bar equipment would be scarce, which means that most of the mixed drinks were *highballs:* simple booze-and-soda (or booze-and-water) combinations poured directly over ice in tall glasses. Ungarnished and far from fancy, the highball still strikes us as a sophisticated libation. And so we offer you recipes for three classic highballs, the first of which is *the* capital-H Highball, if you want to get technical about it.

CLASSIC HIGHBALL

 "Made in a hurry" is what *highball* means, since the drink, which originated among nineteenth-century railway men, was named for a railroad signal (a green ball, held up high) that meant "Pass. Proceed swiftly."

2 ounces Canadian blended whisky
ginger ale or club soda

Fill a highball glass with ice. Pour in the whisky and top with
the ginger ale or soda. Stir briefly.

7 AND 7

This variation on the Highball takes its name from the brands
of Canadian whisky and lemon-lime soda used.

2 ounces Seagram's 7 Crown whisky
7-Up

Fill a highball glass with ice. Pour in the whisky and top with
the 7-Up. Stir briefly.

BOURBON AND BRANCH

Would most bartenders today even know what to do if asked to
make a Bourbon and Branch? The truth is, this old-fashioned,
refined-sounding name disguises an utterly simple drink. *Branch*
is short for *branch water,* which literally means water from a
small creek (a branch, or tributary, of a larger stream). Since
most bars don't stock water from small creeks (and haven't for
ages!), plain, still spring water will do.

2 ounces bourbon
still spring water

Fill a highball glass with ice. Pour in the bourbon and top with
the water. Stir briefly.

THE SUMMERTIME (CRAB) BUFFET

There were days when the air in downtown Baltimore smelled like cinnamon. There were days when it smelled like cloves. And there were days when the air was redolent with a distinctly curry-like scent—the inimitable smell of Baltimore's own contribution to the world of seasonings, Old Bay.

The fragrances emanated from the old McCormick & Co. spice factory, a hulking monster of a building that sat hard by Baltimore's Inner Harbor, just a few blocks south of the city's central business district. Established in 1889 and now a multinational giant, McCormick has long since relocated its headquarters to the Baltimore suburbs, and that great spice factory has been razed. But those who grew up in the Baltimore of four-plus decades ago well remember the harborside McCormick plant and the way the goings-on there regularly perfumed the city's air.

Why this rhapsody about the McCormick company? Because for Marylanders, the fragrance and flavor of many local crab dishes cannot be divorced from the smell and taste of McCormick's Old Bay seasoning. Old Bay's compound of spices and herbs—which includes black and red pepper, bay leaves, cloves, allspice, ginger, mace, and cardamom, among others—seems calibrated specifically to enhance blue crabs' flavor. (Oh, it's good with many other things, too; see our steamed shrimp recipe on page 70.) On those long-ago days when the scent of Old Bay wafted through downtown Baltimore's atmosphere, it smelled as if the whole city were having a crab feast.

Two of the dishes in our summertime crab buffet—the Maryland Crab Soup and the Crab Imperial—rely upon Old Bay as an essential seasoning. (And we've also created a variation on one very famous mixed drink that, in our version, incorporates Old Bay; see the sidebar on page 216.) Here's the buffet's complete menu.

Crab Buffet

CRAB PUFFS
MARYLAND CRAB SOUP
CRAB IMPERIAL
SOFT CRAB SANDWICHES
MARYLAND FRIED TOMATOES
FRESH CORN SALAD
FRESH PEACH CHIFFON PIE

BLACK-EYED SUSAN
SEYVAL KIR
BLOODY MARY(LAND)

This buffet is meant to serve twelve people. Plan your buffet for a late afternoon or early evening. As usual, here are some strategy notes: The pastry puffs for the crab puffs can be baked several days ahead and either stored in the freezer or, if the weather's dry, simply enclosed in a sealed plastic bag until it's time to use them. The crab soup can be prepared a day ahead of time (some people swear it's better the second day), refrigerated, and reheated just before serving. Start the morning of your buffet day by beginning work on the peach chiffon pie, whose first steps require a couple of hours (mostly waiting—not active—time) and which takes several hours to set once it's been made. In the early afternoon, pick through the crab meat that will be used in the crab-puff filling and Crab Imperial (this is an annoyingly time-consuming but absolutely necessary task), and clean and bread the softshell crabs. The Fresh Corn Salad can also be prepared in the early afternoon, then chilled until serving time. During the two hours or so before guests arrive, make the filling for the crab puffs and assemble them. Prepare the Crab Imperial mixture and place it in ramekins. Cut the tomatoes for the fried tomatoes but refrain from flouring them until just before frying.

Unfortunately, you'll have to spend some time away from your guests and in the kitchen once the soup course is on the buffet table. During the last half-hour or so before serving the main course, flour and fry the tomatoes, sauté the softshell crabs (guests can assemble their own sandwiches), and bake the Crab Imperial.

An additional note: Processed fresh blue-crab meat (which has been removed from the shell and steamed) is generally sold in one-pound containers, in three grades: lump, backfin, and claw. Use lump—the best and most expensive grade—for the Crab Imperial. Use the flakier backfin for the soup and crab puffs. Cheaper, darker, and more strongly flavored, claw meat should not be used for any of these recipes.

CRAB PUFFS

A fitting hors d'oeuvre for this buffet, Crab Puffs also make great finger food for cocktail parties. The recipe will yield about four dozen puffs.

FOR THE PASTRY PUFFS:

1 cup water
½ cup (1 stick) unsalted butter
¼ teaspoon salt
1 cup unbleached all-purpose flour
4 large eggs

FOR THE FILLING:

1 pound fresh blue-crab meat, backfin grade
½ cup finely chopped celery
¼ cup chopped fresh flat-leaf parsley
6 tablespoons mayonnaise
1 tablespoon thinly sliced scallions, green tops only
1 teaspoon Dijon mustard
1 teaspoon fresh lemon juice
¼ teaspoon sweet paprika
dash of Worcestershire sauce
salt and freshly ground black pepper to taste

Make the pastry puffs: Preheat the oven to 400° F and line a baking sheet with parchment paper. In a small saucepan, heat the water, butter, and salt over high heat until the mixture boils and the butter melts. Lower the heat and add the flour all at once. Beat vigorously until the mixture pulls away from the sides of the pan and forms a ball. Remove from the heat. Add the eggs one at a time, beating until smooth after each egg is added. Drop the batter by the teaspoonful onto the prepared baking sheet, spacing 2 inches apart. Bake for 35 to 40 minutes, until the puffs are golden brown and dry. Remove from the oven and place the sheet on a wire rack. When the puffs are cool, make a slit in the top or side of each. Remove any soft or spongy dough inside the puff.

Make the filling and assemble the puffs: Carefully pick through the crab meat, removing any bits of shell. In a medium-size bowl, combine the crab meat with the remaining ingredients and mix well. Fill a pastry bag or a resealable plastic bag with the filling, cut off the tip or corner, and squeeze filling into each puff.

MARYLAND CRAB SOUP

Ramona amazed James with this recipe, which tastes exactly like the crab soup of his youth. (Let other writers have their madeleines; James has his crab soup.) Tomatoey and beefy, Maryland crab soup is very unlike other seafood soups. Marylanders often add broken pieces of whole crab and crab claws to their crab soup—to be contentedly sucked on when the soup's been eaten. We thought that practice rather too messy—barbaric, even—for your polite buffet, so this crab soup uses shelled crab meat only.

1 pound fresh blue-crab meat, backfin grade

¼ cup (½ stick) salted butter

1 medium-size onion, diced

3 quarts water

1 (14½-ounce) can beef broth

1 (28-ounce) can diced tomatoes, drained

¾ cup pearl barley

1 cup corn kernels, fresh or frozen

1 cup lima beans, fresh (shelled) or frozen

1 cup string beans, fresh or frozen, cut into 1-inch pieces

1 cup thinly sliced cabbage

2 stalks celery, chopped

2 carrots, peeled and cut into ¼-inch coins

¼ cup chopped fresh flat-leaf parsley

1 tablespoon Old Bay seasoning

1 tablespoon fresh marjoram leaves

1 teaspoon sweet paprika

salt and freshly ground black pepper to taste

Carefully pick through the crab meat, removing any bits of shell. Melt the butter in a large pot over medium heat, add the onion, and sauté until translucent, 6 to 7 minutes. Add the water, broth, tomatoes, barley, and crab meat. Reduce the heat to medium-low, cover, and simmer for 30 minutes. Add the remaining ingredients. Cover and simmer until the vegetables are tender. Ladle into mugs or small, deep bowls (rice bowls work beautifully for a buffet), about 1 cup per person. Serve with a good sliced white bread and butter.

CRAB IMPERIAL

Less is more: That minimalist aesthetic dictum applies better to Crab Imperial than to any other dish we know. Crab Imperial should taste mostly of crab meat—and because blue crab can so easily be overwhelmed by other tastes (even that of egg), it is essential that seasonings be used sparingly and that only enough egg be used to vaguely bind the lumps of crab meat together. The same goes for the mayonnaise and butter: They're meant to subtly flavor the dish and to keep it just moist enough to endure baking. We bake our Crab Imperial in vintage crab-shaped glass ramekins (a flea-market treasure), but any small ramekins (capacity: about ⅔ cup) will do. That portion may seem small, but the dish is so lusciously rich that a little goes a very long way.

THE CRAB-SHAPED RAMEKIN

2 pounds fresh jumbo lump blue-crab meat
1 extra-large egg
⅓ cup mayonnaise
2 teaspoons grated onion
2 teaspoons very finely minced green bell pepper
½ teaspoon Coleman's dry mustard
½ teaspoon Old Bay seasoning
¼ teaspoon Worcestershire sauce
⅛ teaspoon salt
pinch of freshly ground black pepper
½ stick unsalted butter, cut into 12 pats
sweet paprika

Preheat the oven to 350° F. Carefully pick through the crab meat, removing any bits of shell but leaving the lumps as intact as possible. In a medium-size mixing bowl, combine the crab meat, egg, mayonnaise, onion, green pepper, dry mustard, Old Bay, Worcestershire sauce, salt, and pepper and gently mix until the crab meat is lightly but evenly coated. Spoon the crab mixture into 12 small ramekins and dot each with a pat of butter. Lightly sprinkle paprika over each, then bake for 20 minutes or until lightly browned. Serve immediately.

SOFT CRAB SANDWICHES

Moving to New York City was a shocking experience for James. It wasn't the noise, the dirt, or the tumult that distressed him; it was that you can hardly find an NYC restaurant that prepares softshell crabs properly. New York chefs do all manner of *wrong* stuff to what Marylanders call "soft crabs"—often loading them down with almond- or caper-heavy sauces that drown softshells' fragile deliciousness. For a native Baltimorean, it's a travesty to do much more to a soft crab than to bread it lightly and quickly sauté it in butter (or, as in the following recipe, a combination of butter and oil).

This just-right recipe comes to these pages courtesy of James's stepfather, Ken Frederick. Its Maryland bona fides cannot be gainsaid. Note: When buying fresh softshell crabs, make sure that they're alive when you purchase them. (Though molting has sapped their energy, live soft crabs do move, though sluggishly.) Try to get crabs measuring between three and a half and four and a half inches, point to point. If you're squeamish, have the fishmonger clean them for you; cleaning softshell crabs is not difficult, but it does amount to the torture of poor, defenseless creatures. Here's how to do it: First, using a sharp knife or kitchen shears, cut off the crab's "face" (its eyes and mouth parts). Now, lift the points at both ends of the crab's body and, using a paring knife or your fingers, scrape or pull off the gills (the grayish, feathery organs) beneath. Finally, turn the crab over and pry up and remove the pointed flap (called the "apron") attached to the bottom shell; it should break off easily. Rinse the crab in cold water and pat dry. Once they're deceased, softshell crabs spoil rapidly; refrigerate them after cleaning and cook them within a few hours.

12 softshell crabs, cleaned
salt and freshly ground black pepper
2 cups all-purpose flour
4 egg whites, beaten until just frothy
2 cups panko (Japanese-style bread crumbs)
1¼ cups extra-virgin olive oil, plus more if needed
½ cup (1 stick) salted butter, plus more if needed
sliced white bread, romaine lettuce leaves, sliced tomatoes, and mayonnaise for sandwiches

Lift the points of each crab's shell and lightly salt and pepper the interior. Lightly dredge each crab in the flour, then dip it into the egg whites and then into the panko, lightly but evenly coating it with the crumbs. In a large (13-inch), heavy-bottomed frying pan, heat the oil over medium-high heat until it just begins to smoke. Add the butter, giving it a moment to melt before proceeding. Add 6 crabs to the pan, bottom shell down. Sauté for 5 minutes, then turn and sauté for an additional 3 minutes, or until the top shells are a rich reddish brown and the crabs are firm to the touch. (Cooking time will vary depending on the size of the crabs.) Repeat with the other 6 crabs, replenishing the oil and butter if necessary.

The crabs can be eaten by themselves, but provide your guests with sliced bread, lettuce, tomatoes, and mayonnaise so that they can make sandwiches if they wish.

Doubtless, some guests will recoil at eating the shells, claws, and legs, but exert some stiff peer pressure and they'll soon learn to enjoy the experience.

Maryland Fried Tomatoes

Folks farther south fry their tomatoes green. For Maryland fried tomatoes, however, you should use tomatoes that are ever so slightly ripe—just at the point when a pale pink-orange hue has begun to mottle the skins and flesh but the tomatoes are still quite firm. If possible, use large beefsteak tomatoes (four to five inches at their longest diameter and weighing about half to three-quarters of a pound apiece). This recipe should provide two slices of fried tomato for each of twelve guests—plenty for a buffet like this.

6 large, semi-ripe tomatoes
3 cups all-purpose flour
½ teaspoon salt
¼ teaspoon freshly ground black pepper
1¼ cups extra-virgin olive oil, plus more if needed
sugar

Slice the tomatoes into thick (½-inch) slices, discarding slices from the stem ends and bottoms. (Each slice must be cut on both sides.) In a large, shallow bowl, whisk together the flour, salt, and pepper. Dredge the tomato slices in the flour mixture and set aside. Heat the oil in a large (13-inch), heavy-bottomed frying pan over medium-high heat. When the oil just begins to smoke, add a batch of floured tomato slices to the pan, arranging them in a single layer and leaving about ½ inch between the slices. Fry until brown and slightly crunchy on the bottom, 4 to 6 minutes, then carefully turn and fry until browned on the other side, another 3 to 5 minutes. Carefully remove from the pan (the tomatoes may fall apart, slightly) and drain on paper towels. (You may wish to keep the already-fried tomatoes warm in the oven while frying the rest.) Repeat with additional batches, replenishing the oil if necessary and draining on paper towels when done. Transfer to a serving platter and lightly sprinkle each slice with sugar.

FRESH CORN SALAD

People usually identify corn with the Midwest. But the mid-Atlantic region of the United States—Maryland especially—enjoys a climate that's just about ideal for growing sweet corn. Corn season, which extends from July into October, coincides with peak crabbing season, and crabs and corn are inextricably linked in Marylanders' minds. For years, the white corn variety called Silver Queen ruled Marylanders' corn-loving palates, but we're given to understand that Silver Queen has recently been knocked off her throne by several other white varieties that are even sweeter. No matter. Any variety of sweet corn—white, bicolored, or yellow—can be used in the following recipe. The fresher the corn, the better the salad will be.

8 ears sweet corn (any color), husked
1 cup minced red bell pepper
¼ cup extra-virgin olive oil
1 tablespoon unflavored brown rice vinegar
1 clove garlic, finely minced
¼ cup fresh basil leaves, thinly sliced
¼ cup chopped fresh flat-leaf parsley
2 tablespoons chopped fresh oregano leaves
2 tablespoons minced fresh chives
salt and freshly ground black pepper to taste

Bring salted water to boil in a large stockpot. Drop in the ears of corn and cook until just tender, 5 to 6 minutes. Drain in a colander and immediately spray the corn with cold water to stop the cooking process. Pat the ears dry with paper towels and, using a sharp knife, cut the kernels from the cobs. Combine the corn kernels and bell pepper in a medium-size mixing bowl. In a separate bowl, combine the remaining ingredients and whisk them until the mixture emulsifies. Pour this dressing over the corn mixture, mix, toss to combine, and refrigerate for 1 to 4 hours before serving.

DOG DAY QUENCHERS

The dog days of August—which in Maryland often extend well into September—are crab feast season. Beer and, more recently, white wine are the usual beverages of choice. (French whites from the Loire Valley, especially Muscadet, Vouvray, and white Touraines partner marvelously with crab dishes.) But there's no reason *Drinkology EATS* can think of not to whip up some refreshing summertime cocktails, as well. Here are three suggestions.

BLOODY MARY(LAND)

We had to try it, and we're glad we did. Old Bay seasoning does indeed make a fine addition to a classic Bloody Mary.

♒ lemon wedge
2 ounces vodka
4 ounces tomato juice
½ ounce fresh lemon juice
½ teaspoon Old Bay seasoning
¼ teaspoon Tabasco sauce
2 or 3 dashes Worcestershire sauce
♒ celery stalk

Rim a highball glass with the lemon wedge and fill the glass with ice cubes. Combine the vodka, tomato juice, lemon juice, Old Bay, Tabasco sauce, and Worcestershire sauce in a cocktail shaker, with ice. Shake well, then strain to the glass. Squeeze the lemon wedge into the drink, and drop it in. Garnish with the celery stalk.

SEYVAL KIR

This version of the classic Kir celebrates a white-wine grape widely grown in Maryland's vineyards and, in fact, up and down the East Coast. Called Seyval Blanc, it's one of the class of grapes known as French hybrids—crosses between European *Vitis vinifera* vines and native American vine species that were developed in response to the *Phylloxera* epidemic that ravaged French vineyards in the nineteenth century. (For a synopsis of this desperate chapter in wine's history, see this book's companion volume *Drinkology WINE: A Guide to the Grape,* pages 122–125.) Though disparaged by many wine snobs, dry Seyval Blanc wines, at their best, can resemble dry Rieslings in their combination of crispness and lush fruitiness.

♭ lemon twist
½ teaspoon crème de cassis
chilled dry Seyval Blanc
2 or 3 ice cubes (optional)

Rim a chilled white wine glass with the lemon twist. Pour the crème de cassis into the glass and top with the wine. Stir briefly and garnish with the twist. If you wish, you may plunk a few ice cubes into the glass.

BLACK-EYED SUSAN

Botanically speaking, the daisy-like black-eyed Susan is Maryland's official state flower. Mixologically speaking, the swizzle-like Black-Eyed Susan is Maryland's unofficial state mixed drink. It's the drink served at Baltimore's Pimlico race track each May during the running of the Preakness Stakes, the second "jewel" in horse racing's Triple Crown. But there's no need to confine it to one afternoon in May; it's a formidable summertime heat-quencher.

🍸 lime wedge
crushed ice
¾ ounce Cointreau
¾ ounce dark rum
¾ ounce vodka
2 to 3 ounces orange juice
2 to 3 ounces pineapple juice

Rim a highball glass with the lime wedge. Fill the glass loosely with crushed ice. Pour in the liquors, then top with equal amounts of orange and pineapple juice (2 to 3 ounces each). Stir briefly, then garnish with the lime wedge.

Fresh Peach Chiffon Pie

Boy, do we ever jump back to yesteryear with this recipe. Does anyone even make the creamy confections known as chiffon pies any more? Well, yeah. Ramona does—and after you've made it once, this peach chiffon pie with graham cracker crust will become a standard of your summertime repertoire, too. (If you want to save yourself a bit of trouble, use a store-bought graham cracker piecrust.)

FOR THE PIECRUST:

1¼ cups finely crushed graham cracker crumbs (about 22 squares)
2 tablespoons sugar
6 tablespoons (¾ stick) salted butter, melted

FOR THE FILLING:

1 envelope (1 tablespoon) unflavored gelatin
¼ cup warm water
¼ cup very hot water
2 cups (about 4) very ripe, soft peaches, peeled, pitted, and finely chopped
¾ cup sugar
1 tablespoon fresh lemon juice
1 large egg white
⅛ teaspoon salt
1 cup heavy cream

Make the piecrust: In a medium-size mixing bowl, mix together the graham cracker crumbs and sugar. Pour in the melted butter and mix well. Transfer to a 9-inch pie plate, firmly pressing the crumb mixture onto the bottom and sides to form an even crust. Chill for at least 1 hour before filling.

Make the filling: In a small bowl, soften the gelatin in the warm water. Pour in the hot water and stir until the gelatin is completely dissolved. In a large mixing bowl, combine the peaches, ½ cup of the sugar, and the lemon juice and let stand for 30 minutes. Pour the gelatin into the peach mixture and mix until well combined. Chill until the mixture begins to thicken, about 1 hour. When the peach mixture has begun to set, beat the egg white together with the salt until soft peaks form. Gradually add the remaining ¼ cup sugar and beat until stiff peaks form, then fold the egg-white mixture into the peach mixture. Whip the cream until stiff peaks form and fold it into the peach mixture until thoroughly incorporated. Pour into the graham cracker crust and refrigerate until firm, at least 3 hours.

CHAPTER NINE

¿Comida No Problema?

A MEXICAN COCKTAIL PARTY/BUFFET

RAMONA COMES BY HER TALENT FOR MEXICAN COOKERY NATURALLY. As we told you in chapter 7, Ramona is part German, but her father's side of the family is Mexican—meaning that chiles were as common as sauerkraut in her girlhood household.

In her catering gigs, she's often served Mexican and Southwestern-style food. A few years back, Ramona catered a Tex-Mex–themed holiday party for a New York company; the party was held at the firm's offices, which occupied a floor of an office tower in midtown Manhattan. She was told to prepare food for about 150 people, but as always in such situations, she took the client's head-count as a low estimate and prepared enough to feed, she figured, 200 or so. And she engaged the services of a small crew of waiters, including her sister Rachel.

From Ramona's point of view, the party looked like trouble from the moment she arrived, a couple of hours before the event was to begin. She and her helpers were ushered into a small room, which they were told would be their prep area. The room—an unused office—had no stove, no refrigerator, no sink. In fact, it had *no* furniture at all: not even a desk to serve as a table. It was, however, equipped with a small microwave oven, conveniently parked *on the floor.*

Ramona has an undeniable talent for calmly making the best of a bad situation. By the time the party began, she'd organized a scheme for getting the food heated, arranged on serving trays, and out the door and into the hands and mouths of the hungry, holiday-spirited revelers. For the first hour or so of the party, things went well.

Too well. Looking alarmed, the waiters returning to Ramona's makeshift kitchen began reporting to her that the crowd was swelling.

Things went well—too well

Apparently, word had rapidly circulated among office workers elsewhere in the building that there was a great shindig—with great food—happening on the whatever-it-was floor. What had been planned as an intra-company fête was quickly exploding into a building-wide free-for-all.

The food supplies dwindled. Pretty soon, all the pre-prepped canapés had disappeared, and Ramona found herself down to the basics: some extra tortillas, refried beans, cheese, and pickled hot peppers that—who knows why?—she'd had the foresight to bring along. And so she began churning out a slapdash version of a Tex-Mex standard, chalupas. (Slather some refried beans on tortilla wedges, sprinkle a little grated cheese on them, dot them with hot pepper slices, and microwave them till the cheese melts.)

By this time, the waiters were, let us say, *over it.* The burgeoning size of the party and the intensity of the work were much more than they'd bargained for, and they were feeling harried and tired—and in no mood to suffer fools. Equipped with yet another tray of tossed-together chalupas, Ramona's sister Rachel was making her umpteenth foray into the crowd when she was cornered by a lawyer-broker-accountant type, who began shoveling the chalupas from her tray into his besotted maw. "Man, these are delicious!" he exclaimed. "What do you call this?"

Fixing him with an icy deadpan the likes of which only Rachel can summon, she responded, "Oh, this? We call this *comida no problema.*

¿Comida no problema? In truth, the recipes presented in this chapter—or many of them—require a good deal of time and attention. On the other hand, these dishes are *fun* to make (assuming you like to cook, that is). If you've never eaten prickly pear cactus—never even considered such a thing—prepare yourself for an unusual treat. (We provide two recipes employing prickly pear "pads"—called *nopales* in Mexico.) If you've never made your own tamales—or tortillas, for that matter—get ready to learn some interesting and useful skills. If it's never occurred to you that fish might be raw and "cooked" at the same time, say *buenas dias* to the extraordinary dish called ceviche. And the original *comida no problema*—chalupas? We've got those, too—though this more finely crafted version uses fresh corn tortillas and homemade refried beans. So where's the problem, anyhow? Here's the menu:

The waiters were *over it*

Menu

STARTERS AND DIPS
CHILES TOREADOS
SALSA CRUDA
NOPALITOS DIP
MEXICAN-STYLE GUACAMOLE

FINGER FOODS
Jicama Canapés
Chicken Cubes with Mole
Chorizos/Quesa Fresca with Salsa Verde
Chalupas

BUFFET
Ceviche
Nopalitos Salad
Tamales with Shredded Pork and Chile Filling
Refried Beans
Homemade Corn Tortillas
Salsas and Crema for Dipping

DESSERT
Buñuelitos
Flan Napolitano

DRINKS
Tequila Shots
Sangrita
Iced Hibiscus Tea
The Easiest, Best Frozen Margarita Ever
TNT Coffee

Now, granted, this is quite a spread. (We've calibrated the recipes to feed a hungry party of twelve.) Here are some strategy notes:

First, when shopping for the party, be sure to buy *lots* of limes. Fresh lime juice is an essential ingredient in many Mexican dishes and mixed drinks, and you'll need lime wedges for garnishes, as well. So play it safe and lay in at least three dozen.

Plan your cocktail party/buffet for early evening. Begin your work *two evenings earlier* by soaking the pinto beans for the refried beans and the corn husks for the tamales. The day before the party, make the flan, the refried beans, and the tamales (which can be refrigerated and then resteamed before serving).

On the morning of the day of the party, squeeze the limes for all the fresh lime juice you'll need. Make the ceviche, the nopalitos dip, and the nopalitos salad. In the late morning/early afternoon, mix up the sangrita, infuse the hibiscus tea, make the tortillas, and make and fry the buñuelitos (which can be rewarmed in the oven before serving). In the mid- to late afternoon, make the salsas, the guacamole, the jicama canapés; fry the tortillas for the chalupas; and prepare the mole sauce for the chicken, setting it aside and reheating it just before you need it.

Two hours before the guests arrive, assemble the chalupas; broil the chicken and chorizo slices. During the final half-hour before the party begins, assemble the chicken cubes with mole and plate up the quesa fresca and chorizos with salsa verde. When the guests arrive, make the chiles toreados and broil the chalupas (to serve immediately), and begin resteaming the tamales for the buffet. Reheat the refried beans just before setting the buffet table. Rewarm the buñuelitos just before serving dessert. And throughout the party, make up batches of the Easiest, Best Frozen Margarita Ever as your guests demand.

STARTERS AND DIPS

Warm up the party (in more ways than one) by presenting your just-arriving guests with freshly grilled chiles toreados; bowls of salsa cruda, nopalitos dip, and guacamole (with plenty of tortilla chips on the side); and shots of a good white (*blanco*) tequila. Among the *blanco* tequilas we

STOVETOP ROASTING

Several of the recipes in this chapter call for roasted and seeded hot chiles (jalapeños or serranos) and/or tomatoes. It isn't hard to roast chiles and tomatoes directly over a stovetop burner's flame, but it must be done carefully. Here are Ramona's suggestions:

To roast and clean a chile: Spear the chile with a fork. Turn the burner on high. Hold the speared chile very close to the flame—even within the top part of the flame. As the chile heats, you will hear it pop and crackle as its skin splits and chars. Rotate the chile very slowly, exposing all of its skin to the flame. When the chile's skin has been roasted all over, place the chile in a resealable plastic bag, seal the bag, and let it sit for 5 to 10 minutes. (The chile will continue to steam while inside the bag, and the seal will prevent the hot-pepper fumes from leaking out and stinging your eyes.)

Remove the chile from the bag and hold it under cold *running* water. With a paring knife, slit the chile lengthwise and, continuing to hold it under the running water, pull out the seeds and ribs. Pull off the stem and remove the skin, which should slip away easily from the flesh. (If any small bits of skin adhere to the flesh, just scrape them off.)

To roast and clean a tomato: Spear the tomato with a fork, and, as with a chile, hold the fruit as close to the burner's flame—turned on high—as possible. Because a tomato's skin is thinner and more fragile than a chile pepper's, hold each spot to the flame only until the skin wrinkles and loosens—don't char it. Rotate the tomato until its entire surface has been exposed to the flame and all the skin is wrinkly and soft. Place the tomato on a cutting board and pull off the skin, which should slip away easily. Cut the tomato into quarters and remove the seeds with a paring knife or your fingers.

especially like are the Chinaco and El Tesoro Platinum brands. Also offer your guests the Sangrita and the (non-alcoholic) hibiscus tea. (See the Bar Associations sidebar on page 253.) Save yourself some trouble and use store-bought tortilla chips for this part of the party.

CHILES TOREADOS

This starter is a favorite snack in the bars and grills of the northeastern Mexico city of Monterrey. It's breathtaking—in the literal sense. (Whew!) Grill only as many as you think your guests can handle. Four per person should do—unless, of course, your guests are macho types committed to proving the imperviousness of their palates. If so, make more—but ask yourself why you continue to hang out with such people.

4 serrano chiles per person
corn oil
salt to taste

Flatten the chiles with the side of a butcher knife or small cleaver. Rub each with corn oil. Heat a grill pan or large cast-iron skillet over medium-high heat and throw on the chiles, turning them until charred on all sides, about 12 minutes. Transfer to a serving plate with a small bowl of salt, for dipping, on the side.

SALSA CRUDA

Salsa cruda literally means "raw sauce." It's the absolutely basic salsa to serve with tortilla chips. For instructions on roasting and seeding the chiles, see the Technicalities sidebar opposite.

4 very ripe medium-size tomatoes, peeled and seeded
2 jalapeño or serrano chiles, roasted, peeled, and seeded

1 large white onion
1 cup fresh cilantro leaves
2 tablespoons extra-virgin olive oil
2 tablespoons fresh lime juice
½ teaspoon salt
⅛ teaspoon black pepper

Finely chop the tomatoes, chiles, onion, and cilantro and combine in a bowl. Add the oil, lime juice, salt, and pepper and mix well.

NOPALITOS DIP

Nopales are the young, tender, bright-green pads of the prickly pear cactus; when diced or cut into strips—as in this recipe—they're called *nopalitos*. One wonders, of course, what could have been going through the mind of the first person who decided to try to eat a cactus. (He or she must have been extremely hungry.) Setting aside that unsolvable food-history riddle, we can report that nopales/nopalitos are actually quite good, with a subtle flavor that resembles that of string beans. Nopales are commonly available at produce markets that serve a Latin American clientele; if possible, choose medium-size pads, about five inches long. The vegetable seller will usually remove the thorns for you; if, perchance, you must buy the nopales with thorns attached, remove them by laying each pad flat on a cutting board, holding the base firmly with a pot holder, and shaving off the thorns with a sharp knife.

Besides the thorns, nopales have another noteworthy and somewhat unpleasant characteristic: When cut, the pads ooze a clear, slimy substance similar to the slime released by okra. By slicing the nopales into thin strips and boiling them as directed in this recipe, you'll get rid of most of the slime.

This dip's other ingredients include a tomatillo, a Mexican fruit whose name and appearance (once its parchment-like husk is removed) recall a tomato's. Tomatillos are indeed related to tomatoes (they're both members of the nightshade family), but the tomatillo's subtly herbal taste is all its own. The recipe also calls for a red (that is, a ripened) jalapeño. As always when seeding and chopping raw jalapeño chiles, remember to protect your hands by wearing rubber gloves or sheathing them in plastic bags.

4 medium-size nopales, thorns removed
1 tomatillo, husked, cored, and halved
1 cup crema (Mexican sour cream)
2 red jalapeño chiles, seeded and chopped
1 small red onion, finely minced
½ red bell pepper, seeded and finely minced
⅔ cup fresh cilantro, chopped
2 teaspoons fresh lime juice
⅛ teaspoon ground cumin
salt to taste

Bring a large pot of salted water to boil over high heat. Cut the nopales crosswise into ½-inch strips. Add the nopales strips and the tomatillo halves to the boiling water. Remove the tomatillos when tender, about 5 minutes, and set aside. Boil the nopales strips for an additional 10 minutes. Drain the nopales, rinse in cold water, and dry the strips with paper towels, wiping away any residual slime. Dice the tomatillo halves when they have cooled.

Combine the crema, jalapeños, onion, bell pepper, cilantro, lime juice, and cumin in a food processor and pulse until fairly smooth. Add the diced tomatillo and the nopales strips and pulse until the mixture is just slightly chunky. Transfer to a serving bowl, add salt, and mix well. Serve with tortilla chips.

Mexican-Style Guacamole

Dios only knows how many thousands—millions?—of recipes exist for guacamole, the quintessential Mexican avocado salad/dip. (We ourselves provide you with yet another, in chapter 10; see page 330.) The following version is simpler, chunkier, and less creamy—more faithful to the Mexican original—than many other guacs. Because avocados, once they're peeled, oxidize so quickly, guacamole is notoriously difficult to keep. Add the lime juice if you make the guacamole more than two hours before you serve it; it isn't needed for taste, but it will lessen the discoloration. Be sure to use the smaller, pebbly- and black-skinned Hass avocados for this (and all other!) avocado dishes; they're much more flavorful than the larger, smooth- and green-skinned Fuerte variety.

1 medium-size onion, diced
1 jalapeño chile, seeded and finely minced
¼ cup fresh cilantro leaves
1 teaspoon salt
2 medium-size ripe tomatoes, diced
4 ripe Hass avocados
1 tablespoon fresh lime juice, if needed

In a large mixing bowl, combine the onion, jalapeño, cilantro, and salt. With the back of a large spoon, press the mixture against the sides of the bowl until the onions begin to glisten. Add the tomatoes and mix. Cut the avocados in half lengthwise, remove the pits, peel them, and dice the flesh. Add the avocados to the onion-tomato mixture and gently mix until just combined. If you are making the guacamole more than 2 hours before serving, add the lime juice, mix again, transfer the guacamole to a container that can be tightly covered, and refrigerate until serving. Serve with tortilla chips.

FINGER FOODS

All the guests have arrived, and it's time to begin passing around the finger foods. We like this selection because it's so varied—ranging from the crisp, light, crunchy jicama canapés to the cheesy, greasy (greasy is good) chalupas. Because our chalupas require refried beans and home-made tortillas, we provide those recipes in this section.

JICAMA CANAPÉS

The large, light brown–skinned root vegetable called the jicama (HEE-kah-mah) is so commonly used in Mexican cookery that it's sometimes referred to as the "Mexican potato." When used raw, as in this recipe, jicama has a mild flavor and crunchy texture reminiscent of water chestnuts. Jicamas are no longer hard to find in American supermarkets.

¾ cup fresh lime juice
½ cup superfine sugar
1 medium-size jicama (about 1½ pounds)
3 medium-size oranges
48 fresh mint leaves

In a medium-size nonreactive mixing bowl, combine the lime juice and superfine sugar and stir until the sugar dissolves. Peel the jicama and cut the flesh into ¾-inch cubes. (The goal is to end up with 48 cubes altogether.) Cut the peels and white pith off the oranges and section them with a sharp paring knife, removing the white tissue between sections as well as any seeds. Cut each section in half crosswise. (You should be able to get 16 half-sections from each orange, for a total of 48.) Add the jicama cubes and orange pieces to the lime-sugar mixture, stir briefly, and let macerate for 30 minutes. Drain. Set each jicama cube on a work surface, top the cube with an orange section, place a mint leaf atop the orange, and spear with a cocktail pick. (Picks with colorful cellophane frills are especially appropriate for this canapé.) Arrange the canapés on a serving tray.

CHICKEN CUBES WITH MOLE

This dish really is *comida no problema.* Because doing so can be an all-day-long affair, Ramona wisely balks at the idea of making her own mole—the Mexican sauce that combines chiles, chocolate, and (in its more elaborate manifestations) many other ingredients. There are some excellent commercial moles on the market; we used the Doña María brand, whose sultry, complexly spicy flavor is offset by just a hint of sweetness. Like other commercial moles, Doña María mole is condensed; you must reconstitute it with water or chicken broth. Just half of an 8¼-ounce jar combined with two cups of broth make more than enough sauce for this recipe. If you use a different brand, follow the instructions on the label.

about 4 ounces condensed commercial mole, such as Doña María
2 cups chicken broth

2 large chicken breasts, about 1½ pounds
¼ cup sesame seeds

In a small saucepan, combine the condensed mole and chicken broth. Cook over low heat, stirring constantly, until the sauce is thickened, even-textured, and hot.

Broil the chicken breasts until cooked through, about 7 minutes on one side and 4 minutes on the other. (Slice one of the breasts at its thickest part to make sure it is completely cooked; if still pink in center, return breasts to broiler for 1 to 2 additional minutes.)

Allow the breasts to cool slightly before handling. Cut them into 1-inch cubes, discarding any irregular pieces. (You should end up with at least 24 cubes.) Spear each cube with a cocktail pick, dip it into the mole, and arrange the mole-coated cubes on serving trays. Sprinkle with sesame seeds and serve.

Salsa Verde

Both of the following two, utterly simple appetizers are served with salsa verde (that is, Mexican-style "green sauce"), so we give you the salsa recipe first. Double this recipe if you want to make enough salsa verde so that you can set a bowlful (for tortilla-dipping) on the buffet table, as well.

1 cup water
6 medium-size tomatillos, husked
1 small onion, chopped
2 jalapeño or serrano chiles, roasted, peeled, and seeded
4 medium-size cloves garlic
½ cup packed fresh cilantro leaves
salt to taste

In a medium saucepan, bring the water, tomatillos, onion, 1 chile, and 2 cloves garlic to a boil. Reduce the heat and simmer for 15 to 20 minutes, until the tomatillos burst and are completely soft. Remove from the heat, set aside, and let cool almost to room temperature. (If not cooled, the mixture will cook and discolor the cilantro when finishing the sauce.)

Meanwhile, place the remaining 1 chile and 2 cloves garlic in a mortar and, using a pestle, pulverize into a paste. Scrape the paste into a blender, add the cilantro, and pulse until smoothly pureed. With a slotted spoon, remove the cooled solids from the saucepan, add them to the blender, and pulse until smooth. The sauce should be only slightly thick. If too thick, add small amounts of the cooking liquid until the desired consistency is achieved. Add salt. Use as soon as possible, as the salt will begin leaching the brilliant green color from the salsa within just a few hours.

CHORIZOS WITH SALSA VERDE

Salsa verde performs beautifully as a dipping sauce for the chile-laden sausages called chorizos. We prefer Spanish-style chorizos, which use smoked pork and are firmer than Mexican-style chorizos, which use ground pork. Make sure that you buy *fully cooked* chorizos for this quick-to-assemble appetizer.

3 fully cooked chorizos
salsa verde (see recipe above)

Cut the chorizos into ½-inch slices and broil until heated through and just slightly browned, no more than 2 minutes per side. Spear the slices with cocktail picks and arrange around the circumference of a serving plate. Puddle salsa verde in the center of the plate, for dipping.

Quesa Fresca with Salsa Verde

And this appetizer is even simpler. Quesa fresca is Mexican fresh cheese (that's what the Spanish means) that's very close to feta in taste and texture. It's available in the dairy section of most large supermarkets. It often comes in 12-ounce, 1-inch-thick rounds; it's one of these that we use in this recipe.

1 (12-ounce) round of quesa fresca
salsa verde (see recipe on page 233)

Cut the round of cheese into 1-inch cubes. (It should yield at least 24, and possibly more, cubes.) Spear the cubes with cocktail picks and arrange around the circumference of a serving plate. Puddle salsa verde in the center of the plate, for dipping.

Homemade Corn Tortillas

Taste- and texture-wise, fresh, homemade tortillas are a world away from the packaged, store-bought variety. Making your own tortillas is neither difficult nor especially time-consuming—that is, once that you get the hang of it. The trick is to create a dough that's neither too stiff nor too pliant, neither too dry nor too moist.

To make her tortillas, Ramona uses a traditional wooden tortilla press (like the one pictured on the following page), which consists of two boards, hinged together, and a lever that enables you to press the top board very forcefully down onto the bottom board. Other types of tortilla presses—including circular metal presses—are widely available, but the instructions below explain the procedure when using a wooden press. (Wooden tortilla presses are sold at virtually all Mexican groceries and by many Internet purveyors.)

Masa harina, the special flour used for corn tortillas, is actually ground hominy—that is, corn kernels that have been treated with lye. Masa harina is available in the flour section of most supermarkets.

Special equipment: wooden tortilla press

2 cups masa harina, plus more if needed
1½ to 2½ cups water

Heat 1 or 2 (or more) nonstick frying pans or well-seasoned and lightly greased cast-iron frying pans over medium-high heat until water drops flicked onto the surface bounce around and scatter. (Keep the pans very hot, adjusting the heat as necessary, as you make the tortillas.)

In a medium-size mixing bowl, combine the masa harina with 1½ cups water. Add more water, if necessary, to make a soft dough that can easily be flattened without cracking but that is firm enough to be rolled into balls that do not flatten by themselves when set on a flat surface.

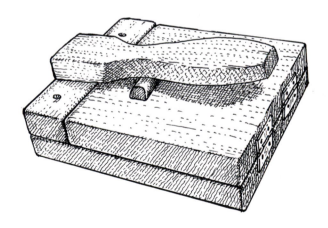

Scoop up about 1 tablespoon of the dough and roll it into a ball. You'll test the dough's consistency one tortilla at a time, until you achieve the correct ratio of masa harina to water.

Open the tortilla press and cover both boards with a clean, thin dishtowel (no terry cloth towels!) or a double length of paper towels. Place the dough ball in the center of the bottom board, fold the dishtowel or paper towel over it, close the press, put the lever in place, and press down on the lever, exerting as much pressure as you can on the top board. (Note: When making lots of tortillas, Ramona rarely uses the lever, which takes a little time to position. She prefers simply pressing down on the top board with her hands.)

The flattened tortilla should be less than ⅛ inch thick but firm enough to hold its shape and pliant enough not to crack at the edges. If the ball of dough will not flatten easily, the dough is too dry. Add more water to the dough and try again. Once you've flattened the tortilla, open the press and peel the towel from one side of the disc. If cracks appear around the edge of the tortilla, the dough is still too dry. If the towel does not peel easily off the tortilla, the dough is too moist. Adjust the proportion of masa harina to water accordingly, and try again.

When the towel peels away easily from both sides of the disc and the tortilla, when turned onto your hand, does not fall apart and yet is soft and pliant enough to sag slightly, you're very close to succeeding—but there's still one more test to go. Immediately turn the tortilla onto one of heated pans. It should sizzle briefly but should not stick to the pan, nor should steamy bubbles form underneath. If it sticks or bubbles, the dough is still too soft and wet. Add a little more masa harina to the dough and try again.

Once you've got the consistency just right, form all the dough into balls, flatten them one at a time in the press, and turn the discs onto the heated pan(s). Cook each tortilla for about 1 minute, until the edges begin to lift slightly from the pan, then quickly and carefully turn the tortilla over and cook the other side for about 1 minute. Do not let the tortilla brown or smoke. To test for doneness, turn the tortilla over again—it should puff up immediately. (Once you're reasonably certain you have the timing right, you do not need to do this with every tortilla.) Transfer the cooked tortillas to a plate or a flat-bottomed bowl lined with foil or a towel and keep warm until ready to serve.

Note: As you flatten the tortillas, the dishtowel or paper towel will absorb some water. Eventually, it will become too damp to peel away easily from the tortillas. When this happens, replace with a fresh dishtowel or paper towel.

Tortillas can be stacked by the several dozen. They can be refrigerated or frozen and reheated either in the oven (wrapped in foil) or in a microwave oven.

Refried Beans

Now we come to the second constituent of the chalupas you'll be making—the refried beans, or, as they're called in Spanish, *frijoles refritos.* For the chalupas, you'll use about 1 cup of the refried-bean paste. Serve the remainder of the beans in a bowl on your buffet table.

1 pound dried pinto beans
2 medium-size onions, chopped
10 to 12 cloves garlic, minced
1 teaspoon ground cumin
1 pound sliced bacon

1 teaspoon salt, or to taste
½ teaspoon freshly ground black pepper, or to taste

The night before cooking, rinse the beans, place them in a heatproof bowl, and cover with boiling water to a depth of 2 to 3 inches above the beans. Soak overnight.

The next day, drain the beans and rinse them again. Transfer them to a large pot and add 1 chopped onion, the garlic, and the cumin. Add enough water to just cover the beans, bring to a boil, then reduce the heat and simmer until the beans are very tender, 1 to 1½ hours. Let the beans cool in the cooking liquid. When cool, drain the beans and reserve the liquid.

In a large frying pan, fry the bacon until crisp. Remove the bacon from the pan and set aside. (Crumble it when cool.) Over medium heat, fry the other chopped onion in the bacon fat until translucent, about 7 minutes. Reduce the heat to low, add the beans to the pan, and mash and stir them while continuing to cook over low heat until heated through. The mashed bean paste should be slightly chunky and about the consistency of peanut butter. If it's too dry and thick, add some of the reserved cooking liquid until the right consistency is achieved. Add salt and pepper.

When serving the beans, garnish with the crumbled bacon.

CHALUPAS

Chalupas are a Mexican appetizer made with corn tortillas. Recipes for chalupas vary widely (some employ shredded beef, pork, or chicken), but our relatively simple, nacho-like chalupas use only tortillas, refried beans, cheese, and green chiles. James learned to make them years ago, from his Tejana friend Marvi Arredondo. These toothsome hors d'oeu-vres also make an easy snack for TV watching. (If you want to make them in a hurry, use packaged corn tortillas and canned refried beans.) This recipe yields two chalupas each for twelve guests.

about 1¼ cups corn oil
4 corn tortillas (see page 235)
1 cup refried beans (see page 238)
1 cup (about 4 ounces) grated longhorn-style cheddar cheese
24 slices canned green chile peppers

Cut each tortilla into 6 wedge-shaped chips. Heat the oil in a large (13-inch) frying pan over medium-high heat until it begins to smoke. (The oil should be ¼ to ½ inch deep.) Working in batches of 6 or 8, add the tortilla chips to the hot oil and fry until crisp, turning once (about 1 minute per side). Drain on paper towels and let cool.

Spread some refried beans on each chip and sprinkle with cheese. Dot each with a chile slice. Arrange on a broiling pan and broil until the cheese has melted, about 2 minutes. Let cool slightly before serving.

THE BUFFET TABLE

Besides the fresh tortillas and the refried beans, the buffet-table offer-ings include a ceviche (fish or scallops "cooked" in lime juice), a nopal-itos salad, and—the main dish—a pile of tamales with shredded pork and chile stuffing. Also offer your guests several condiments for dipping the tortillas and tamales: a bowl of crema (Mexican sour cream) and bowls of salsa verde (see page 233) and salsa roja (see page 247). The tamales recipe is the most difficult and labor-intensive in this chapter.

In fact, it's one of the hardest recipes in this book, so do prepare the tamales a day in advance—and enlist the help of a friend (or friends!) in making them.

CEVICHE

Marinating fish and some other seafoods in citrus juice has an effect very similar to that of cooking: Over the course of several hours in the marinade, the flesh solidifies and becomes opaque. This Mexican-style ceviche (seh-VEE-chay) recipe is suitable for either a firm, white-fleshed fish or small bay scallops. (For instructions on roasting and seeding chiles, see the Technicalities sidebar on page 226.)

2 pounds very fresh white-fleshed fish, such as red snapper, or 2 pounds bay
  scallops
2 cups fresh lime juice
1 clove garlic, crushed and minced
4 teaspoons salt
¼ teaspoon freshly ground black pepper
1 large white onion, chopped
2 serrano or jalapeño chiles, roasted, seeded, and minced
½ cup fresh cilantro leaves, chopped

Cut the fish into ½-inch cubes. (If using scallops, leave whole.) Place the fish or scallops in a glass or ceramic bowl or wide-mouthed mason jar. Add the lime juice, garlic, salt, and pepper. Refrigerate for 4 to 6 hours, until the fish pieces or scallops are opaque. Place the onion in a sieve or colander and lower it into a pot of boiling water, blanching for 5 seconds. Immediately refresh in cold water. Add the onion, chiles, and cilantro to the ceviche and refrigerate until ready to serve.

NOPALITOS SALAD

Ramona and James don't know what got into us the day we planned our Mexican party. We just couldn't get enough of those prickly pear cactus pads called nopales (or, when, diced or cut into strips, nopalitos). The distinctive flavor of the nopalitos comes through much more forcefully in this salad than in the comparatively mild nopalitos dip.

FOR COOKING THE NOPALITOS:

4 medium-size nopales, thorns removed
husk of 1 large tomatillo
¼ cup chopped onion
1 clove garlic
⅛ teaspoon baking soda
½ teaspoon salt

FOR THE DRESSING:

¼ cup extra-virgin olive oil
2 tablespoons cider vinegar
½ teaspoon salt
¼ teaspoon black pepper
1 ripe Hass avocado, peeled, pitted, and chopped
½ cup grape tomatoes, halved
½ cup fresh cilantro leaves, finely chopped
1 serrano chile, roasted, peeled, seeded, and sliced into thin strips

Cook the nopalitos: Slice the cactus pads into ⅜-inch strips. Place in a large saucepan with the tomatillo husk, onion, garlic, baking soda, and ½ teaspoon salt; cover with water; and bring to a boil. Reduce the heat and simmer for about 30 minutes, until the cactus is tender. Drain. Pluck out the cactus strips and place them in a medium-size bowl. (Discard the other solids.)

Make the dressing: In a small bowl, whisk together the oil, vinegar, salt, and pepper and pour the mixture over the hot cactus. Cover and marinate for 1 hour. Add the remaining ingredients, toss to combine, and serve.

TAMALES WITH SHREDDED PORK AND CHILE FILLING

Ah, tamales. Among Mexican families, making tamales is often a group effort—with the older children joining in when it comes time to assemble the little corn-husk packets. You'll lessen your anxiety considerably if you make the tamales a day in advance of your party. (Once they've been steamed, they can be refrigerated and then resteamed—just long enough to heat them through—before serving.) And the job will be much more fun (and, yes, will require much less effort from you, individually) if you enlist the help of a spouse, partner, friend, or older child—or a small group of such persons!—in putting the tamales together.

An admission: We really don't have an exact idea of how many tamales this recipe makes. (You thought cookbook writers were supposed to know this sort of thing? Well, we are, but . . . .) The precise number will depend on just how much dough and filling you load into each tamale. In any case, you'll have plenty for your party—somewhere between 50 and 70—and probably leftovers, besides.

Use a pasta pentola—a "multipurpose" stockpot with a deep basket insert—for steaming the tamales. The water in the pot will probably have to be replenished during the long steaming time, and a pentola, whose steamer basket is easily removable, will make this job much easier.

Special equipment: pasta pentola ("multipurpose" stockpot with steamer-basket insert)

about ½ pound dried corn husks

about 2 pounds pork loin or fresh pork shoulder, including bones
1 medium-size onion, cut in half
6 cloves garlic
7 whole cloves
1 cinnamon stick

8 dried ancho chiles
4 dried guajillo chiles
1 large onion, diced
6 large cloves garlic, crushed and minced
2 tablespoons extra-virgin olive oil
2 bay leaves
1 tablespoon ground cumin
2 teaspoons salt
½ teaspoon freshly ground black pepper
½ teaspoon ground cayenne pepper
¼ teaspoon ground allspice

4 cups masa harina
2 cups rendered pork fat (lard), at room temperature
1 teaspoon salt

Soak the corn husks: The night before making the tamales, remove the corn husks from their package, place them in a large stockpot, and cover with water. Soak overnight.

Cook the pork: Place the pork, onion, garlic, cloves, and cinnamon stick in a large pot, cover with water, and boil for 2 to 3 hours, until the meat is very tender. Let cool in the liquid. Remove the pork from the pot, discard any bones, shred the meat, and set aside. Strain the cooking liquid (discarding any solids), skim it to remove any fat, and set aside.

Make the filling: Remove the seeds, stems, and ribs from the dried chiles. Place the chiles in a heatproof bowl, cover them with boiling water, and let stand for 30 minutes. Drain the chiles, put them in a blender, and pulse until smoothly pureed. Set aside.

In a large saucepan, sauté the onions and garlic in the oil over medium heat until soft, about 4 minutes. Add the shredded pork and stir, cooking until just heated through. Add the chile puree, bay leaves, cumin, salt, pepper, cayenne, allspice, and 2 cups of the reserved pork cooking liquid. Bring to a boil over high heat, reduce the heat to medium-low, and simmer, uncovered, for about 1 hour, until the liquid has largely evaporated, the sauce has thickened, and the meat is well coated. Remove from the heat and set aside.

Drain the corn husks, separate them, and place them on a bed of paper towels to dry. (It's fine if they remain slightly moist.)

Make the dough and assemble the tamales: Mix the masa harina with the rendered pork fat and salt. Stir in just enough water—½ to 1 cup— to form a light, easily spreadable dough.

To make each tamale, tear a corn husk in half lengthwise. (The piece should be 4 to 5 inches wide at the bottom.) Using a spreading knife or small spatula, spread about 2 tablespoons of the masa dough on the *lower half* of the husk. (Leave the top portion of the husk bare.) Spread the dough as thinly and evenly as possible, but do not spread it all the way to the outer edges of the husk—leave about ¼ inch bare at either side. Spoon 1 tablespoon of filling in the center of the dough. (The drawing on the next page shows the corn husk spread with dough and topped with filling.)

Now fold the sides of the husk inward over the filling, overlapping the edges of the dough and completely enclosing the filling. Then fold the lower, filled half of the husk up and over the top, tapering portion of the husk.

Steam the tamales: Fill a pentola pot with water to a level just below the bottom of the steamer basket. Remove the basket from the pot and bring the water to a boil. As the water is heating, fill the steamer basket with the tamales, standing them on their ends, fold side down. Do not pack them in too tightly. Place the steamer basket in the pot and cover the tamales with a layer of corn husks. Steam for 1½ hours, or until the corn husks can be easily peeled away from the cooked dough inside. While steaming, check the water level at intervals and replenish if necessary.

Tamales should be served hot, with refried beans and with crema (Mexican sour cream) and green and red salsas for dipping. If you make the tamales a day ahead, allow them to cool after steaming, transfer to an airtight container, and refrigerate. Before serving, put them back in the pentola's steamer basket and steam until heated through, about 30 minutes. Leftover tamales may be frozen; when ready to use, thaw them and steam again, or—if you're heating just a few tamales—heat them in a microwave oven at high power for about 1 minute.

Salsa Roja

Made with fully ripened jalapeños or serranos, this traditional red salsa is only mildly hot. To intensify the heat, use habanero or scotch bonnet chiles instead. For instructions on roasting the tomatoes and chiles on the stovetop, refer back to the Technicalities sidebar on page 226.

4 medium-size very ripe tomatoes, roasted, peeled, seeded, and chopped
1 small onion, chopped
4 cloves garlic, crushed and minced
2 tablespoons extra-virgin olive oil
2 red (ripe) jalapeño or serrano chiles, roasted, peeled, and seeded
½ teaspoon salt

In a blender, puree the tomatoes, onion, and garlic. Heat the oil in a saucepan and add the pureed mixture, the roasted chiles, and salt. Cook over medium heat until the sauce boils, then reduce the heat to low and simmer, stirring occasionally, for 5 to 10 minutes. The sauce should be only slightly thick; if too thick, add a little water and stir. Remove the peppers before serving.

Desserts

One dessert is good. Two desserts are very good. If you only have time and stamina to make one of these traditional Mexican treats, however, choose the flan, which can be prepared a day in advance. (Those buñuelitos are awfully tempting, though.)

Buñuelitos

It seems as if just about every culinary culture has a fried-dough confection, and Mexico is no exception. Buñuelitos (also called *buñuelos*) resemble doughnuts (in this recipe, we even give them holes), but they're lighter and fluffier.

Special equipment: deep fryer or candy thermometer

½ cup milk, room temperature or slightly warmed
1 envelope (1 tablespoon) active dry yeast
½ cup (1 stick) unsalted butter, softened
¼ cup sugar
6 large eggs, beaten until light and frothy
about 4 cups unbleached all-purpose flour
½ teaspoon cinnamon
½ teaspoon salt
hot water
corn oil
confectioners' sugar and additional cinnamon, for dusting

Combine the milk and yeast in a small bowl and let the mixture stand for about 5 minutes, until it begins to bubble. In a large mixing bowl, cream the butter together with the sugar. Add the eggs and the yeast mixture and stir until well incorporated. Add the flour, cinnamon, and salt and stir. In very small amounts, add hot water, stirring well after each addition, until a sticky dough has formed. Turn onto a floured board and knead until elastic. Lightly grease the dough, put it back in the bowl, cover, and set in a warm place to rise until doubled in volume, 30 to 60 minutes.

If using a deep fryer, fill the fryer to the maximum level with oil and set the temperature to 360° F. If frying on top of the stove, fill a heavy pot 3 to 4 inches deep with oil, insert a candy thermometer, and heat the oil over high heat to a temperature of 360° F.

Form the risen dough into 1½-inch balls. Lightly grease your hands. On waxed paper, press each ball out with your fingertips to form a paper-thin round 4 to 5 inches in diameter.

Using a doughnut-hole cutter or thimble, cut a hole in the middle of each round. As the rounds are made, carefully slip each into the hot oil. Fry, turning once, until crisp and golden, about 2 minutes total. Drain on paper towels. Serve warm, dusted with a mixture of confectioners' sugar and powdered cinnamon. (The mixture should be about 10 parts sugar to 1 part cinnamon.)

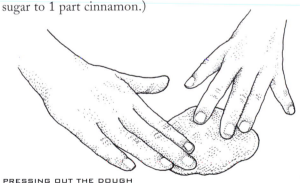

PRESSING OUT THE DOUGH

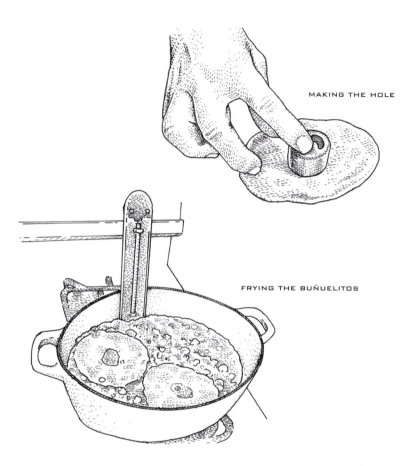

MAKING THE HOLE

FRYING THE BUÑUELITOS

Note: The buñuelitos can be prepared several hours in advance. Rewarm in a 200° F. oven for 20 minutes before serving. Do not dust with the cinnamon sugar until ready to serve.

FLAN NAPOLITANO

The Spanish-style custard known as *flan* is a popular dessert in Mexico and, indeed, throughout Latin America. This Yucatán flan, traditionally called flan Napolitano (Neapolitan flan), uses evaporated milk—a staple of Mexican cookery—and is baked in a bain-marie (see instructions in the Technicalities sidebar on page 117). The first step in creating the flan is to make the caramel that will coat the flan's surface. If you've never caramelized sugar, proceed carefully. As the sugar heats, it becomes a clear syrup that turns progressively darker shades of brown, and the color changes more swiftly toward the end of the process. It's extremely important to remove the pan from the heat just as the caramel turns a rich, chocolaty brown; if left on the heat just a moment longer, it will begin to blacken and burn. (If that happens, begin again. The burned caramel will have an unpleasant, bitter taste.)

FOR THE CARAMEL:

1 cup sugar
1 tablespoon light corn syrup

FOR THE CUSTARD:

2½ cups milk
1½ cups evaporated milk
8 ounces cream cheese, softened
6 large eggs
6 large egg yolks
¾ cup sugar
1 tablespoon vanilla extract

Make the caramel: Place the sugar and corn syrup in a medium-size (12-inch) frying pan (preferably one with curved sides) and heat over medium-high heat. Stir with a wooden spoon, at first just occasionally and then more frequently as the sugar melts and begins to change color. Remove the pan from the heat as soon as the caramel is a deep, rich, even brown, and immediately pour the caramel into a 9-inch round cake pan. Swirl the caramel around the cake pan to coat the bottom evenly. (Use oven mitts when handling the cake pan, which will become very hot as soon as the caramel is poured into it.) Let cool. When cool, lightly butter the sides of the pan.

Make the custard: Preheat the oven to 350° F. Boil water for the bain-marie. Combine the milk and evaporated milk in a medium-size saucepan and heat over medium heat until the milk just begins to boil. Immediately remove from the heat and set aside. In a large mixing bowl, cream the cream cheese with a fork, then add the eggs, egg yolks, and sugar and beat with an electric mixer until smooth. (It's OK if tiny flecks of cream cheese remain in the mixture at this point.) While continuing to beat, gradually add the scalded milk to the egg mixture. Add the vanilla and beat until smooth.

Pour the custard mixture through a strainer into the prepared cake pan. Lightly skim the surface with a spoon to remove any bubbly foam. Place the cake pan in a bain-marie and bake for 1¼ hours or until a knife inserted in the center comes out clean.

Carefully remove the cake pan from the bain-marie and set on a wire rack to cool. When cool, run a knife around the edge of the pan. Place a large serving plate (with a deep well) upside down atop the cake pan and carefully invert the two; tap lightly on the bottom of the cake pan to release the custard. (Some of the caramel will have liquefied and will pool around the flan—this is the desired effect.) Chill until serving.

THE HOT, THE COOL, AND THE FROZEN

Except for the TNT Coffee, all the mixed drinks for your Mexican cocktail party/buffet can be prepared in batches. The selection includes a sangrita, traditionally served as a chaser for shots of tequila; a refreshing, dramatically colored (and nonalcoholic) herbal infusion for quenching thirsts; and, of course, a frozen Margarita.

SANGRITA

Don't confuse *sangrita* with the wine-based drink called *sangria*; they couldn't be more different. This spicy-sour-sweet tomato-and-orange-juice beverage can be served, in small portions, along with shots of tequila *or* the tequila can be added directly into the mix. (Note that if you add in the tequila, you'll need a pitcher that holds at least 2½ quarts.)

1 quart tomato juice
1 cup freshly squeezed orange juice
4 tablespoons fresh lime juice
3 tablespoons green Tabasco sauce
2 tablespoons sugar
½ teaspoon salt, or to taste
3¾ cups white tequila (optional)

Mix all the ingredients in a large glass or ceramic pitcher. Chill. If you add the tequila to the sangrita, serve in old-fashioned (rocks) glasses, about 4 ounces per serving. If, however, you're serving the tequila separately, serve both the tequila and the sangrita in large shot glasses: A shot of tequila should be chased with a shot of sangrita. (The beverage can also be drunk by itself, without alcohol.)

THE HOT, THE COOL, AND THE FROZEN

ICED HIBISCUS TEA

This "tea"—actually an infusion of flower petals—is called *agua de jamaica* in Spanish, and it belongs to the category of soft drinks that Mexicans call *aguas frescas*. (*Agua fresca* means "fresh water"; other agua frescas call for the addition of crushed fruit, such as mangoes or watermelon, to a mixture of water and sugar.) This hibiscus iced tea's color—a vivid reddish-purple—is more pronounced than its mildly, pleasantly herbal taste.

2 quarts water
1 cup sugar
2 cups dried red hibiscus flowers
2 tablespoons fresh lime juice

Combine the water and sugar in a saucepan and bring the mixture to a boil. Remove from the heat, add the hibiscus flowers, and stir. Let steep for about 20 minutes, or until the color has mostly leached from the flower petals. Strain into a large glass or ceramic pitcher, add the lime juice, and chill. Serve in highball glasses, over ice.

THE EASIEST, BEST FROZEN MARGARITA EVER

This fabulous frozen Margarita recipe comes our way via Ramona's friends Joseph Ligammari and Frank Verlizzo. Because it uses frozen limeade (which is very sweet), the recipe calls for a smaller proportion of Cointreau (which is also very sweet) than do most Margarita recipes. Use whole ice cubes *only* if you have a commercial-grade blender capable of crushing ice; otherwise, you must crush the ice before adding it to the blender carafe. (Take this warning very seriously! If you put whole ice cubes into a regular blender, you'll end up with a drink that's full of ice fragments—and you risk burning out the blender's motor, to boot.)

Note, too, that the quality of a Margarita depends, in large part, on the quality of the tequila; we therefore strongly recommend you use a premium white *(blanco)* tequila in this drink. The number of drinks this recipe makes depends entirely on the size of your glasses: If you're serving it in standard-size (four-ounce) cocktail glasses—which we recommend—it should yield about ten drinks. If you're serving it in large Margarita glasses, not only will you get fewer drinks per batch, but your guests will become much drunker much quicker. (The Margaritas go down *very* easy, so be careful.)

⚜ lime wedges
salt
1 (12-ounce) container frozen limeade concentrate
about 8 ounces white tequila
about 4 ounces Cointreau
2 standard trays of ice cubes

Rim each glass with a lime wedge and salt. (Reserve the lime wedges.) Spoon the frozen limeade into the carafe of a commercial-grade blender. (Do not thaw the limeade beforehand.) Fill the limeade container about two-thirds full with tequila, add Cointreau to fill the container completely, then pour the liquor into the carafe. Add the ice cubes and blend until smooth. Pour into the prepared glasses, and garnish each with a lime wedge.

TNT COFFEE

For this meal-ending hot coffee drink, we recommend using the Jamaican coffee liqueur called Tía Maria rather than the Mexican liqueur Kahlúa. We like both of them a lot, but we find that the sharper- and more herbal-flavored Tía Maria holds its own better when combined with coffee. (And, besides, if we used Kahlúa, we'd have to call the drink KNT Coffee, which just doesn't have the same ring.)

1 ounce Tía Maria
½ ounce white tequila
hot coffee
whipped cream
cinnamon

Pour the Tía Maria and tequila into a warmed Irish coffee glass or ceramic mug. Add the coffee (almost to the brim), and stir. Top with a dollop of whipped cream and dust very lightly with powdered cinnamon.

CHAPTER TEN

The D.I.Y. Bash

COCKTAIL PARTIES FOR
TWENTY TO ONE HUNDRED

MANY HOME-ENTERTAINING GUIDES ARE, WE'VE NOTICED, EXER-CISES in cheerleading. ("Giving a cocktail party? Fabulous! Just follow our advice and you won't have any problems whatsoever.") Well, we're all for shaking the pom-poms and yelling Go, Team, Go! And we really do think that throwing a sizable, successful home cocktail party carries a significant emotional reward, but we're going to say something right up front, and we're not going to make any bones about it:

Giving a large cocktail party in your home—and doing all the planning, all the shopping, and most or all of the food preparation yourself—may be the most difficult entertaining job you could take on.

Oh, you *can* do it—and you can do it in a way that shows your guests a rollicking good time. But you've got to proceed carefully, put all the necessary time and thought into planning the event, and be ready to give over all your time during the several days preceding the party to working on it and nothing else. You'll also need some significant help. (We're using the term *D.I.Y.* somewhat loosely.)

There. With those stern caveats out of the way, let us continue.

A cocktail party is, to misquote Karl Marx (of all people), a strange home-entertaining entity. It's a much more complicated affair than, for example, a dinner party, whose size is necessarily limited to the seating capacity of your dining room. But a cocktail party's complexity goes well beyond the number of guests invited, because the key to a vibrant, scintillating cocktail party is *variety*—the variety of the people who come and the variety of the drinks and foods on offer. A cocktail party's rhythm is also very different from that of a party based on a meal, which

proceeds according a regular, course-by-course scheme. To a guest, a cocktail party may seem amorphous, but cocktail parties, too, go through a series of stages that are more or less predictable, and understanding the way that cocktail parties typically evolve can be of great benefit to your planning.

Start your planning five weeks ahead

Ramona is of the strong—almost adamant—opinion that you ought to begin working on a home cocktail party a full five weeks in advance of the event, *especially* if you're planning your party for the holiday season, when you'll be competing for resources (and guests!) with other party givers. So let's use her schedule to define your tasks—and the timetable you should try to abide by in performing them.

WEEK ONE

Obviously, the earliest tasks you must undertake are to choose a date and time for the event and to draw up a guest list. The date part is usually easy, especially if the party is meant to coincide with, and celebrate, a milestone of some sort—a birthday, an anniversary, the launching or completion of an important project. (Not that a cocktail party needs to commemorate anything; we're all for parties whose only purpose is the gathering itself.) Do note, however, that holding a cocktail party on a "school night" is a risky proposition, since work obligations may prevent many guests from attending (or may delay their arrival or foreshorten their stay).

The time part is just a little more complicated: Will it be an afternoon or an evening party? When will it begin, and how long will it last? We think it's wise to decide on the length of the party in advance, since the amount of work you'll do depends partly on how many hours the party will go on. Note that if you want to give an evening party that will go on for more than two hours, you *must* feed your guests the equivalent of dinner—which usually means setting out a full buffet as well as preparing a range of finger foods to be passed among the crowd.

THE GUEST LIST

Anyone who's ever planned a party (of whatever sort) knows that the second of the preliminary tasks—deciding whom to invite—can be daunting. The size of the party is the first factor to consider: How many people can your house (or, rather, the rooms in which the party will be held) comfortably accommodate? And what do you mean by "comfortably," anyhow? In New York—a city of cramped apartments—we're well used to standing-room-only cocktail parties in which the crush of people is part of the party's appeal. (Think of Holly Golightly's mobbed party in the classic movie *Breakfast at Tiffany's*.) But a crowded party at which only a small number of people can actually sit down might be disastrous if, say, more than a few of your guests are elderly or have physical disabilities (or if any are claustrophobic!).

The size of the guest list also depends on the amount of effort you can devote to the party and the money you can afford to spend. These may seem obvious considerations, but there are some subtleties involved. We'll come back, in the following pages, to the topic of servers and other helpers, but let's just say here that the larger the party, the more people you'll have to hire to help you—and labor costs can add greatly to a party's expense. Let us also stipulate that, in our opinion, a gathering of one hundred people constitutes the absolute upper limit of a cocktail party that you can plan and execute yourself. If you try to do a larger party, you are *crazy*. Oh, you might pull it off, but you'll spend so much time running the show that you won't have a chance to *be* at your party. And that's no fun at all.

Of course, we cannot tell you *whom* to invite, but we can offer a couple of pointers. First, because there are few things more embarrassing than throwing a party that seems under-attended, you should definitely invite more people than you want to show up. Just how many more is a good question. Ramona and James are popular (and lucky) hosts; the parties we've given have, without exception, been well attended. Still, it's our experience that at least a **20 percent won't show** fifth of those invited won't show. (Even some who say they'll *definitely* be there won't appear. Go figure.) So we'll hazard the following rule: Invite 20 percent more people than you think you can handle. And if you're holding the party during peak party season (Thanksgiving through New Year's Day), think about increasing that percentage at least slightly, since it's likely that a fair share of the invitees will receive competing invitations.

And now we come to some delicate matters. First: If any of your friends has a serious problem with alcohol—especially if they become angry and belligerent when drunk—you might think twice before including them on the guest list. This is a hard thing to say. We, too, worry about those among our friends who can't handle their liquor. We don't want to hurt their feelings—or risk losing their friendship—by excluding them. (An indisputable truth: People *always* find out that they weren't invited.) But we also know that even a single bad drunk can *ruin* a cocktail party. We've seen it happen. A party at which two ill-matched lovers—both bad-tempered drunks—began loudly bickering, then violently arguing, and ultimately progressed to throwing their drinks at one another in the middle of a crowded room stands out particularly clearly in James's memory. It was the kind of situation that is amusing only in long retrospect.

The second delicate matter: Should guests be permitted to bring young children to the party? This is obviously your call, and may depend on how well or ill behaved your friends' little terrors (er, kids) are. But it's our considered opinion that a cocktail party—especially an evening party that extends over several hours—should be an adults-only event. If you do decide to welcome children to an evening-long cocktail party, make sure there are enough beds into which the tykes can be comfortably tucked when they grow sleepy and irritable. If you, more sensibly, opt for the adults-only policy, specify this on your invitation.

There is one way in which compiling the guest list for a large cocktail party is easier than deciding whom to invite to other sorts of at-home gatherings. At a sizable cocktail party, the guests are mobile—and there are lots of them. Nobody's trapped into having to interact with anyone else, which means that you, the host, don't have to worry about your guests' compatibility to the same extent you would when planning an intimate dinner party.

THE INVITATION

By all means, send out invitations to your party. Note that by "send," we mean *send through the mail*. Remember the U.S. Postal Service? Yes, it's still there, still functioning. Email is dandy for many sorts of communications, but to our antiquated minds, party invitations are not among them. (One note: If you're planning a party for the holiday season, you may want to send a "save the date" email to invitees as far in advance as two months before the party—and then follow up with a mailed invitation. Doing so obviously requires beginning the planning process even earlier.)

Of course, you can buy cocktail party invitations at card shops—and we've seen some that are clever and attractive. Even so, store-bought invitations necessarily have a generic feel, so we encourage you to create your own invitations if you have the inclination. The biggest drawback is the amount of time it takes to print invitations using your computer's printer: Set aside at least one whole evening for this task, and expect things to go wrong (the printer to run out of ink, the card stock to jam, and the like).

If you do design your own invitation, be sure to include the following information, at a minimum: (1) the purpose of the celebration (if any); (2) the name(s) of the host(s); (3) the date, day of the week, and time of the party (including the time the party will end); (4) the address; (5) the proviso "Adults Only," if that is indeed your party policy; and (6) the instruction to RSVP and a telephone number and/or email address to which invitees can respond. Personally, we don't grasp the usefulness of the phrase "Regrets Only," which seems to be gaining ground as an alternative to "RSVP." The older, time-honored injunction *répondez s'il vous plaît* asks prospective guests to definitely decide, one way or the other, whether they'll attend. Do note, however, that the inclusion of RSVP on the invitation hardly guarantees that everyone will contact you (my, how manners have deteriorated!), but it does increase the likelihood that you'll have a good-enough idea, in the days immediately preceding the party, of just how many people to expect.

Some invitations also include an insert giving a map and travel directions—a good idea if you live in an out-of-the-way place or a large, geographically complex city. (Alternately, you might post a map and directions on a personal Web site—and include the site's address on the invitation.) If the cocktail party is a housewarming, or a birthday or anniversary party, or any other sort of celebration to which people are likely to bring gifts *and* you do not want any gifts, don't forget to include the line "No gifts, please" on the invitation. (Some people will still bring gifts, but the amount of stuff you'll have to dispose of at a future garage sale will be reduced.) Needless to say, if you *would* like to receive presents, don't include this instruction. Make peace with your greed.

An aside: During the weeks before the party, some guests will call or email to ask what they can bring. Your answer: *Nothing.* A cocktail party is not a potluck supper, and it is very bad form to ask your guests to provide any of the potables or edibles. Despite your intransigence on this score, however, some people will bring along gifts of wine, liquor, or flowers. Accept them graciously—and be sure to have extra vases on hand to accommodate the inevitable bouquets.

> ## It's a cocktail party, not a potluck supper

Finally, it is essential that you proofread, proofread, proofread your invitation before printing and sending it. Better yet, have someone else—preferably someone who majored in English in college—proofread it for you. Take this suggestion very seriously. It is mortifying to discover that you've mailed out invitations on which the word "Saturday" is misspelled.

To be safe, send out the invitations four weeks before the day of the party.

WEEKS TWO THROUGH FOUR

Although you won't go into high gear until the final few days before the party, use the weeks following the mailing of the invitations to do all the necessary advance work. Securing the services of the bartender(s), server(s), and other helpers you'll need is of first-order importance; do this as soon as possible. Make preliminary decisions about the menu; pre-shop to make sure that you can get all the ingredients and equipment you'll need for the dishes you want to prepare; and test *every* recipe beforehand.

Recipe Testing

That last suggestion may seem rather odd for cookbook writers to make. Aren't the recipes we provide trustworthy? Well, we've certainly tried them all, and we can vouch that they worked for us. But every kitchen, and every cook, is different—as is each person's taste. Things that sound good on the printed page may not please you on the plate and palate. And even if you *like* everything you try, you may find that certain dishes simply take too much time to prepare, or that combinations of dishes that you thought might work together are actually incompatible. In any case, we think it's insane (that's right: the sheerest insanity) to plan on serving your guests dishes that you've never tried cooking before.

As you test the dishes—which you can do gradually over weeks two through four—carefully note how much active time each requires. Decide on the order in which the dishes will be prepared and served. Make sure, if you decide to serve several dishes that must be prepared simultaneously, that you have enough kitchen equipment and workspace—including staging space—to accomplish this. Try to figure out how many extra hands you may need in the kitchen when it comes time to cook for the party itself. In other words, develop a game plan.

Menu Planning

Of course, you're not testing recipes randomly; you're planning a menu that will satisfy—and, you hope, delight—a large and diverse group of people. *Diverse* is the most important word in the previous sentence. In planning your menu, don't forget that some of your guests' tastes and dietary requirements will differ from your own. At the two full-scale cocktail parties that James and Ramona threw while researching this book—one for forty people, the other for a hundred—the guests included (1) vegetarians (all, mercifully, were lacto-vegetarians, who also eat dairy products); (2) people who eat more or less everything except red meat; (3) people with food allergies, including allergies to wheat, potatoes, peanuts, and shrimp; (4) a goodly number of omnivores (phew!). We knew a little about some of our guests' dietary preferences/restrictions in advance, and we made it our aim to create menus that ensured that each person, no matter what their proclivities or requirements, would be able to eat at least some of the foods presented. (Even vegans would not have gone absolutely hungry.) The goal, of course, is to ensure that everyone would feel well taken care of, and we recommend that you follow a similar approach, even if you don't know all your guests' tastes and dietary strictures. (Or perhaps *especially* if you do not have this information.)

Other important considerations in menu planning include the following:

Timing. It's critical that you work out a scheme that allows you to prepare some of the food during the day or days preceding the party and, especially, one that restricts the number of dishes that must be cooked during the party itself. For example, Ramona and James just love hot hors d'oeuvres, but we recognize that the number and quantity of hot hors d'oeuvres that you can serve during a several-hour-long cocktail party is limited by (1) the capacity and number of ovens at your disposal,

(2) the number of kitchen helpers you have, and (3) the amount of time you're willing to spend in the kitchen and away from your guests during the party. (If you serve scads of hot hors d'oeuvres, be prepared to miss most of your own party, since you'll constantly be tending the hearth.)

Serving. Another crucial menu-planning issue concerns how the food will be distributed. Your goal, when planning, should be to strike the right balance between finger foods that will be passed on trays by servers and "stationary" dishes that will be placed on tables at various locations throughout the party space. How the food will be served and where it will be placed are the principles we used when putting the recipes in this chapter in order (see pages 295 and following). We've organized the recipes and other menu suggestions into five basic categories:

- *Snacks,* including coated nuts and other munchies to be set on tables throughout the space.

- *An appetizer spread,* consisting of cheeses, fruit, pâtés/mousses, crudités, and dips set out on one table or counter.

- *Finger foods,* to be passed, on trays, by servers. (This, the largest category, is further broken down into types of finger foods: deviled eggs, bruschette, vegetarian hors d'oeuvres, and so on.)

- *The main table*—a "carve 'n' carry" buffet at which guests prepare their own plates.

- *Desserts,* to be placed on the main buffet table near the end of the party, after the other dishes have been cleared away.

Amount. Without knowing the specifics of your party—the number of guests, the time of day, and the length of the party—we can't advise you on the amount of food to serve. But we can supply you with one over-arching principle: *Don't be stingy*. A party at which the food runs out midway through is, by definition, a lousy party. Much better that you should have too much food (and that you should live for days after on the leftovers) than that you serve too little. As the givers of Roman debauches and Kwakiutl potlatches knew, parties are about showering guests with *abundance*. And there are just some principles that are trans-cultural and eternal. We supply a few other pointers—of a minimal sort—when we discuss cheese (see page 302), the passed finger foods (page 316), and the main buffet table (page 342).

Don't be stingy

One other word of advice: Take the party's *pace* into account when deciding on how much food to buy and serve. We spoke earlier about a cocktail party's "rhythm," and that rhythm will partly determine how much food is consumed—and when. For a several-hour-long evening party, plan on serving relatively many passed finger foods during the first hour or so. Then reduce the number of finger foods that servers are circulating through the crowd, and send the trays out at slightly longer intervals. Do keep the finger foods flowing—though fewer of them, and at increasingly longer intervals—until the party's final stage so that even the latest-arriving guests get something to eat (there will always be such stragglers).

Pricing. Don't be miserly with the food, but don't bust your budget, either. Ramona, an old hand at the catering trade, watches over every party's food budget by employing a simple Excel spreadsheet that enables her to closely estimate the total cost of the food as she develops the party's menu and does her pre-shopping. The spreadsheet lists (1) each of the dishes she thinks she might like to serve, (2) each of the ingredients (and the amount) required by that dish, (3) the unit price of each ingredient, and (4) the cost of each ingredient when the amount is multiplied by the unit price. In a final column, Ramona lists the store where each ingredient will be purchased. By keeping a running total, she can immediately see how close to her budget she's coming. If any particular dish threatens to distort the entire budget, she can eliminate it, substituting one with cheaper ingredients. (It's a great tool—and one that James, well known for throwing budgetary caution to the winds, refuses to learn.) Note that Ramona's spreadsheet also doubles as a complete shopping list when it comes time to buy all the food for the party.

Don't bust the budget, either

EQUIPMENT AND SUPPLIES

Also use the weeks leading up to the week of the party to lay in all the equipment and non-food party supplies you'll need—or to make arrangements for their delivery. Ramona and James aren't high and mighty folk (hardly!), but we snootily believe that a proper cocktail party requires real glassware, real (i.e., metal) cutlery, and real (i.e., ceramic) plates, coffee cups, and other dinnerware. (We compromise our principles when it comes to napkins: Paper dinner napkins and, of course, paper bevnaps are OK.) Unless you have such items on hand, in the quantities required, you'll have to buy them or rent them.

If you intend to become a regular thrower of cocktail parties (nothing would please us more) *and* if you have adequate storage space, it probably makes sense to buy all your glasses, flatware, and china rather than renting them. A restaurant-supply house is the place to go for such items. Most outlets, though they're geared toward the trade, are perfectly happy to sell their wares to ordinary retail customers. Not only are prices low, but the product lines carried by such stores are seldom discontinued; because the glasses, flatware, and dishes you buy will remain in stock virtually forever, you will be able to replace or add to them as needed for future parties.

If, instead, you decide to rent, begin exploring the possibilities as early as possible. Most towns of any size have one or more party-supply rental outfits, and these days most such companies maintain Web sites on which you can view the products they offer. (The Web sites also commonly quote prices, so you can do some comparison shopping before contacting a particular firm.) If your party will occur during the holidays or the peak wedding season (that is, the month of June), it's especially important to make rental arrangements as far in advance as possible, since party supply companies do run out of stock and may not be able to fulfill a last-minute order. When making rental arrangements, make certain that the company's delivery and pickup times accord with your scheduling needs. (Ramona says, "And find out how long you can keep the stuff, in case you have to nurse your hangover and can't face the thought of cleaning up the day after the party.") Also find out whether the rental company prefers that glasses and dishes be returned washed or unwashed. (Rental companies usually prefer the latter, since it cuts down on breakage—and it will make your post-party cleanup less oppressive, too.)

EQUIPMENT SPECIFICS

Forgive us if what we say in this section seems too obvious to need saying. But we've been through this drill often enough to know that you're bound to get yourself in trouble if you don't—with due care and deliberation—map out every last thing ahead of time.

Regarding kitchen equipment, make sure that you've got every piece of equipment required for the making of every dish. That's the easy part. The hard part is determining which pieces of equipment you'll need in duplicate, triplicate, or larger quantities. To illustrate the problem simply: If you've only got one large saucepan, you can't make two dishes, each of which requires a large saucepan, simultaneously. In our experience, it's hard to have too many of the following items when mounting a large cocktail party: stainless-steel mixing bowls of various sizes; baking sheets for heating hot hors d'oeuvres (commercial-grade jelly-roll pans, which heat evenly and can withstand a lot of wear and tear, are best); and wooden spoons, metal spoons (both slotted and unslotted), wire whisks, and spatulas. You're also likely to need several cutting boards, several paring knives (and, possibly, multiples of other knives, as well), and—very important!—several kitchen timers.

An aside: The size of the party you can give and the kinds of dishes you can prepare are also dependent on the capacity of your refrigerator and the number of ovens you have to work with. (It's also a good idea to clean your oven or ovens and to test their accuracy during the pre-party weeks.) The variety and quantity of foods are also limited by the amount of staging space you have in your kitchen (and perhaps an adjacent room given over to this purpose); if your kitchen is small or has very limited counter space, do *not* plan on serving a huge variety of finger foods, the preparation of which requires significant staging space.

There's the cooking, and then there's the serving. Do *not* make the mistake of believing that you or your helpers will be able to do much in the way of dishwashing during the party itself. Make sure, therefore, that you have an appropriate and attractive serving dish (and an appropriate serving utensil) for *each* of the foods you intend to present to your guests. (Lay all the dishes and utensils out on a table and count them, and then count them again.) Serving dishes, of course, include the trays on which the passed canapés and other finger foods will be arranged; if some of these foods are accompanied by a dipping sauces, you'll also need enough small, stable bowls to hold the sauces.

At a cocktail party that includes a buffet and dessert table, you'll need at least one dinner plate per guest; one dessert plate (or, if you're serving a pudding or other semisolid dessert, one small bowl) per guest for *each* dessert; and one coffee mug per guest. Actually, treat these as minimum numbers and buy or rent at least a few extras to cover breakage. You'll also need one dinner fork, one dessert fork (and/or spoon), and one teaspoon (for the coffee) per person. Avoid serving any dishes that require table knives; at a crowded party, there simply won't be enough table space for guests to set down their plates in order to cut up their food. Soup bowls and soup spoons? Forget it! Soups may be fine at smaller buffets, but *under no circumstances* should you serve a soup at a large cocktail party. Believe us: Nobody wants mulligatawny spilled down the front of her little black dress. (We deal with glassware—types and numbers of glasses—in the section on the bar; see page 286.)

Finally, if you're giving a cold-weather party, don't forget that you'll need to do something about people's coats. Of course, you can follow time-honored practice and simply designate a bed on which coats can be thrown. As commonplace as this strategy is, however, it's not the wisest (especially if it rains or snows). We therefore gently urge you to consider investing in a coat rack or racks—or renting them, if you're already arranging with a party supplies rental company for the leasing of other equipment. One caution: If you buy a coat rack, go for the highest quality. Cheap coat racks can't take a lot of weight, and they tend to fall over—creating more of a mess than the coats-on-the-bed solution. (Believe us, we've been there.)

THE HIRED HELP

We've already mentioned the importance of securing the services of a bartender (or bartenders), servers, and other helpers very early on in the planning process. As with so many aspects of cocktail-party planning, acting early is especially important if you're throwing your party during the holidays, when you'll be competing for help with many other party givers.

The first issue to resolve is how many helpers you'll need. As you might guess, this mostly depends on the number of people attending the party. We propose the following rules of thumb, which assume that you (and perhaps a co-host) will be doing the lion's share of the food preparation:

Number of Guests	Helpers Needed
20 to 40	1 kitchen helper 1 bartender 1 server
40 to 60	1 kitchen helper 1 bartender 2 servers
60 to 80	2 kitchen helpers 1 or 2 bartenders 2 servers
80 to 100	2 kitchen helpers 2 bartenders 2 servers

Note that there is an upper limit to the number of people (including yourself) whose work you can successfully supervise in an immediate, hands-on way. (Ramona informs James that this issue has actually been studied by the military.) That upper limit is *seven*—and this assumes that every team member is possessed of a hard-working, motivated, "self-starter" personality. Five is a more workable number, so if you're giving a very large party requiring more than five helpers, it's a good idea to appoint a second-in-command who can answer helpers' questions and solve any problems that arise.

Note, too, that the number of bartenders you'll need partly depends on the kinds of drinks you'll be serving. If your party features a full bar and you expect that a fair number of guests will order mixed drinks that require effort and attention to make, hire two bartenders even for a party of as few as thirty or forty people.

The next question: How do you go about finding the help? First, ask friends who've given large parties if they can recommend people. We've found that people tend to keep, and treasure, the names and phone numbers of good party helpers, and it is much wiser to hire people who come with personal references than to try your luck with an agency. Second, if perchance you're on friendly terms with bartenders or waiters at restaurants you frequent, ask them if they might be available on the date of your party—or if they can recommend people they know. (We've had very good luck with this strategy.) Third—and as a last resort—contact an agency. Agencies that provide bartenders, waiters, and other party helpers are listed in the Yellow Pages under "Bartending Services" and "Party Planning Services." Do not take our hesitancy to rely on agencies the wrong way. We like to

Ask your friends for recommendations

believe that most such businesses are well run and that they take care in screening their employees. But it's a sad truth that an incompetent or lazy bartender or server can spell disaster for a party. (Even worse, perhaps, are servers who like to believe that they are *guests* at your party, and who neglect their duties to mingle with the crowd.)

An aside: If you are intending to offer a variety of mixed drinks, try to make sure that the bartender(s) you hire actually know how to make a fairly wide range of standard cocktails. There are, unfortunately, lots of bartender *poseurs* out there who don't know a Margarita from a Tom Collins, and who are of the (untutored) opinion that a Dirty Martini is one that's made without washing the hands.

When contracting with individuals or with agencies, make sure to specify exactly when you want the helpers to arrive and how many hours you'll need each person to work. Bartenders and servers should be at your house at least an hour in advance of the party's starting time, so that they can receive instructions, change clothes if necessary, and do whatever last-minute setup work is needed. The scheduling of kitchen help depends on the size of the party and how many dishes (and what kinds) you're serving. As you develop your cooking game plan, try to figure out how much help you'll need in the kitchen the day before the party, on the party day itself, and during the party.

If your party will be open-ended, make sure that this is acceptable to anyone who might be asked to stay beyond the contracted hours. (You might entice helpers by offering to pay for a taxi or car home if they're asked to stay past a certain hour.) You should also specify how you wish the bartender and servers to dress.

Prevailing rates for bartenders, servers, and other helpers differ from one area of the country to another, so we're afraid we can't offer much help on that score. If you're negotiating with individuals rather than an agency, however, do make sure that each person you hire understands and agrees to the hourly rate or flat fee you offer. Be generous enough to make your helpers *want* to work for you.

Should you tip? Whether or not you should present bartenders and servers with a tip in addition to the agreed-upon fee is an interesting question. There's certainly nothing wrong with tipping anyone who provides exemplary service. But you should definitely tip any bartender or server who comes to you through an agency—if, that is, their work is acceptable—since the agency will be taking a substantial cut of whatever fee you pay.

THE BAR

The pre-party weeks are also the time to make decisions about the bar—and to order all the booze you'll need. These are among the most difficult party-planning decisions you'll make, so let's go through this carefully.

Placement. We've all been to home cocktail parties at which the bar was placed in a particularly awkward spot—one guaranteed to create bottlenecks and to frazzle the nerves and exhaust the patience of thirsty guests. Our (brilliant) advice: Think about traffic patterns when deciding where to put the bar; don't stick it in a nook, small room, or other out-of-the-way place that will limit its accessibility. Take into account that guests will tend to congregate at the bar, meaning that the area in front of the bar should be fairly spacious and free of furniture and other obstructions. Also: The bar should be dedicated solely to the making and serving of drinks. If you place food on the bar or, worse, make the bartender share a table at which food is also being served, you're asking for trouble. The space will get mobbed, and everybody—those who want a drink, those who want food, and the bartender—will be frustrated and unhappy.

If at all possible, also try to locate the bar reasonably near a sink. Spills requiring cleanups *will* occur, and—no matter how many bar tools you provide—the bartender will have to perform a certain amount of equipment-washing over the course of the party. A nearby sink will make his or her job much easier, and—just as important—it will cut down on the amount of time the bartender must spend away from the bar. (Of course, if you're lucky enough to have a suitable wet bar in your house, your problem's solved.)

Bar height and size. Ever notice that real bars—*bar* bars—are waist-height or slightly higher? Ever thought about why this is so? It's because the bartender must stand while doing his or her job, and a waist-height counter makes for a much more comfortable (and therefore efficient) workstation than a thigh-high table.

The size of the bar, however, is even more important than its height. In a word, it should be as *capacious* as possible—large enough to hold all the straight liquor, bar condiments, and red wine (beer, white wine, and champagne can be held in ice-filled tubs or chests behind the bar); all the bar tools; and a fair number of glasses—as well as providing adequate space for the bartender to work. There's no need to set out all the glasses at once—the bartender can replace them as needed—but do make sure that the additional glasses are located in a convenient spot behind the bar. The purpose of putting most things—most of the booze, the bar tools, a goodly number of glasses—on the bar rather than stashed away behind it is twofold: (1) it allows guests to immediately survey the range of choices offered, and (2) it greatly cuts down on the number of times the bartender will have to turn away from the guests in order to retrieve this or that item. Particularly during the earliest phase of the party—when arriving guests will all be lining up for drinks at once—this is an extremely important consideration.

The booze: types and amounts. Ay, here's the rub. To order the right amounts—and right kinds—of liquor and other alcoholic beverages (and nonalcoholic beverages, for that matter), you've got to know at least a little something about your guests' tastes. If the invitees include a lot of beer drinkers but you go heavy on the wine, you'll have an unhappy crowd on your hands. If you invite a goodly number of scotch drinkers but—knowing nothing about whiskey yourself—decide that a bottle of bourbon will probably do, your party may end disappointingly early. But even if you can guess, more or less accurately, what people are likely to drink, how can you possibly figure out how much booze to buy? We can't answer your plaintive question with anything approaching absolute certainty, but we can provide a few suggestions.

First (and foremost): A cocktail party is a party at which *cocktails* (among other beverages) are served. A few years back, wine and spirits writer James Villas wrote a trenchant column for *Gourmet* magazine in which he bemoaned the absence of hard liquor and mixed drinks at too many of the "cocktail parties" he attended. He'd begun resorting, he said, to carrying a flask of liquor with him to all such events. (James Waller has sometimes adopted such a stratagem himself.) We're gonna give it to you straight: If you invite people to what you call a cocktail party but serve them only beer and wine, you are *lying,* and you're going to anger your hard liquor-drinking guests.

So what sort of hard liquor should you buy, and how much? It's our experience that if hard liquor is offered, more people will choose to drink it—either straight or in mixed drinks—than you might think.

Even people who otherwise stick to beer and wine will, at a party, have a "real" drink (or several) if given the option. You don't have to go overboard with the variety of liquors you offer, however. As a basic rule, provide just enough variety (of liquor, mixers, condiments, and garnishes) to enable the bartender to make a reasonable range of "standard" mixed drinks—Martinis, Manhattans, Screwdrivers, and the like. The Bar Associations sidebar on page 287 offers specific suggestions.

You might also consider offering one or (at the most) two *special* cocktails at your party—unusual mixed drinks that your guests are unlikely to have had before or "signature" drinks geared to your cocktail party's theme. Some simple examples: If you throw a Kentucky Derby party on the first Saturday of

Consider offering a "signature" cocktail

May, serve Mint Juleps. If you're giving a birthday cocktail party and happen to know that the guest of honor's favorite liqueur is amaretto, include a special, amaretto-based cocktail among the elbow-bending options. But note this proviso: Do *not* limit the hard liquor/mixed drink offerings to this special cocktail. (Not everyone will like it.) If you do offer a special, signature cocktail, give your bartender a break and choose a mixed drink that can be made up in batches beforehand. (This eliminates any cocktails that must be individually shaken.) For a few ideas regarding special cocktails you might consider serving, consult the Bar Associations sidebar at the end of this chapter (see page 362).

An aside: Another, somewhat similar notion is to include a party punch or (for wintertime gatherings) a hot mulled wine among the alcoholic-beverage options. Once again, however, we must insist: If you serve a punch or mulled wine, do so *in addition to* the other offerings. (Not everyone adores punch.) Do not make your bartender responsible for the punchbowl's replenishment; he or she will have plenty enough to do taking care of the bar. Include the making of the punch among the food-preparation duties (but don't add fizzy ingredients until you're about to serve it), make sure you have the ingredients on hand for more than one batch, and put one of your servers in charge of checking the punchbowl at intervals and refilling it as necessary. There's nothing drearier than a seven-eighths empty punchbowl. (The sidebar at the end of the chapter also includes just a couple of punch and mulled wine ideas.)

We've strayed. Let's get back to the topic of the *amount* of booze you should stock. Ramona (whose knowledgeability in this area constantly awes James) points out that there's a predictable pattern to the way that people drink at cocktail parties—a rhythm that can help you estimate now much hooch to lay in. During a party's first hour, she says, you can count on each person having two drinks; after that first hour—once they've lubricated themselves sufficiently and have gotten involved in conversations (and in eating)—people tend to slow down significantly. For each subsequent hour of the party, estimate that each person will have just one drink. Thus, the total number of drinks (of all kinds) that you'll need is expressible in the following equation, in which P equals the number of people at the party, H equals the party's length in hours, and D equals the total number of drinks:

$$P + (P \times H) = D$$

(In case you can't follow its logic, the first P in the equation stands for the additional drink that each person is likely to have during the party's first hour.) Thus, for a party of forty guests that will last four hours, you get the following result:

$$40 + (40 \times 4) = 200$$

You didn't know that planning your bar needs could be reduced to pure mathematical science, did you? Well, in truth, it can't, since this equation neglects a number of variables, including, of course, the kind of liquor your guests will be drinking, as well as the number of drinks in each bottle of liquor (or wine), the generousness (or lack thereof) with which your bartender pours, and the fact that, throughout the party, a fair number of guests will set their drinks down, forget where they put them, and return to the bar "prematurely."

Do the math

Nevertheless, the equation does have the "ballpark" virtue of letting you know how much booze would be much too little and how much would be much too much. Think about it. Let's say you guesstimate that, of the forty guests at your four-hour-long party, half will mostly drink wine, one-quarter will mostly drink hard liquor or mixed drinks, and one-quarter will mostly drink beer. Each bottle of wine contains five or six glasses' worth, depending on how liberally they're poured; each liter of hard liquor contains fifteen or sixteen drinks' worth, if you figure that each mixed or straight drink will contain about two ounces of booze. Needless to say, beer drinkers' drinks are measured in individual bottles or cans. Following these guidelines, we come up with the following baseline estimates:

For the wine:

(20 guests × 5 drinks each) ÷ 5 drinks per bottle = 20 bottles of wine

For the hard liquor:

(10 guests × 5 drinks each) ÷ 15 drinks per liter = 3.3 liters of liquor
(i.e., 4 liters)

For the beer:

> 10 guests × 5 drinks each = 50 bottles or cans of beer

These results provide you with a *floor*, not a ceiling. You don't want to chance running out of booze, so you've got to pump the figures up. But, working from these calculations, you can see that the following purchases will, in all probability, be more than sufficient for your forty-guest, four-hour-long party:

- 2 cases of wine (24 bottles). Not knowing how many of your wine-drinking guests prefer red and how many prefer white, let's just say that you'll order a case of each.

- 5 or 6 liter bottles of hard liquor. Since individual guests will prefer different kinds of hard liquor, you must order more than the four liters the baseline calculation requires. Two liters of vodka (the most popular spirit nowadays) and one liter each of gin, scotch, and bourbon might suffice. If you want to give guests an additional choice, throw in a liter of an additional spirit—say, light rum or white tequila. If you want your guests to be able to order cocktails, you'll also have to provide small (350ml) bottles of sweet and dry vermouth and perhaps other auxiliary liquors and liqueurs, as well. (See page 290.)

- 10 six-packs of beer (cans or bottles). You could probably get away with eight six-packs, but buying ten will give you a comfortable cushion.

See how easy it is? (Yeah, right.) To further your confusion, let us mention four factors that are likely to throw off all your beautiful arithmetic:

1. If you're serving Champagne or another sparkling wine, realize that the majority of guests—even many of those who ordinarily drink

beer or hard liquor—will opt for the Champagne. Booze-wise, Champagne comes close to being the universal solvent. Assume that at least half your guests will drink nothing else, and lay in enough cases to permit this. (Reduce the amounts of the other booze you buy accordingly).

2. If you're giving a New Year's Eve party, assume that your guests will drink substantially more than they would on other occasions (perhaps three drinks each during the first hour and one drink each for every forty minutes thereafter) and adjust your liquor order accordingly.

3. Some guests won't drink at all. You must, of course, accommodate them with soft drinks, fruit juices, and still and sparkling water, though it might also be nice to stock some nonalcoholic wine and beer—and perhaps even to advise your bartender to offer some nonalcoholic mixed drinks. (See *Drinkology: The Art and Science of the Cocktail*, pages 362–370 for recipes.)

4. Guests who've driven to the party will limit their alcohol consumption to one or two drinks over the course of the party—if, that is, they're being responsible. (It's one of your duties as host to try your best to make sure that no one drives drunk. Keep a list of taxi company and limousine service telephone numbers handy in case you need to make arrangements to get someone home.)

If all this begins to sound just a little too complicated, comfort yourself with the following fact: If you goof and estimate something wrongly, you're in good company. Restaurants, bars, and professional catering services all have trouble with this stuff. They all run out of things, at least occasionally. Do your best. Try to over- rather than underestimate. If you flub a couple of the details, you'll do better next time. (Or you'll flub something else.) Relax. No, wait a minute, don't relax, 'cause you've still got to take care of . . .

Bar tools. If you're offering guests cocktails, you've got to equip the bartender with the tools needed to make them. And you've got to supply some of the tools in multiples, to reduce the amount of time the bartender must spend washing up. Here's a *minimum* list for a midsize cocktail party (forty to sixty people). The list also includes tools for opening beer and wine, for cutting fruit garnishes, and for cleaning up spills:

1 or 2 barspoons

many bar towels

bowls (or other vessels) for garnishes
(twists, citrus wedges, cherries, olives, etc.)

1 bottle opener

3 cocktail shakers

3 cocktail strainers (Hawthorne or julep variety)

1 corkscrew ("waiter's friend" variety)

1 cutting board

1 ice bucket

ice tongs

2 or 3 jigger-pony measures

1 measuring cup

1 set of measuring spoons

BAR SPOON

HAWTHORNE STRAINER

JULEP STRAINER

STANDARD COCKTAIL SHAKER

3 mixing glasses
1 paring knife
1 pitcher (for water)
1 sponge

JIGGER-PONY

WAITER'S FRIEND

And don't forget the beverage napkins and swizzle sticks. Note that if you're serving special cocktails, you may also need specialized bar tools. (Mint Juleps, Mojitos, and other drinks require a muddler; Margaritas require a small plate to hold the salt for rimming glasses.) If some cocktails are being prepared in batches beforehand, you'll need pitchers for those. (Another thing to keep in mind: If you're intending to offer cocktails that require fresh citrus juices, the lemons, limes, and/or oranges should be squeezed ahead of time and kept chilled, in pitchers, until the party begins.)

Behind the bar, you'll need an ice chest or a large bucket dedicated *solely* to holding the ice that will replenish the ice bucket on the bar. (This is in addition to the ice-filled chests/buckets in which the beer and white and sparkling wines will be kept cool.) And the bar area should be equipped with two trash cans: a larger one behind the bar, for the bartender's use, and a smaller one in front of the bar (discreetly positioned, but visible) for the guests.

Some notes about blenders and blended drinks: Think *very* carefully before you decide to serve blended, frozen drinks at a large cocktail party. Here are the factors you need to weigh: (1) Blenders create a great deal—a *great* deal—of noise. If the bar is located outside, that might *(might)* be OK. If the bar's indoors, consider the acoustical repercussions before going ahead. (2) Frozen drinks, even when made in largish batches, take a lot of attention and effort to make; if you're hiring just a single bartender, don't burden him or her with this additional duty. (3) To be made rapidly and properly, frozen drinks require a commercial-grade blender capable of crushing ice. If your blender is of the ordinary, home-kitchen variety, forget it. (4) In fact, forget it if you can't equip the bar with at least two commercial-grade blenders; otherwise the bartender will spend too much time washing the carafe between batches. 'Nuff said?

Glassware. Like dinnerware and flatware, the glasses for your party can be bought at a restaurant-supply house (that is, if you're into saving money) or rented from a party-supply rental firm. If you're serving beer, wine, cocktails and other mixed drinks, and Champagne (or another sparkling wine), you'll need the following five kinds of glasses:

· Highball glasses (a.k.a. tumblers) for beer, highballs, and tall nonalcoholic drinks

· Wine glasses (Choose 13-ounce stemmed glasses, which are suitable for both red and white wine.)

· Double rocks glasses (a.k.a. double Old Fashioned glasses) for on-the-rocks straight and mixed drinks

· Cocktail glasses (a.k.a. Martini glasses) for shaken or stirred cocktails that are served "up"

· Champagne flutes

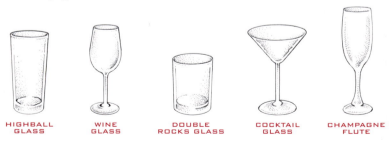

HIGHBALL
GLASS

WINE
GLASS

DOUBLE
ROCKS GLASS

COCKTAIL
GLASS

CHAMPAGNE
FLUTE

Can you make do with fewer types? Well, it's a free country (or so we'd still like to think), so you can do whatever you please. You can serve beer in the can or bottle. (Yuck.) You can serve straight, on-the-rocks drinks in wine glasses. (Double yuck.) You can even serve Champagne in wine glasses. (Yecch!) Be our guest—just don't make us be yours.

The same rule applies to glassware as applied to dinnerware and serving dishes and utensils. Don't make the error of believing that your helpers will have time to wash glasses during the party itself. To be safe, buy or rent one glass for each drink you think will be consumed. (Again, estimate how many guests are likely to drink beer, wine, cocktails, and so on, and gauge your glassware totals accordingly.) That's a lot of glasses. Will all of them be used? Probably not. But as we keep saying, it is much better to have too much—food, liquor, glasses, whatever—than to risk running out.

BAR ASSOCIATIONS

SOMETHING FOR (NEARLY) EVERYONE

Selecting the *types* of beer, wine, and hard liquor and the other provisions with which to stock your cocktail party's bar isn't nearly as difficult as deciding on the amounts of booze you'll need. If you follow our suggestions here, you can't go wrong. Er, that is, you *almost* can't go wrong. We've all got friends (mercifully few of them) who only drink one particular thing—be it Guinness Stout, Cabernet Sauvignon, or white crème de menthe on the rocks. Our basic bar recommendations won't satisfy such persnickety characters. Take pains to accommodate such a person's narrow palate only if he or she is a guest of honor.

Note that the recommendations that follow do not include ingredients for special, signature cocktails or a party punch. If you want to offer such potables, see the sidebar at the end of the chapter (page 362) for some ideas, and add the necessary additional ingredients to your bar shopping list.

SOMETHING FOR (NEARLY) EVERYONE

Beer. You'll want to choose a beer that *most* beer drinkers will find acceptable—and that means a lager, a pilsner, or a pale ale. (Most dark-beer and -ale drinkers will settle for a good pale, lighter-bodied beer, but the opposite is not the case.) Forget "light" beers; make your "lo-cal" beer–drinking chums go off their fake diets for a few hours. As we've said elsewhere, we're particularly fond of a number of Asian lagers, including, to name a few, Kingfisher (from India), Singha (from Thailand), Kirin (from Japan), Tsingtao (from China), and Efes Pilsen (from Turkey—Wait! Is Turkey in Asia or Europe?). But these are just some possibilities among a *world* of possibilities.

Wine and Champagne. Again, the main object is to please the most people. (Or is it to offend the fewest?) An important secondary (?) goal is to keep the cost of the booze within reason—and the wine, whether still or sparkling, can easily bust a party's budget. Our wine suggestions are made with this reality in mind. You should buy and taste various wines before deciding on the two or three you'll stock for the party. Better yet, have a few friends by (a pre-party party!) to help you do the tasting and decision making. And when you do buy, buy by the case. Virtually all wine merchants offer at least a 10 percent discount—and some take as much as 20 percent off—a "solid" case (a case containing only one kind of wine).

About reds: If it seems to you that your red wine–drinking pals generally prefer full-bodied, robust wines, consider choosing a Malbec from Argentina or one of the red wines of Spain's Jumilla region (made mostly from a grape called Monastrell in Spain and Mourvèdre elsewhere). You can find *excellent* Malbecs and Jumillas for less than $15 a bottle.

If you'd rather go with a lighter-bodied red (likely to be compatible with a wider range of foods), you might choose one of the Beaujolais Cru wines, which are named for the particular French villages they come from. (There are ten such villages in all; Brouilly, Fleurie, Juliénas, and Morgon are the names you're likely to encounter most often.) Again, you should be able to find a range of Beaujolais Crus for under $15 a bottle. (For more information on these exceptional and underrated wines, see *Drinkology WINE: A Guide to the Grape,* page 277.)

Regarding white wine, the versatility of a dry Riesling cannot, in our judgment, be matched. (Also, virtually everyone likes it.) The best Rieslings are from Germany's Mosel-Saar-Ruwer region; although they're undervalued, you might find even the cheapest of them a bit pricey for a large party. But there are alternatives, including dry Rieslings from Germany's Rheingau and Pfalz regions, from Austria, and from Washington State. (A week before writing this sentence, James had an eight-buck Riesling made by the Washington producer Covey Run; it wasn't what you'd call complex, but it was delicious—and it struck James as a nearly perfect party white.)

About sparklers: If you've decided to serve French Champagne—which, to get technical about it, is the only kind of *Champagne* there is—you've already blown your budget, and more power to you. But be aware, in case such things matter to you, that there are many, many excellent sparklers besides Champagne—and that many of these can be had for a fraction of Champagne's price. If you have time during the weeks preceding your party, you might taste-test a cava (a Champagne-method wine from Spain), a Prosecco (from Italy), and perhaps a Champagne-method bubbly from California or elsewhere. (There are some good South African sparklers on the market today.) In putting together your taste-test contestants, ask a manager or salesperson at your local wine shop for advice.

Cocktail makings. By choosing wisely, you can create an extremely versatile bar from a limited number of basic liquors (that is, the liquors that constitute mixed drinks' main alcoholic ingredients), "auxiliary" liquors (subsidiary ingredients in mixed drinks), mixers, condiments, and garnishes. If you buy just the items on the following lists, your bartender will be able to make these well-known (and often-ordered) mixed drinks, among others: Cape Codder, collinses (several kinds), Cosmopolitan, Cuba Libre, Daiquiri, fizzes (several kinds), Gimlet, Gin and Tonic, Highball (Classic), Manhattan, Margarita, Martinis (gin and vodka), Old Fashioned, rickeys (several kinds), Rob Roy, Rum and Tonic, Salty Dog, Screwdriver, Sidecar, slings (several kinds), sours (several kinds), Tequila Sunrise, Vodka and Tonic. That's quite a variety for a reasonably small bar. (The selection of sodas and juices should also satisfy your non-alcohol-drinking guests. Note, though, that diet sodas can lend "off" tastes to mixed drinks; if you want to include diet sodas among your offerings, do so *in addition to* the sugar-sweetened sodas.)

Here are the lists. Note that we're not giving you the *amounts* you need—just the types of liquor and the other necessary items. (Refer back to pages 280–283 for general advice on amounts.) Well, maybe we can offer just one suggestion vis-à-vis amounts: Buy twice as much vodka as any other hard liquor, since it's likely that guests these days will order more vodka-based drinks than other kinds.

Main Liquors

bourbon *or* blended
  Canadian whisky
gin
light rum
scotch (blended—*not* single malt)
white tequila
vodka (plain and lemon-flavored)

"Auxiliary" Liquors

brandy or cognac
Cointreau
dry vermouth
sweet vermouth

Mixers

club soda or seltzer
cola

ginger ale
tonic water
cranberry juice
grapefruit juice
orange juice
bottled water (sparkling and still)

Condiments
Angostura bitters
grenadine
Rose's lime juice

kosher salt
simple syrup
superfine sugar

Garnishes
green (Spanish) olives, stuffed
  with pimientos
lemons
limes
maraschino cherries
oranges

A word about ice. The word is *lots.* To ensure freshness, you shouldn't buy the ice until the day of the party. (You probably don't have freezer space to store it, anyway.) But you should try to calculate the amount of ice you need before purchasing it. The *Drinkology* series' rule about ice for parties is simple: Estimate how much you'll need, then buy *double* that amount. We're not kidding. Your party will survive if you run out of a particular food or particular liquor. If you run out of ice, however, you're sunk. When estimating your ice requirements, take into consideration that a single shaken or stirred cocktail requires the equivalent of a full standard tray's worth ice cubes (that's at least half a pound *per drink*), and that you'll also need oodles of ice to chill the beer, white wine, and (if you're serving it) Champagne. If it's a large cocktail party you're throwing, think about arranging for delivery with an ice wholesaler. These businesses typically supply retail customers as well as the trade—and it's a whole lot easier to have the ice delivered than to lug it all home from the supermarket.

Week Five—Party Week (and Party Day)

OK, let's synchronize our watches.

You've spent the previous four weeks taking care of all the preliminaries. Now, all you've got to do is buy all the food, set everything up, do all the cooking—or, rather, all the cooking and food-prep work that can be done before the party begins—and, of course, worry and fret.

You're doing your own menu planning for this one, so we can't really advise you, as we have in some previous chapters, about the order in which you should prepare the dishes. But we can offer this one—perhaps obvious—suggestion: Prepare as much of the food as far ahead of time as recipes permit. If you're serving snacks such as coated nuts, which can be made days ahead, get those out of the way early in the week. Many dips, pâtés/mousses, and terrines can be prepared a full day ahead—and may even benefit from a little "ageing" in the fridge. And then there are some dishes—including, for example, the gravlax we present on page 349—that *must* be begun days before they're to be served. We talked earlier about putting together a game plan; now's the time to develop a *detailed schedule* for accomplishing all the cooking.

Let us give you just a few more pointers (for last-minute matters) before setting you loose.

Décor: The Non-Decorative Aspects

Notice that we haven't supplied you with any ideas on how to outfit your lovely home for the party. The flowers, the piñatas, the disco balls, the balloon animals, the crêpe-paper garlands—they're all your concern. But there are just a few things you should consider as you set up, no matter what your decorating scheme:

Clear the decks. At large cocktail parties, things get broken, so put away all the frangible bric-à-brac. But there's another reason for removing all nonessential objects from tabletops, mantels, and other surfaces: Your guests will need places to rest their drinks and plates. Which leads us to another suggestion: If any of your tabletops are susceptible to glass rings, protect them with tablecloths (or remove that furniture from the party space). Do *not* expect guests to use coasters; even if you have enough coasters to go around (which is doubtful), guests won't remember to use them.

Provide enough trash cans. Don't make your guests hunt around for places to dispose of their garbage. Put one trash can somewhere in each party room (more than one if the space is especially large), locating the cans in spots that are both discreet and visible.

Clean your house. But you knew to do this, yes? (One detail that's too often neglected: Make sure that there's plenty of extra toilet paper—clearly visible and conveniently placed—in each bathroom just before the party. Hand towels, too!)

And don't forget those extra vases. We mentioned it earlier, but we'll say it again: Some guests may be bring flowers as "hostess gifts." Make sure you have vases on hand to accommodate the bouquets. (Glass vases from the florist's shop are just fine.)

DEALING WITH THE STAFF

You'll be unbelievably busy during the last hour before the party begins, but you should take sufficient time to give instructions to the bartender(s) and server(s) when they arrive. Take the servers on a whirlwind tour of the house, so that they'll understand the lay of the land and will be able to direct guests to the bar, coat room, and bathrooms. Apprise the bartender of everything he or she needs to know—especially if you're serving a special, signature cocktail—and equip him or her with a cocktail recipe handbook in case a guest should request an unfamiliar drink. (*Drinkology: The Art and Science of the Cocktail* would be the perfect choice.) Advise the bartender not to be too, too generous when pouring hard-liquor drinks—not because you're being parsimonious but because you want to guard against guests becoming too quickly intoxicated.

Appoint a team leader—someone to whom all problems and questions are to be taken. (This leader may, of course, be you.) If you're working with more than four helpers, appoint a second-in-command.

The servers should also be told the ingredients of each dish, though it makes more sense to provide them with this information as the individual dishes are being served (otherwise, they'll forget). Guests will certainly ask diet-related questions about the food (or they'll simply be curious about the ingredients of dishes they like and dishes they don't), so it's a good idea to equip the servers with this knowledge.

Enjoin everyone to do as much cleaning up as possible while the party is in progress. When servers' hands are free, they should pick up every empty glass, stray plate, and bit of trash they spy. This ongoing "busing" of the party will not only make your post-party cleanup easier, but it will keep the party space from becoming littered-looking as the hours go on.

Pay the helpers at the end of the party, but prepare the payments ahead of time. If you've contracted with individuals (as opposed to an agency), prepare an envelope for each helper (with that person's name on it). Pay the helpers *in cash*. Make sure that you also have a wad of cash, in appropriate denominations, for tips. (For advice on tipping the help, refer back to page 276.)

Are we forgetting anything? *Undoubtedly.* But we think it's high time to progress to the recipes that are, believe it or not, this chapter's main reason for being. Once again: Each recipe is calculated to provide one dish (out of many dishes) for at least twenty people, and the recipes are arranged according to how they'll be served—whether on tables throughout the space; on larger, dedicated tables or counters; or on serving trays passed among the crowd.

And, lest we forget: Good luck!

SNACKS

Especially for a very large cocktail party occurring in several rooms, James and Ramona feel that at least some of the food should be distributed throughout the space—on occasional tables or at other stations—so that guests can help themselves wherever they happen to be and whenever they feel like munching. These snacks should be of a very simple, no-fuss kind—nuts, crackers, cheese straws, and the like—that require little, besides the serving dishes they're placed in, in the way of serving "apparatus." Sure, you may want to place a small pile of (small) napkins wherever you're locating such foods. And if you're serving olives—a favorite party snack—you should also position small dishes for the discarded pits next to the olive bowls. (While we're on the subject, let us mention that we *love* spicy Tunisian olives, marinated in red pepper–infused oil.)

Several of the recipes given in chapter 1—the various kinds of coated nuts (pages 19–23), the ice-box crackers (page 40), and the parmesan cheese crisps (page 42)—make terrific cocktail-party snacks. Ramona and James's enthusiasm for coated nuts knows no bounds, so we offer three more recipes in the following pages, as well as recipes for cheese straws and a similar snack fashioned from store-bought frozen puff pastry.

CRYSTAL COCKTAIL NUTS

This and the next two coated-nut recipes are simpler than the ones presented in chapter 1. All three are very sweet, but don't let that put you off. The sweetness, in each case, is balanced by other flavors—in this recipe, by salt and by the umami taste of the nuts themselves. (*Umami* is the so-called "fifth taste"—beyond sweet, salty, sour, and bitter—that characterizes many savory, protein-rich foods.) Despite their sweetness, these make superb cocktail nuts. Note that the simple syrup you'll make for this recipe is a bit thicker and more viscous than the two-parts-sugar, one-part-water syrup ordinarily used in cocktail recipes.

1½ cups granulated sugar
½ cup water
1 pound unsalted roasted cashews or almonds
1 cup superfine sugar
4 teaspoons fine sea salt

In a saucepan, stir together the granulated sugar and water. Bring to a boil, reduce the heat to low, and simmer for 10 minutes, stirring occasionally. Remove from the heat and let stand until cool enough to be touched.

Put the nuts in a large kitchen strainer or sieve and place the strainer in a bowl that is just a bit bigger than the strainer. Pour the syrup over the nuts and shake or stir gently to make sure they are all coated with the syrup.

Combine the superfine sugar and salt in a resealable plastic bag, seal, and shake until well integrated. Drain the nuts, but do not let them dry. Add them to the plastic bag, seal, and shake gently to coat completely. Spread on a plate or tray to dry. After drying, the nuts may be stored in an airtight container for up to 1 week.

CINNAMON-COCOA COCKTAIL NUTS

Unsweetened cocoa powder gives these coated nuts a sultry chocolate flavor that's just right for cocktails.

1½ cups granulated sugar
½ cup water
1 pound unsalted roasted cashews, almonds, or hazelnuts
¾ cup superfine sugar
6 tablespoons unsweetened cocoa powder
1 teaspoon cinnamon

In a saucepan, stir together the granulated sugar and water. Bring to a boil, reduce the heat to low, and simmer for 10 minutes, stirring occasionally. Remove from the heat and let stand until cool enough to be touched.

Put the nuts in a large kitchen strainer or sieve and place the strainer in a bowl that is just a bit bigger than the strainer. Pour the syrup over the nuts and shake or stir gently to make sure they are all coated with the syrup.

Combine the superfine sugar, cocoa powder, and cinnamon in a resealable plastic bag, seal, and shake until well integrated. Drain the nuts, but do not let them dry. Add them to the plastic bag, seal, and shake gently to coat completely. Spread on a plate or tray to dry. After drying, the nuts may be stored in an airtight container for up to 1 week.

Hot Chocolate Nuts

Despite this recipe's simplicity, we felt quite adventurous creating it. Could we actually pull off a chocolate-coated nut suitable for serving with cocktails? The addition of the chili powder did the trick.

8 ounces bittersweet chocolate
1 pound unsalted roasted cashews or almonds
1 cup confectioners' sugar
8 tablespoons unsweetened cocoa powder
1 teaspoon chili powder

Melt the chocolate in the top of a double boiler over gently simmering water. When the chocolate has melted, stir it until it is smooth. Remove the double-boiler top from the heat, add the nuts, and stir gently until all the nuts are completely coated.

Combine the confectioners' sugar, cocoa powder, and chili powder in a resealable plastic bag, seal, and shake until well integrated. Spoon the nuts into the plastic bag, reseal it, and shake gently until all the nuts are evenly coated with the powder. Spread on a plate or tray to harden and dry completely. After drying, the nuts may be stored in an airtight container for up to 1 week.

Herbed Cheese Straws

Easy to make, cheese straws have long been a favorite American cocktail snack. This recipe and the variation that follows each yield about three dozen straws.

1 cup unbleached all-purpose flour
1½ teaspoons baking powder
½ teaspoon salt

¼ teaspoon onion powder
¼ teaspoon dried oregano
¼ teaspoon dried thyme
⅛ teaspoon ground cayenne pepper
⅛ teaspoon garlic powder
⅛ teaspoon sweet paprika
1 cup (about 4 ounces) finely grated extra-sharp cheddar
½ cup (1 stick) unsalted butter, cut into pats
6 teaspoons milk

Preheat the oven to 375° F. Line a baking sheet with parchment paper. In a medium-size mixing bowl, whisk together the dry ingredients, including seasonings. Add the cheese and butter and cut into the flour mixture with a pastry blender or fork until the mixture resembles coarse meal. Add the milk and stir until an elastic dough forms.

Scoop out very small amounts of dough (about ½ teaspoon per straw) and, using your hands, roll each into a very thin, 8-inch-long straw. Place the straws on the prepared baking sheet and bake for 10 to 12 minutes, until golden. Cheese straws may be made 2 to 3 days ahead of time; when the straws have cooled, transfer them very carefully (they are fragile) to an airtight plastic container.

GARLIC CHEESE STRAWS

1 cup unbleached all-purpose flour
1½ teaspoons baking powder
½ teaspoon salt
¼ teaspoon garlic powder
⅛ teaspoon ground cayenne pepper
⅛ teaspoon sweet paprika

1 cup (about 4 ounces) finely grated extra-sharp cheddar
½ cup (1 stick) unsalted butter, cut into pats
6 teaspoons milk

Preheat the oven to 375° F. Line a baking sheet with parchment paper. In a medium-size mixing bowl, whisk together the dry ingredients, including seasonings. Add the cheese and butter and cut into the flour mixture with a pastry blender or fork until the mixture resembles coarse meal. Add the milk and stir until an elastic dough forms.

Scoop out very small amounts of dough (about ½ teaspoon per straw) and, using your hands, roll each into a very thin, 8-inch-long straw. Place the straws on the prepared baking sheet and bake for 10 to 12 minutes, until golden. Cheese straws may be made 2 to 3 days ahead of time; when the straws have cooled, transfer them very carefully (they are fragile) to an airtight plastic container.

PUFF PASTRY TWISTS

Made with the prepared puff pastry you can find in your grocer's frozen foods case, these twists are light and crisp. Thaw the puff pastry to room temperature, but do not allow it to sit around in a warm kitchen for too long before using. This recipe yields about four dozen twists.

1 package (1 pound) prepared puff pastry, thawed
1 cup finely grated Parmigiano-Reggiano
½ teaspoon freshly ground black pepper
½ teaspoon garlic powder
½ teaspoon onion powder
½ teaspoon sweet paprika

Preheat the oven to 400° F. Line two baking sheets with parchment paper. Carefully unfold the prepared puff pastry. Cut the sheet in half to make 2 rectangles of equal size.

In a small bowl, combine the cheese and spices thoroughly. Sprinkle the mixture evenly over one of the rectangles of pastry. Carefully lay the other rectangle on top. Using a pizza cutter, carefully cut the rectangle into ½-inch-wide strips. Cut the strips in half crosswise. (Each should be 5 to 6 inches long.) Twist each strip to form a loose corkscrew, taking care not to separate the layers. Lay the twists on the prepared baking sheets. Bake for 15 to 18 minutes, until golden and crisp. The twists may be made 2 to 3 days ahead of time; when the twists have cooled, transfer them to an airtight plastic container.

THE APPETIZER SPREAD

Besides the snacks placed here and there throughout the party space, a full spread of other appetizers grouped on one or more large tables or counters should greet the arriving guests. Do not, however, use the same table as that on which you lay the main buffet; the appetizer spread should remain "up and running"—and should be tidied and replenished as necessary—throughout the party, or at least until dessert is served.

The appetizer spread can be as simple or elaborate as you wish, though (as always) Ramona and James cast their ballots for a spread that conveys the impression of variety and abundance. Among the kinds of foods such a spread might include are cheeses, fresh fruit, crudités (bite-size pieces of raw and blanched vegetables), dips, pâtés or liver mousses, and deviled eggs. (Since deviled eggs can also be passed on trays, we include deviled-eggs recipes at the beginning of the following section; see page 317.) The appetizer spread should also include a selection of crackers, bakery-fresh breads, and potato chips (and perhaps corn chips and other vegetable chips, as well).

Cheese. Here's a sensible rule of thumb: Buy about three ounces of cheese per guest. For a party of twenty people, this translates to about four pounds; multiply this amount as necessary for larger gatherings. Variety is, as we've continually stressed, important, but no matter how large your party, limit the variety to perhaps six different kinds of cheese. A diverse-enough selection might, for example, consist of the following:

- One semi-soft cheese, such as Edam, fontina, Gouda, or Havarti
- One blue cheese, such as Stilton or one of the other English blues (see page 182), the superb Spanish blue called Valdeon, or even that good old supermarket standard, Saga Blue (from Denmark)
- One soft-ripened cheese, such as Brie, Camembert, or Saint André
- A sharp, aged cheddar
- A chèvre
- One semi-firm cheese, such as Gruyère or manchego, or a sliceable hard cheese such as the Spanish cheese called Idiazabal

Remove all cheeses from the fridge about an hour and a half before the party's kickoff time, so that they have a chance to grow fragrant and tasty. (You may want to keep them wrapped, however, until just before the party starts.) Soft-ripened cheeses should be served *ripe*—soft, gooey, and smelly. If you don't buy your cheese from a first-rate cheese-monger (that is, a shop that knows not to sell Bries, Camemberts, and similar cheeses before their time), buy soft-ripened cheeses a week in advance of the party and let them mature in your refrigerator. (The other cheeses should be bought within a few days of the party day.) When setting out the cheese, make sure that each wedge or round is accompanied by an appropriate cheese knife or spreader.

Fruit. Most of the fruit on your cheese-and-fruit board should be "finger fruit"—fruit that guests can pick up and eat with a minimum of struggle. Seedless table grapes are de rigueur. Depending on the season, other fruits you might consider include strawberries; cherries (make sure you provide small dishes for the pits); tangerines, clementines, and mandarin oranges; seckel pears; and lady apples. In general, avoid fruit that must be cut, sliced, or seeded—although setting out a few larger pears and apples (with cutting board and paring knife handy) isn't such a bad idea, since a few guests might like to accompany their cheese with apple or pear slices. (But don't overdo this; most guests won't go to the trouble.) If you're afraid you'll be able to find only unripe fruit in local markets, buy your fruit a few days in advance and force-ripen it in plastic or brown-paper bags.

Ramona adores dried fruit—and she's even managed to convince James, whose dried-fruit intake was formerly limited to the raisins in an occasional bowl of raisin bran, that the stuff is edible. (Well, maybe better than edible: He's even taken to eating granola with dried cherries in it. What has this world come to?) At any rate, she advises including a scattering of dried fruits—figs, dates, peaches, pears, pineapple rings, apricots, and even smaller dried fruits like cherries and cranberries—among the fruit offerings.

Bread, crackers, and chips. For the cheese-and-fruit board, lay in one loaf of bakery-fresh bread for every ten to fifteen people. Again, aim at diversity, providing a selection of different kinds of breads, including whole-grain varieties. Don't slice or set out all the bread at once, however. It's highly unpredictable how much will be eaten, so keep some in reserve with which to replenish the table as necessary. (After the party, freeze leftover loaves for future use.) Baguettes are especially appropriate for a party, since their small diameter yields slices of just the right size for cheese, tapenades, and pâtés or mousses. (Slice baguettes, on a slight diagonal, into ½-inch slices; if you're serving tapenades and mousses, toast some baguette slices to serve with these dishes.) More sizable loaves should be sliced into half-slices (full slices are too large), and the half-slices arranged in baskets.

Large flatbreads make attractive "platforms" for cheese-and-fruit spreads. If you have a Middle Eastern bakery in your locale—or an Italian bakery that produces long, flattish focaccia loaves—consider buying an oversize flatbread on which to heap all the cheese and fruit offerings. (One Italian bakery we know will knock out six-foot-long focaccias on order; you just have to call twenty minutes ahead.) Note that this platform serves a decorative purpose only; don't count it when figuring the total number of loaves needed to feed your guests.

One package of crackers for every ten or fifteen guests should also be sufficient. Again, aim at variety, and be sure to include non-wheat crackers (rye crispbreads, rice crackers) for your gluten-allergic friends. If you're serving dips, accompany them with crudités as well as potato chips or other vegetable chips. But take our advice and use store-bought chips; you're unlikely to have time in the busy days preparing for the party to make your own.

Crudités. The word *crudités* means "raw [things]," though, technically speaking, not all the vegetables on a crudité platter should be absolutely raw. Some should be briefly microwaved or blanched in boiling water to soften them slightly and—more important—to intensify their flavor. Ramona, whose enthusiasm for crudités approaches that of a ravenous bunny for a well-tended vegetable garden, suggests that you choose a variety of differently colored and shaped veggies when putting together your crudité selection. Here are her pointers on what to look for when buying some of the vegetables that might be included, as well as some notes on preparation:

· *Asparagus.* Small spears are best. The lower ends of asparagus spears are usually tough and fibrous and should be cut off (to find out where the tender part ends, bend the spear until it breaks) or their outer layer shaved off with a vegetable peeler. For crudités, asparagus should be microwaved, covered, on high power for two to three minutes (depending on size) or blanched in boiling water for two minutes and then immediately plunged into ice-cold water. Brief microwaving or parboiling will turn the stalks brilliant green and bring out the asparagus flavor.

· *Cucumbers.* Unwaxed "hothouse" cucumbers (sometimes called English or Japanese cucumbers), which come individually shrink-wrapped, and the small, unwaxed pickling cucumbers called Kirbys are best. When buying cucumbers, make sure they have no soft spots or wrinkling at the ends. Hothouse cucumbers need not be peeled or seeded—simply washed and sliced into ¼-inch-thick rounds. If you buy Kirbys, choose those that are no more than 1½ inches in diameter; quarter them, lengthwise, into spears.

· *Carrots.* We know they're popular, but we strongly advise against using those bagged, pre-peeled industrial products misleadingly sold as "baby" carrots for your crudité platter. (They're not really babies; they're adult carrots that have been mechanically abraided until they are all the same size and shape.) So-called baby carrots usually possess an unpleasant, slightly bitter "off" taste," so use honest-to-God *carrot* carrots instead. Peel them, then cut them into slices or ⅜-inch-square sticks. (Note: Avoid using the purple carrots sold in the produce sections of fashionable markets. They taste weird. How's that for culinary sophistication?)

· *Celery.* Celery sticks are the hoi polloi of any crudité platter, but there's no reason you can't be a tad more creative, for instance by cutting the stalks into three- to four-inch sections and filling them with cream cheese, peanut butter, or a thick-textured dip. (Either of the Stilton cheese dips whose recipes appear in chapter 1—see page 33— would work beautifully.) Do not throw away the stalks at the center of the head—the little ones with the pretty, pale leaves; reserve them for use as garnishes.

· *Squash.* Zucchini and yellow squash are crudité staples when in season. Yellow squash cannot tolerate rough handling—any cuts or bruises turn brown overnight. Select squash whose skins are smooth and undamaged and that are no more than about 1½ inches in diameter. Wash them carefully and slice into rounds. If you choose baby yellow or white squash or baby zucchini, take pains to avoid damaging the squashes' delicate skins; the spiky-textured stems should be cut off and the blossom ends trimmed. If the baby squash are small enough to be consumed in a couple of bites, serve them whole.

· *Broccoli.* After cutting off and discarding the woody, fibrous stem, break or cut each head of broccoli into bite-size florets, then microwave or blanch them in boiling water for two minutes to intensify the color and flavor. After blanching, immediately plunge the florets into ice-cold water and pat them dry with paper towels before adding them to the crudité platter.

- *Cauliflower.* Make sure the head of cauliflower has no blackish spots. Cut out the hard center and break or cut the head into bite-size florets. No blanching is required.

- *Bell peppers.* A range of different-colored sweet bell peppers—green, red, orange, yellow, purple—really dresses up a crudité platter. Choose only firm, unwrinkled peppers. Wash the peppers carefully; seed them and remove any white, pithy ribs from their interiors; then cut them into tiles or sticks.

- *Tomatoes.* Bite-size tomatoes—cherry tomatoes, grape tomatoes, or baby pear tomatoes—are essential members of the crudité congress. When buying, examine the tomatoes (usually packaged in net bags or plastic baskets) as carefully as possible to make certain that they are fresh and unwrinkled. During tomato season, all the varieties are reliable; out of season, Ramona has had good luck with grape tomatoes, which are generally sweet whenever you buy them. Just rinse and drain, then pile them on the platter.

- *Scallions.* Many people—fearing "onion breath," we suppose—won't touch the scallions on a crudité platter, but a few people really love them. (And they really look great on the plate.) Choose small, very fresh scallions. Cut off the roots (but leave a few inches of the green tops), peel away any drying layers, rinse, and serve.

- *String beans and their relatives.* String beans, yellow wax beans, and the French green beans known as haricots verts are all suitable candidates for the crudité platter. (Intensely flavorful and easy to prep, haricots verts have only one drawback: They're usually about twice as expensive as the other varieties.) No matter which kind of beans you choose, cut off the ends and rinse. Microwave or blanch haricots verts for thirty seconds; string beans or wax beans for one minute. Immediately plunge them into ice-cold water, and pat them dry before adding to the platter.

· *Snow peas.* A limp snow pea is an old and tired snow pea, so make sure the snow pea pods are quite firm when purchasing. Blanch or microwave for ten seconds, then plunge into ice-cold water, patting the pods dry before serving.

· *Radishes.* Among crudité lovers, radishes have a fanatical following. Make sure that the radishes you buy are very fresh—not woody or split. Cut off the tops, stems, and roots, and wash carefully. Small radishes may be presented whole. Larger ones may be cut into quarters or sliced like cucumbers. Very long radishes ("French breakfast" radishes and that ilk) should definitely be sliced.

· *Mushrooms.* Raw mushrooms are iffy, since they cause some people gastric distress. If you do decide to include them, select small, white button mushrooms that are super fresh and have not yet begun to split under the cap. Clean the mushrooms extremely carefully and cut off most of each mushroom's stem before putting them on the plate. Spindly enoki mushrooms add an exotic touch to a crudité platter; cut the stalks from the base (discard the base) and break them apart if necessary, but do not cut the stalks into pieces.

Certain vegetables are simply inappropriate for crudités: Brussels sprouts' too-powerful flavor overwhelms that of any dip; hot peppers (no matter how pretty) will cause unwary guests unwonted suffering; avocados oxidize too readily; freshly shelled raw peas are just too tiny. You can save yourself a little bit of trouble by buying packaged, pre-cut celery and carrot sticks, but proceed with caution: If the veggie sticks are packed in water, check to make sure that the water is clear and that the celery isn't curled or splitting. If the carrots and celery are packed dry, make sure that the carrots do not have an ashen appearance and that the celery sticks aren't shrunken-looking at their ends.

When deciding on which dips and tapenades to include in your appetizer spread, don't limit yourself to the selection that follows. Elsewhere in *Drinkology EATS*, you'll find equally suitable dips, tapenades, and other spreads. For the crudités, also consider the Stilton dips on page 33; for potato chips, the faux caviar dip, also on page 33; and, for corn chips, the nopalitos dip on page 228. All of the "instant" cocktail party recipes in chapter 3—including those for tapenades and bean spreads—will be equally at home at a larger, planned gathering.

Hot Artichoke Dip

This beautifully colored, soufflé-like dip is an old war horse, but it remains ever battle-ready. It's especially good with crudités.

1 jar marinated artichoke hearts (about 1 cup)
1 cup mayonnaise
1 cup grated Parmigiano-Reggiano
1 finely clove garlic. finely minced

Preheat the oven to 350° F. Place the artichokes and their liquid in a blender or food processor and pulse until well chopped. Add the other ingredients and blend until thoroughly mixed. Pour the mixture into an oven-proof ramekin. Bake for 15 to 20 minutes, until puffy and golden. Serve hot. (The ingredients may be blended and stored in the refrigerator for up to 1 week. Bring to room temperature before baking.)

SPINACH DIP

Another war horse, likewise ready for combat. This slightly chunky, colorful concoction is one of our favorite potato-chip dips.

1 (10-ounce) package frozen chopped spinach, thawed
1 (8-ounce) can water chestnuts, drained and finely chopped
½ cup finely chopped red bell pepper
1 scallion, thinly sliced (about 3 tablespoons)
1 cup mayonnaise
1 cup sour cream
½ teaspoon Coleman's dry mustard
½ teaspoon salt, or to taste
¼ teaspoon celery seed
¼ teaspoon freshly ground black pepper
¼ teaspoon garlic powder
⅛ teaspoon ground cayenne pepper
⅛ teaspoon sweet paprika

Squeeze as much liquid as possible from the spinach and chop it finely. In a medium-size bowl, combine the spinach and the remaining ingredients and mix until well integrated. Transfer to one or more serving bowls, cover, and refrigerate for at least 1 hour before serving.

MUSHROOM TAPENADE

In chapter 3, we offer recipes for olive- and sundried-tomato–based tapenades, any of which would be suitable for a large cocktail party (see pages 81–83). Here's another of these Provençal-style spreads—one based on several varieties of mushrooms.

6 tablespoons extra-virgin olive oil
6 large cloves garlic, minced
½ pound white mushrooms, cleaned and chopped
¼ pound cremini mushrooms, cleaned and chopped
¼ pound shiitake mushrooms, cleaned and chopped
1 teaspoon dried thyme
¼ teaspoon salt
¼ teaspoon freshly ground black pepper
⅛ teaspoon dried oregano
pinch of ground cayenne pepper
½ cup dry red wine
½ cup chopped fresh flat-leaf parsley
⅓ cup Kalamata olives, drained, pitted, and chopped
2 tablespoons fresh lemon juice
lemon slices

Heat 4 tablespoons of the oil in a medium-size frying pan over medium heat. Add the garlic and sauté until fragrant, about 1 minute. Increase the heat to medium-high and add the mushrooms, thyme, salt, pepper, oregano, and cayenne. Cook, stirring frequently, until the mushrooms soften and release their liquid, 2 to 4 minutes. Add the wine and cook the mixture, continuing to stir frequently, until most of the liquid has evaporated and the mushrooms have acquired a rich, deep brown color. Remove the pan from the heat and set aside to cool.

When it has cooled to room temperature, transfer the mushroom mixture to a food processor and add the parsley, olives, lemon juice, and remaining oil. Pulse until the mixture is of a spreadable though just slightly chunky consistency. Transfer to a shallow serving dish and garnish with lemon slices. Serve with toasted baguette slices and/or crackers.

CHICKEN LIVER MOUSSE WITH SAGE

Ramona and James are partial to strong, unapologetic tastes, which means we love virtually every sort of liver. In this and the following recipe, humble chicken livers are used to create explosively flavored mousses. No, these dishes haven't the subtlety or exquisiteness of a foie gras pâté, but they're damned good (not to mention that a pound of chicken livers is about one-fiftieth of the price of a pound of foie gras). The purpose of the bacon fat, which is poured over the completed mousse, is to protect it from oxidation.

1 pound chicken livers

FOR POACHING THE LIVERS:

2 cups chicken broth
½ large onion
2 large cloves garlic, crushed and coarsely chopped
1 bay leaf
½ teaspoon dried rosemary or 1 sprig fresh rosemary
½ teaspoon salt
⅛ teaspoon dried thyme or 1 sprig fresh thyme
⅛ teaspoon ground allspice
⅛ teaspoon freshly ground black pepper

FOR COATING THE MOUSSE:

4 slices bacon

FOR SEASONING THE MOUSSE:

¾ teaspoon coarsely ground black pepper
¼ teaspoon ground sage

¼ teaspoon salt
additional coarsely ground black pepper

Separate the lobes of the livers and remove any fat, membranes, and blood vessels. Place the broth, onion, garlic, bay leaf, rosemary, salt, thyme, allspice, and pepper in a large saucepan and bring to a boil. Add the livers and poach until slightly firm but still pink inside, about 5 minutes. Remove the pan from the heat and let cool to room temperature, about 1 hour.

Fry the bacon until crisp. Reserve the bacon for another use. Strain the bacon fat and let it cool slightly.

When the livers are cool, pour the mixture into a sieve set over a bowl; discard the poaching liquid and bay leaf. Put the livers and other solids in a food processor and pulse until smooth. Transfer to a bowl and add the ¾ teaspoon pepper, the sage, and the ¼ teaspoon salt. Mix thoroughly, scrape into a large ramekin, and smooth the top. Sprinkle with the additional coarsely ground pepper. Carefully pour the bacon fat on top and spread to thinly cover the entire surface of the mousse. Refrigerate the mousse until firm, 2 to 3 hours. (The flavor will improve if the mousse is given 12 to 24 hours to mature.)

CHICKEN LIVER MOUSSE
WITH CURRANTS AND MADEIRA

This delicious mousse, which may be decorated with a floral design (see the drawing on page 315), is protected from the air by a coating of aspic. To make the aspic, you must first clarify the reserved poaching liquid to rid it of all suspended solids. We use a traditional egg white fining method for clarifying the liquid.

1 pound chicken livers

FOR POACHING THE LIVERS:
2 cups chicken broth
½ large onion
2 large cloves garlic, crushed and coarsely chopped
1 bay leaf
½ teaspoon dried rosemary or 1 sprig fresh rosemary
½ teaspoon salt
⅛ teaspoon dried thyme or 1 sprig fresh thyme
⅛ teaspoon ground allspice
⅛ teaspoon freshly ground black pepper

FOR FLAVORING THE MOUSSE:
2 tablespoons dried currants
2 tablespoons Madeira
¼ teaspoon salt
¼ freshly ground black pepper

FOR THE ASPIC:
1 egg white
1 envelope (1 tablespoon) unflavored gelatin

fresh chives, herb leaves, and red bell pepper (optional)

Separate the lobes of the livers and remove any fat, membranes, and blood vessels. Place the broth, onion, garlic, bay leaf, rosemary, salt, thyme, allspice, and pepper in a large saucepan and bring to a boil. Add the livers and cook until slightly firm but still pink inside, about 5 minutes. Remove the pan from the heat and let cool to room temperature, about 1 hour.

Place the currants and Madeira in a small saucepan and bring the mixture to a boil. Immediately remove from the heat and let cool to room temperature.

When the livers are cool, pour the mixture into a sieve set over a bowl; reserve the poaching liquid and discard the bay leaf. Put the livers and other solids in a food processor and pulse until smooth. Transfer to a bowl and add the plumped currants and their soaking liquid and stir to combine. Scrape into a large ramekin and smooth the top. If you wish, decorate the mousse with a floral design made from chive stems, herb leaves, and flower shapes cut from red bell peppers. (Gently press the decorations into the surface of the mousse so that they are not dislodged when the aspic is poured into the ramekin.) Cover and refrigerate while making the aspic.

Make the aspic: Pour the strained poaching liquid into a saucepan. In a small bowl, beat the egg white until foamy. Add the beaten white to the poaching liquid and bring the mixture to a simmer over medium heat. Do *not* stir. Watch carefully until all the egg white has cooked.

(Much of it will rise to the top of the liquid, though some will stick to the bottom of the pan.) Line a fine-mesh sieve with several layers of cheesecloth, set the sieve above a bowl, and carefully pour the liquid through it. Discard the solids left in the pot. Squeeze the cheesecloth gently to extract as much liquid as possible, then discard.

Sprinkle the gelatin into the clarified liquid and allow it to soften, then stir until it dis-

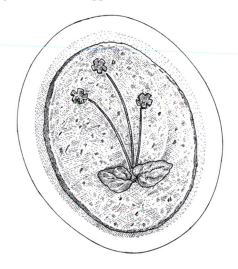

solves. Let cool until the aspic coats a spoon, then carefully pour it over the top of the mousse. Chill until firm, 2 to 3 hours. (The flavor will improve if the mousse is given 12 to 24 hours to mature.)

FINGER FOODS: DEVILED EGGS

We begin our disquisition on finger foods with deviled eggs, but there are prior questions that must be settled first: How many different finger foods should you prepare—and in what quantities? As we've already said, the answers obviously depend on the number of guests and the party's length. But let us make the following suggestion: If your party will also include a main buffet, serve *at least three* different kinds of passed finger foods, and prepare one and a half to two pieces of *each kind* of finger food per guest.

Take the suggestion above as a minimum; if you want the finger foods to keep flowing throughout the party, you'll have to make more. And if your party does *not* include a main buffet—and the party goes on for more than two hours or so—you'll have to prepare *many* more trays of food to pass. (In this case, the greater quantity of finger foods will compensate for the lack of "dinner.") Note that increasing the variety of finger foods and their quantity logarithmically enlarges your workload (assembling canapés and other hors d'oeuvres takes a phenomenal amount of time) and can add greatly to your party's cost (which includes the increased wages of extra kitchen helpers and servers), so try to map all this out carefully. And if you do decide to serve a great quantity of finger foods, limit their variety to no more than six to eight different kinds. Make sure, too, that the majority of finger foods you serve can be substantially prepped before the party begins.

Now, on to the deviled eggs.

We're sure there are a few people—including those with egg allergies—who are averse to deviled eggs, but these folk represent an *extremely* small fraction of the human race. To accommodate everyone else, we offer three different and distinctive deviled eggs recipes. We also solve the one problem that arises when you try to pass deviled eggs on trays: Cut lengthwise, hard-boiled eggs slide around. If, however, you cut very thin slices from both tips of each egg and then slice the egg in half crosswise, you create two cups that stand up by themselves—and that won't slip off your serving tray. Another pointer: To ensure that the filling is as free of lumps as possible—a real advantage if you're piping the filling into the egg-white cups—crumble the yolks by gently but firmly mashing them with a wire whisk until they have the consistency of a coarse, even meal. (Then add the other filling ingredients and mix.) Each of these recipes makes twenty-four pieces; multiply as needed.

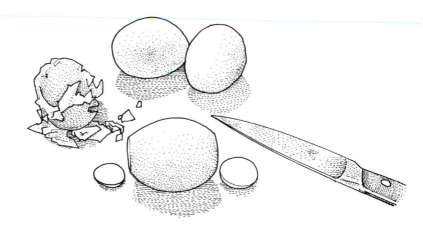

Mexican Deviled Eggs

1 dozen medium eggs
¾ cup (about 3 ounces) grated Monterey Jack cheese
3 tablespoons hot chili sauce
3 tablespoons mayonnaise
2 tablespoons minced onion
2 tablespoons sour cream, plus additional if needed
2 jalapeño chiles, sliced thin, for garnish

Cook the eggs according to our all-but-foolproof method (see page 26). Cool and peel the eggs. Cut a very thin slice from each end of each egg, then cut the eggs in half crosswise. Pop out the yolks into a medium-size mixing bowl and crumble the yolks by mashing them with a wire whisk.

Add all the other ingredients except the jalapeños and mix thoroughly. If the filling is too dry, add more sour cream. Fill the egg-white cups using a spoon or a pastry bag fitted with a wide nozzle. Slice the jalapeños crosswise into very thin circles. Remove any seeds, and garnish each egg with a jalapeño slice.

Mediterranean Deviled Eggs

This deviled egg recipe is unusual in more than one way: It contains no mayonnaise, and the filling is a deep red-orange color.

1 dozen medium eggs
⅔ cup extra-virgin olive oil
½ cup sundried tomato paste
½ cup regular tomato paste
1 medium-size red onion, minced
salt and freshly ground black pepper to taste

ground cumin
24 flat-leaf parsley leaves

Cook the eggs according to our all-but-foolproof method (see page 26). Cool and peel the eggs. Cut a very thin slice from each end of each egg, then cut the eggs in half crosswise. Pop out the yolks into a medium-size mixing bowl and crumble the yolks by mashing them with a wire whisk.

Add the oil, tomato pastes, onion, salt, and pepper to the yolks and stir until the mixture is evenly colored and reasonably smooth. Fill the egg-white cups using a spoon or a pastry bag fitted with a wide nozzle. Sprinkle a little cumin on each, and garnish each with a parsley leaf pressed lightly into the filling.

PICNIC DEVILED EGGS

1 dozen medium eggs
4 tablespoons mayonnaise
1 tablespoon lemon juice
1½ teaspoons chicken broth, plus additional if needed
6 slices bacon, crisply fried and crumbled into small bits
sweet paprika, flat-leaf parsley sprigs, and pimientos

Cook the eggs according to our all-but-foolproof method (see page 26). Cool and peel the eggs. Cut a very thin slice from each end of each egg, then cut the eggs in half crosswise. Pop out the yolks into a medium-size mixing bowl and crumble the yolks by mashing them with a wire whisk.

Add the mayonnaise, lemon juice, and broth to the yolks and mix thoroughly. If the filling is too dry, add more broth. Add the crumbled bacon and mix again. Fill the egg-white cups using a spoon or a pastry bag fitted with a wide nozzle. Sprinkle the eggs lightly with paprika, and garnish with small parsley sprigs and thin strips of pimiento.

FINGER FOODS: BRUSCHETTE

Bruschette (that's the plural of *bruschetta*) are Italian antipasti in which sliced bread is topped with olive oil and/or other ingredients (cheeses, pestos, vegetables) and baked in a hot oven. Bruschette are appropriate for passing on trays, though getting them from the hand to the mouth can be a slightly precarious proposition, so make sure that your servers take a stack of napkins with every tray of bruschette they distribute. Here are two recipes.

UGLY BREAD

Ramona insists that party food "doesn't have to be pretty, as long as it looks sophisticated." This bruschetta—a smash hit at one *Drinkology EATS* bash—certainly qualifies: Its hideousness is highfalutin. (Even if you hate its looks, you'll find the taste redeeming.) Note that this dish *requires* the Italian bread called ciabatta, whose tough crust and spongy interior will prevent the walnut pesto from seeping out during baking.

3 cups shelled walnuts
1½ cups extra-virgin olive oil
⅓ cup clover honey or another mild-flavored honey
3 tablespoons fresh thyme leaves
2 large loaves ciabatta, cut in half horizontally
1½ cups (about 6 ounces) gorgonzola picante, crumbled

Preheat the oven to 450° F. Spread the walnuts evenly on a large baking sheet and toast for 6 minutes. (Be careful not to burn the nuts.)

Allow the toasted nuts to cool, then transfer them to a food processor and add the oil, honey, and thyme. Pulse until smooth.

Spread this walnut pesto on the halved ciabatta loaves. Dot with pieces of crumbled gorgonzola. Arrange the bread on baking sheets, and bake in the 450° oven for about 8 minutes, or until the cheese is bubbling and the edges of the bread have begun to brown. Using a long spatula, carefully transfer the baked ciabatta halves to a cutting board. With a serrated knife or pizza wheel, cut each half-loaf in two, lengthwise. Then cut each quarter-loaf crosswise into 1-inch slices. (Each quarter-loaf should yield about 12 pieces.) Transfer to serving trays. Serve hot.

Note: You may prepare the pesto a day ahead of time, refrigerating it until 1 to 2 hours before use. If the oil separates from the walnut paste during this time, stir the pesto thoroughly before spreading it on the ciabatta.

BRUSCHETTA WITH TWO CHEESES

This delicious bruschetta's topping combines two famous Italian cheeses: the fresh cheese called ricotta (use whole-milk ricotta only) and the semi-soft cheese called fontina.

2 baguettes (each about 2 feet long)
¼ cup plus 2 teaspoons extra-virgin olive oil
1½ cups (about 12 ounces) whole-milk ricotta
1½ cups (about 8 ounces) grated fontina
2 medium eggs, lightly beaten
4 medium-size tomatoes, diced
2 scallions, chopped (white part only)
2 cloves garlic, minced
1 teaspoon dried oregano

½ teaspoon salt
⅛ teaspoon freshly ground black pepper

Preheat the oven to 400° F. Cut the baguettes on a slight diagonal into ¾-inch slices, discarding the ends. (Each baguette should yield 20-plus pieces.) Arrange the slices on baking sheets and toast for 2 minutes, until slightly dry. Remove from the oven, and, using the ¼ cup oil, brush the top of each slice with oil.

In a medium-size mixing bowl, combine the ricotta, fontina, and eggs and mix well. In a separate bowl, combine the 2 teaspoons oil with the tomatoes, scallions, garlic, oregano, salt, and pepper and mix. Spread a generous tablespoon of the cheese mixture on each baguette slice, and top each with a sprinkling of the tomato mixture. Return the bruschette to the oven and bake for 12 to 14 minutes, until the cheese is bubbly and golden. Remove from the oven and transfer to serving trays. Serve hot.

FINGER FOODS:
VEGETABLE AND FRUIT HORS D'OEUVRES

Non-meat hors d'oeuvres aren't just for the vegetarians. All your guests will appreciate the variety that vegetable- and fruit-based hors d'oeuvres bring to the passed foods. Besides the three offered here, you might also consider the apple-Camembert wedges presented in chapter 3 (see page 89) and the jicama canapés in chapter 9 (see page 231).

Serving note: When serving hors d'oeuvres that are held together with toothpicks, cocktail picks, or skewers, include a decoratively carved half-lemon (cut crosswise and trimmed on the end to make it stand up) on each tray, so that guests can stick their used picks into it.

CARROT ROLLS

The combination of fresh herbs snazzes up these brightly colored hors d'oeuvres. They're small, and each guest will probably grab several, so make lots.

3 medium-size carrots, very fresh and firm
1 small log (about 4 ounces) fresh chèvre
3 ounces cream cheese, softened
1 cup finely chopped fresh chives
1 cup finely chopped fresh flat-leaf parsley leaves
1 cup finely chopped fresh tarragon leaves
1 tablespoon fresh thyme leaves

Using a vegetable peeler, cut the carrots lengthwise into very thin, full-width strips. (You should get 25 or more per carrot.) In a small bowl, combine the cheeses. In another bowl, thoroughly mix the chopped herbs. Scooping up about ½ teaspoon at a time, form the cheese into balls, then roll the balls in the herbs to coat them completely. Starting at one end of a carrot strip, roll each herbed cheese ball tightly in the strip and secure with a toothpick. Repeat with the rest of the cheese, herbs, and carrot strips. Carefully cover and refrigerate until ready to serve.

FETA COMPLI

Having invented this hors d'oeuvre, Ramona wondered what to call it. James, who can always be counted on to produce a pun in a pinch, instantly came up with the groan-inducing name. (The hors d'oeuvres themselves, however, will induce ecstatic sighs from artichoke-loving guests.) Depending on the size of the artichoke, this recipe will produce between three and four dozen pieces. For tips on buying and preparing artichokes, see the Technicalities sidebar below.

6 ounces feta, crumbled

juice of 2 lemons

1 tablespoon fresh thyme leaves

1 globe artichoke, tips and top trimmed, steamed and cooled

9 to 12 grape tomatoes, quartered

TECHNICALITIES

THE ART OF ARTICHOKES

There are very few foods on which Ramona and James part ways, but artichokes definitely crown this small list. James can take 'em or (mostly) leave 'em; for Ramona, eating artichokes is only slightly less important than breathing. Choosing and preparing artichokes are somewhat complicated tasks. Here are Ramona's suggestions:

The first thing to know about artichokes is that they are *flower buds*—the immature blossoms of a plant that belongs to the thistle family (and whose magenta-colored full-blown flowers look very much like those of other thistles). As you would if you were shopping for roses, look for (artichoke) buds that are tightly furled. Buds whose leaves—that is, petals—have separated and opened are no longer fresh. The leaves should be bright green, free of brown or purple spots (these indicate bruising in transit), smooth and unwrinkled, and somewhat pliable. (Dry, crisp, straw-like leaves are another giveaway sign that an artichoke is past its prime.) Fresh artichokes feel weighty when held in the hand; if the artichoke seems too light for its size, it was probably picked some time ago and has lost water, and freshness, in the interim. Old or bruised artichokes won't cook properly and may have a bitter taste, so select carefully.

Combine the crumbled feta, lemon juice, and thyme leaves in a small mixing bowl. Let stand for 10 minutes. Pull off the leaves of the artichoke and arrange them on a plate or tray. Remove and discard the choke and the bitter part of the stem. Finely dice the heart and add it to the feta mixture, mixing well. Spoon about ½ teaspoon of the feta mixture onto the base of each artichoke leaf. Garnish each with a tomato quarter.

Most artichokes sold in the United States are of the *globe* variety. The preparation instructions that follow are for full-size (not baby) globe artichokes. Before beginning, place a steamer basket inside a pot, fill the pot with water to the level of the basket's bottom, and bring the water to a boil.

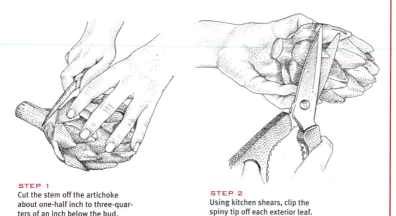

STEP 1
Cut the stem off the artichoke about one-half inch to three-quarters of an inch below the bud.

STEP 2
Using kitchen shears, clip the spiny tip off each exterior leaf.

THE ART OF ARTICHOKES

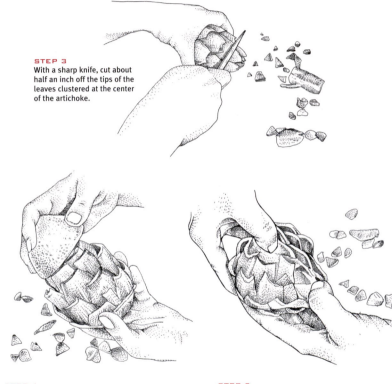

STEP 3
With a sharp knife, cut about
half an inch off the tips of the
leaves clustered at the center
of the artichoke.

STEP 4
Rub a lemon half against all the cut surfaces—
top, leaves, and stem—making sure that every
place you've made a cut is thoroughly moistened
with lemon juice. This essential step will prevent
the artichoke from oxidizing and discoloring.

STEP 5
Work your fingers down into the artichoke and,
gently but firmly, pry apart the leaves so that
the steam will penetrate deeply into the artichoke. If you encounter any spines, also clip
the leaf-tips with shears and rub with lemon.

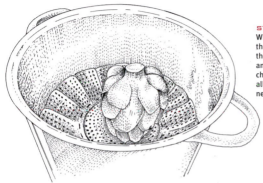

STEP 6
When the water is boiling, place the artichoke upside down inside the steamer basket. Cover the pot and steam for 30 to 40 minutes, checking the water level occasionally and replenishing the water if necessary.

There are two methods for testing for doneness; Ramona uses both. Method number 1: Pull out a leaf from midway down the artichoke; it should come away easily, but pulling it out should not cause the whole artichoke to fall apart. (If it does, the artichoke is overcooked.) Bite down gently on the lower, meaty end of the leaf and scrape the meat off with your teeth; the meat should be soft, but the fibrous outer layer of the leaf should remain intact. Method number 2: Insert the tines of a fork at the base of the artichoke, where the stem begins. (The artichoke's "heart"—from which the leaves radiate outward—lies just inside the skin at this point.) The fork should pierce the artichoke easily, as it would a carrot or potato cooked to doneness. If you feel resistance, the artichoke is not yet done.

If you're using the artichoke for our Feta Compli appetizer (see page 323), let it cool after cooking, then pull off the leaves one by one. Discard any very small, delicate leaves near the center. At the center, you'll encounter the so-called choke—the mass of feathery tissue (the immature thistle florets) that emerges from the artichoke's heart. Cut or scrape away the choke—and also cut off the stem at the base of the heart.

STUFFED DATES

So many finger foods are savory-tasting that it's a fine idea to offset them with at least the occasional sweet hors d'oeuvre. This one fills the bill, though the sweetness of the dates and honey is balanced by the goat cheese stuffing. Use the large, soft Moroccan dates called Medjools; their pits are small and easily removable. And do try to find spreadable goat cheese, which is tangier than ordinary, cow's-milk cream cheese. (A French brand of spreadable goat cheese, called Chevrion, is sold by many specialty shops; if it's unavailable, substitute cream cheese or plain chèvre.)

40 Medjool dates (about 2 pounds)
½ cup (one 5½-ounce package) spreadable goat cheese
thyme honey or other mild-flavored honey

Gently slit each date lengthwise and remove the pit. Stuff each date with a generous ½ teaspoon goat cheese. Arrange the dates on serving trays and lightly drizzle with honey. Serve with napkins.

FINGER FOODS: TORTILLA CANAPÉS

When cut into little flower or star shapes and toasted, wheat tortillas make excellent platforms for canapés topped with guacamole or an ultra-smooth egg salad. Diminutive and light, these canapés have definite "girl appeal"; when we served them at one *Drinkology EATS* cocktail bash, female guests were almost uniformly enthusiastic, while some men found them difficult to handle (the ham-handed klutzes!). Advisory: Make about 10 percent more tortilla cutouts than you'll actually need, since some will split into layers or break while baking. Following this recipe, you should end up with eighty or so intact pieces. (That's enough for each of twenty guests to have four each; multiply the recipe for larger crowds.) Recipes for guac and egg-salad toppings follow.

Special equipment: fluted vegetable/tea cookie cutters (1¼ to 1½ inches in diameter)

10 small wheat tortillas, about 6 inches in diameter

Preheat the oven to 375° F. Using flower-shaped, scalloped-edged, and/or star-shaped cutters, cut the tortillas into small, decorative shapes. (Depending on the size of the cutter, each tortilla should yield about 9 pieces.) Arrange the pieces in a single layer on a baking sheet and toast until crisp but not browned, 6 to 7 minutes. Let cool before adding toppings and garnishes.

Note that the tortillas can be cut and toasted several days in advance; stored in resealable plastic bags, they'll stay fresh and crisp. Storing them will cause more breakage, however, so if you make them in advance, make 20 percent more than you'll need.

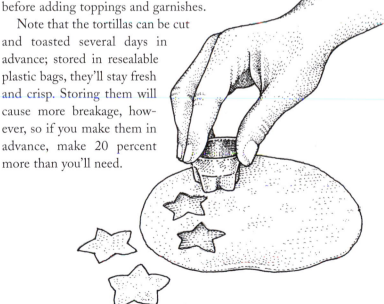

GUACAMOLE TOPPING

This guacamole is *much* smoother than the version presented in chapter 9 (see page 230). The object is to create a smooth paste that can be piped onto the tortilla cutouts.

2 ripe Hass avocados
8 ounces cream cheese, softened
1 cup fresh cilantro leaves, finely minced
1 tablespoon fresh lemon juice
1 tablespoon very finely minced jalapeño chili
½ teaspoon very finely grated onion
¼ teaspoon garlic powder
salt to taste
fresh cilantro leaves or pimientos, for garnish

In a medium-size mixing bowl, combine all the ingredients, and use a fork or potato masher to mash and mix everything together until a smooth paste is formed. Transfer to a pastry bag fitted with a wide nozzle and pipe onto the tortilla cutouts. Garnish each with a cilantro leaf or small piece of pimiento.

Note that this topping *cannot* be prepared more than a few hours before serving, because the guacamole will discolor. Ideally, you'll prepare it just before the canapés are assembled and sent out into the crowd; if you must prepare it a few hours earlier, cover by placing a sheet of plastic wrap directly on the surface of the guacamole and refrigerate.

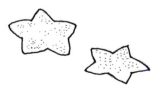

Egg-Mayonnaise Topping

Once again, the goal is to produce an extremely smooth topping capable of being piped.

6 large eggs
½ cup mayonnaise, plus additional if needed
2 tablespoons Dijon mustard
¼ teaspoon celery seed
¼ teaspoon salt
⅛ teaspoon garlic powder
pinch of freshly ground white pepper
a few drops of juice scraped from an onion
capers, salmon roe, or fresh flat-leaf parsley leaves, for garnish

Cook the eggs according to our all-but-foolproof method (see page 26). Cool and peel the eggs. Coarsely chop the eggs, place them in a food processor, and pulse until finely chopped. Transfer to a medium-size mixing bowl, add the other ingredients (except the garnishes), and mix until smooth. If the mixture is too dry, add more mayonnaise. Transfer to a pastry bag fitted with a wide nozzle and pipe onto the tortilla cutouts. Garnish each with a caper, a salmon egg, or a parsley leaf.

Finger Foods:
Polenta and Hominy Cups

Tiny cups made from hardened polenta (corn meal mush) or hominy grits make great vehicles for a variety of fillings. Each of the following recipes makes about twenty cups; we suggest making one batch of each (and filling each with a different filling) for a crowd of twenty. Multiply as needed for larger parties.

POLENTA CUPS

Special equipment: 2 mini muffin tins

corn oil
1 cup water
½ cup finely ground yellow cornmeal
⅓ cup grated Parmigiano-Reggiano or Gruyère
¼ teaspoon salt
⅛ teaspoon freshly ground black pepper

Lightly grease the mini-muffin tins with the corn oil. In a small saucepan, bring the water to a boil over high heat. Reduce the heat to medium and sprinkle the cornmeal into the water, stirring constantly, until it is completely incorporated. Continue to cook until the meal thickens slightly, about 3 minutes. Add the cheese, salt, and pepper and mix. Remove from the heat and immediately fill the muffin-tin cups about half-full with polenta. Let stand until the polenta is cool enough to touch and will hold a shape. Using your fingers or a small spoon, push the polenta up onto the sides of the muffin-tin cups to form cuplike shapes. Let stand until cool, about 1 hour. Unmold the polenta cups and let them dry on a plate or rack for another 60 to 90 minutes before filling. Fill just before serving.

HOMINY GRITS CUPS

This recipe is much the same as the one just given, though the preparation method differs slightly. Hominy grits cups are white; mixing them with the yellow polenta cups when arranging on serving trays (and filling them with a different filling) makes for an attractively variegated presentation. Be sure to use standard, "old-fashioned" grits—not instant or "quick" grits.

corn oil

1 cup water

½ cup hominy grits

⅓ cup grated Parmigiano-Reggiano or Gruyère

¼ teaspoon salt

⅛ teaspoon freshly ground black pepper

Lightly grease the mini-muffin tins with the corn oil. In a small saucepan, combine the water and grits and bring to a boil over high heat. Reduce the heat to medium-low and simmer, stirring occasionally, until the grits thicken, 10 to 15 minutes. Add the cheese, salt, and pepper. Remove from the heat and immediately fill the muffin-tin cups about half-full with grits. Let stand until the grits are cool enough to touch and will hold a shape. Using your fingers or a small spoon, push the grits up onto the sides of the muffin-tin cups to form cuplike shapes. Let stand until cool, about 1 hour. Unmold the grits cups and let them dry on a plate or rack for another 60 to 90 minutes before filling. Fill just before serving.

SHRIMP AND CRÈME FRAÎCHE FILLING

Crème fraîche is thicker and tangier than ordinary sour cream. Most gourmet food shops (and many supermarkets) sell it. If you can't find it, make your own by combining ½ cup heavy cream with 1 tablespoon buttermilk in a glass or ceramic bowl and letting the mixture stand at room temperature, covered, for at least 8 hours, until it becomes very thick. Once it thickens, put it in the fridge, where it will keep for at least a week.

½ pound frozen pre-cooked medium shrimp, thawed and chopped

½ cup crème fraîche

¼ cup finely chopped chives
¼ teaspoon freshly ground black pepper
pinch of ground cayenne pepper
salt to taste

Combine all the ingredients in a small mixing bowl and mix well. Spoon into the polenta or hominy grits cups.

Tomato and Herb Filling

20 grape tomatoes, quartered
1 scallion, very thinly sliced
3 tablespoons fresh basil leaves, very thinly sliced
2 teaspoons extra-virgin olive oil
½ teaspoon balsamic vinegar
pinch of salt
pinch of freshly ground black pepper

Combine all the ingredients in a small mixing bowl and gently mix. Let stand for up to 3 hours, then spoon into the polenta or hominy grits cups.

Mushroom Filling

Use a mixture of white, cremini, enoki, and/or other mild-flavored fresh mushrooms for this filling.

1 tablespoon extra-virgin olive oil
12 ounces mixed fresh mushrooms
1 tablespoon crushed dried morel mushrooms
1 scallion, thinly sliced
1 small clove garlic, crushed and minced
¼ teaspoon salt

⅛ teaspoon freshly ground pepper
¼ cup light cream
½ teaspoon cornstarch
1 teaspoon dry sherry
½ cup sour cream
capers

Heat the oil in a medium-size saucepan, add the fresh mushrooms, dried morels, scallions, and garlic and sauté over medium heat, stirring occasionally, until the mushrooms have shrunken and released their liquid, 2 to 4 minutes. Add the salt and pepper and stir. Combine the cream and cornstarch in a measuring cup and stir until smooth, then add to the mushrooms and stir until thickened. Add the sherry and stir. Cover and keep warm until ready to fill the polenta cups. After filling the cups, top each with a small dollop of sour cream and a caper.

FINGER FOODS:
MEAT AND SEAFOOD HORS D'OEUVRES

James and Ramona talk a good game, but you're about to see just how proletarian we can be. Granted, some of the recipes that follow are pretty darned fancy, . . . but *pigs in blankets*? We do declare.

When selecting meat and seafood hors d'oeuvres for your cocktail party's menu, you might also consider some recipes found in earlier chapters, including buffalo "chips" (see page 49), the two cocktail meatballs recipes in chapter 2 (pages 56 and 60), angels on horseback (page 191), crab puffs (page 207), chicken cubes with mole (page 232), and chorizos with salsa verde (page 234).

Devils on Horseback

This dish is the darker-tempered stable-mate of Angels on Horseback (see page 191). Some people love the li'l devils (one guest at a *Drinkology EATS* bash consumed *seven* all by herself), but others will sniffily forgo this fatty-meaty combo, so a hundred pieces should be more than sufficient for a crowd of twenty to forty people. Be sure to use a premium bacon for this recipe. The devils don't need to be dipped in anything, but, if you can find it, Roasted Yellow Pepper Finishing Sauce made by the Roland Food Company makes a fantastic dipping sauce.

1 pound chicken livers
1 quart chicken broth
½ cup Pedro Ximénez or Amontillado sherry
1 6-inch stalk fresh rosemary
¼ teaspoon fresh ground black pepper
salt to taste (optional)
50 walnut or pecan halves, cut in half lengthwise (100 pieces)
50 large prunes, pitted and halved
25 slices bacon
Roland brand Roasted Yellow Pepper Finishing Sauce (optional)

Separate the lobes of the livers and remove any fat, membranes, and blood vessels. Combine the broth, sherry, rosemary, pepper, and salt (if needed) in a large saucepan and bring to a boil over high heat. (Taste the broth before adding salt; commercial chicken broth can be quite salty enough.) Reduce the heat to medium-high, add the chicken livers and nut pieces, and poach for 5 minutes or until livers are firm. Drain the livers and nuts and let cool.

Preheat the oven to 450° F. Using a sharp paring knife, cut the livers into ¾-inch pieces. Stuff each half-prune with a piece of chicken liver and a piece of nut.

Cut the bacon slices crosswise into quarters. Tightly wrap each prune with a quarter-slice of bacon, and secure with a toothpick. Arrange the assembled devils on jelly-roll pans and roast for 10 minutes or until bacon is crisp. Carefully transfer the devils to serving trays, and, if desired, serve with small bowls of Roland brand Roasted Yellow Pepper Finishing Sauce, for dipping.

Note that the devils may be prepped several hours ahead of time and kept, covered in plastic wrap, in the refrigerator until half an hour before roasting. Make sure to let them to return to room temperature before putting them in the oven.

STEAK ROULADES

"Let's do a sliced steak hors d'oeuvre," proclaimed Ramona (and James, of course, concurred). Ramona consulted various negamaki recipes, but decided we needed something less Asian in flavor, so she marinated the pounded-thin strips of flank steak in red wine. The resulting *roulades* (a hoity-toity term for meat roll-ups) look like negamaki but have a decidedly Continental taste. This recipe makes about 20 roulades.

1 pound flank steak, about 1½ inches thick
1 cup dry red wine
2 cloves garlic, minced
½ teaspoon salt
¼ teaspoon freshly ground black pepper
4 sprigs fresh thyme
3 tablespoons extra-virgin olive oil
2 large portobello mushrooms
1 bunch scallions
½ teaspoon cornstarch

Using a very sharp, narrow-bladed knife, cut the flank steak horizontally into ⅛-inch thick slices. Pound the slices with the flat side of a meat tenderizer until they are very thin, about $1/16$-inch thick. Cut each pounded slice into pieces about 2 inches wide by 6 inches long. Discard any irregular bits.

In a large, shallow bowl (a glass pie plate will do nicely), mix the wine, garlic, salt, and pepper. Submerge the thyme sprigs in the wine mixture, add the steak pieces, and marinate for 30 to 90 minutes.

Meanwhile, bring a small pan of water to boil on the stove. Trim the scallions and cut into even, 3-inch lengths. Plunge them into the boiling water for 30 seconds, then immediately transfer to a bowl of ice water. When cool, drain and set aside.

Clean the mushrooms carefully and cut them into ⅛-inch slices. Heat 2 tablespoons of the oil in a medium-size frying pan, add the mushrooms, and sauté over medium heat until they are soft and have released their liquid, 2 to 4 minutes. Set aside until cool, then drain and reserve the cooking liquid.

Cut 20 lengths of kitchen string, each about 8 inches long. Drain the meat and add the marinade to the mushroom cooking liquid. Pat the meat strips dry with paper towels and lay them out on a work surface. Place a slice of mushroom and one piece of white scallion (or a few pieces of green scallion leaves) crosswise on a short end of each strip of steak. Roll the strips up and tie each with a piece of kitchen string.

Heat the remaining tablespoon of oil in a large frying pan and sauté the roulades over medium-high heat, turning until browned on all sides. Add the reserved marinade and cooking liquids and bring to a boil. Remove the roulades from the pan, place them on a work surface, and cut off and discard the kitchen string. Dissolve the cornstarch in 2 tablespoons of water and stir into the sauce. Cook until thick, about

1 minute. Arrange the roulades on a serving tray, pour the sauce into a dipping bowl, and serve immediately. (Servers should remember to hand out napkins with this hors d'oeuvre.)

PIGS IN BLANKETS

This 1950s standard is, we unashamedly admit, a *Drinkology EATS* favorite. Pigs in blankets (which, if you use all-beef cocktail franks, contain no pig at all) should probably be served *only* with French's mustard. But James found a brand of mustard—Gold's Deli Mustard—that makes a epiphanic dipping sauce for the little non-pork porkers. Important: Do *not* use canned Vienna sausages for your pigs in blankets; they're too squishy, and they have a truly offensive chemical odor/flavor. You can find fresh (if that's the right word) cocktail franks in your grocer's case, right next to the grownup hot dogs. This recipe makes 4 dozen pigs in blankets—just right for a party of twenty guests. People will say, "Pigs in blankets? You've gotta be kidding," and then they'll proceed to scarf them right up.

3 tubes crescent rolls (8 rolls each)
1 (14-ounce) package cocktail franks (contains 48 to 52 pieces)
yellow mustard or Gold's Deli Mustard

Preheat the oven to 350° F. Pop open the tubes of crescent rolls and lay the sheets of dough out on a work surface. Cut the dough into triangles along the perforations and then cut each of these triangles into two smaller, approximately equal triangles. (These two triangles' proportions will differ—one will be more equilateral, the other more scalene in shape—but the dough is so pliable that this doesn't matter.)

Place one cocktail frank atop each small triangle, and wrap it in the dough as if you were diapering a baby: Fold one point down over the center of the frank, then fold the other two points over it. Pinch the edges of the dough together so that the frank is completely enclosed. Arrange the "pigs" on baking sheets and bake for 12 to 15 minutes, until puffy and lightly browned. Transfer to serving trays accompanied by little bowls of mustard, for dipping. Serve hot.

SHRIMP PUFFS

We know: You're much too classy to serve pigs in blankets, but you really would like to present your guests with a puff pastry–based hors d'oeuvre. Here's an option. (It's a variation on our crab puffs; see page 207. We're repeating the puff pastry instructions here so that you don't have to keep referring back.) The recipe will yield about 4 dozen puffs.

FOR THE PUFF PASTRY:

1 cup water
½ cup (1 stick) unsalted butter
¼ teaspoon salt
1 cup all-purpose flour
4 eggs

FOR THE FILLING:

2 (4-ounce) cans of tiny or medium shrimp
8 ounces cream cheese, softened
¼ cup extra-virgin olive oil
2 tablespoons lemon juice
1 tablespoon finely grated onion
1 teaspoon ground fennel seeds

Make the pastry puffs: Preheat the oven to 400° F. and line a baking sheet with parchment paper. In a small saucepan, heat the water, butter, and salt over high heat until the mixture boils and the butter melts.

Lower the heat and add flour all at once. Beat vigorously until the mixture pulls away from the sides of the pan and forms a ball. Remove from the heat. Add the eggs one at a time, beating until smooth after each egg is added. Drop the batter by the teaspoonful onto the parchment-lined baking sheet, spacing 2 inches apart. Bake for 35 to 40 minutes, until the puffs are golden brown and dry. Remove from the oven and place the sheet on a wire rack. When the puffs are cool, make a slit in the top or side of each. Remove any soft or spongy dough inside the puff.

Make the filling and assemble the puffs: Drain the shrimp and reserve the packing brine. In a medium bowl, combine the shrimp, 2 tablespoons of the brine, and the other filling ingredients and mix well. Cover and refrigerate for 1 hour. (Letting the filling stand is essential to meld the flavors.) Then fill a pastry bag or a resealable plastic bag with the filling, cut off the tip or corner, and squeeze filling into each puff.

SMOKED TROUT CANAPÉS

When Ramona and James created these canapés for a cocktail party featuring New York State foods, we used applewood-smoked brook trout from the Catskills, but any good smoked trout will do. (Try to find a smoked-fish producer in your vicinity; small, artisanal producers often sell their products at local greenmarkets.)

If you can't find the Mediterranean-style yogurt that this recipe calls for (try Greek and Middle Eastern specialty shops), you can use drained American-style plain yogurt. (Begin with 2 cups of yogurt. Set a colander over a bowl and line the colander with doubled cheesecloth. Place the yogurt on the cheesecloth and let it drain for 2 to 3 hours, until it has the consistency of sour cream.)

Note that this recipe makes rather a lot of canapés: ninety-six pieces. It's difficult to make fewer, however, since you're using only one small trout.

1 cup thick Mediterranean-style yogurt
3 teaspoons freshly grated horseradish
salt and freshly ground black pepper to taste
24 slices of square, thin-sliced pumpernickel bread
1 small smoked brook trout, about 8 ounces
1 bunch fresh dill

In a small bowl, combine the yogurt, horseradish, salt, and pepper. Set aside.

Carefully peel the skin from one side of the trout. Lift off one fillet, carefully separating it from the fins, tail, and head. Remove the dark, oily meat from the skin side of the fillet. Turn the fillet over and bone it extremely carefully, running your finger over the entire fillet to be sure all the bones have been removed. Lift off the fish skeleton, fins, tail, and head from the other fillet and discard. Trim and bone this fillet as you did the first. Flake the fish, which will separate into chevron-shaped pieces, but do not crumble it.

Spread the yogurt mixture thinly but evenly on the bread slices. After spreading the yogurt, trim the crusts from the bread with a sharp knife. Cut the trimmed slices into quarters. On each quarter-slice, arrange a flake or two of fish and a small sprig of dill.

CARVE 'N' CARRY:
THE MAIN BUFFET TABLE

When it comes to the cocktail party's main table, Ramona and James are dyed–in–the–Shetland wool traditionalists. We like baked ham, roasted turkey, and cured salmon—all served with a minimum of pomp and ready for your guests to carve by themselves and carry away on plates. Most of the sides we suggest—relishes, a pasta salad, a bean dish, dinner rolls—are likewise fairly standard. (The one somewhat unusual dish on our buffet-table menu is a vegetable terrine.) There's a good reason for sticking to the tried-and-true: People like this stuff and are comforted by its familiarity. Feel free to experiment wildly with the finger foods, but think of the main buffet as your guests' home-away-from-home.

Not every cocktail party needs a main buffet. If you're hosting a two- or three-hour-long late-afternoon/early-evening gathering for twenty to forty people, your guests will be more than content with plenty of passed finger foods and an abundant appetizer spread. If, however, your party extends well into the evening (or, as our holiday parties tend to do, into the wee hours and beyond), a main buffet is essential. It also saves you work and money: A large, several-hour-long cocktail party at which only passed finger foods are served requires an army of servers, a sizable militia of kitchen staff, and a mess-hall-size kitchen to pull it off. (If you want to give such a party, call a caterer.)

Gauging the amount of food you'll need to prepare for the buffet is a tricky question. On the one hand, most guests won't load their plates sky-high, and some guests won't visit the buffet table at all. Remember that guests will also be partaking from the appetizer spread and passed finger foods, and many won't feel the need for too much more. Militating against this, however, are two factors: (1) At an hours-long party, some guests will keep returning to the buffet to refuel. (2) We are always surprised—nay, shocked—by how much food some people will consume, if given the opportunity. (It's the skinny ones you've really got to watch out for.)

So here are our tentatively rendered suggestions: For a party of twenty to, say, thirty-five people, prepare one main dish (the ham, the turkey, or the gravlax) and one batch of each the side dishes whose recipes appear in the following pages. For thirty-five to seventy people, prepare two main dishes and double the number of dinner rolls, but stick to one batch of each of the sides. For seventy to one hundred people, make all three main dishes, triple the dinner rolls, and double all the sides. This progression, you'll notice, isn't strictly arithmetic. That's because at larger parties, people tend to eat less (on a per-person basis, that is) for a couple of reasons: For one thing, guests at large parties seem to focus more on the socializing and less on the food. For another, guests at large parties tend to come and go—and only a relatively small proportion arrive at the start and stay for the party's entire length.

Some other pointers: Besides the main dishes and sides, your buffet table should include butter (for the dinner rolls) as well as condiments for those guests who will want to make sandwiches for themselves. Bowls of mustard and mayonnaise are requisite, as are salt and pepper shakers or grinders. (In addition, you'll need a bowl of sour cream and a loaf or loaves of thin-sliced dark rye or pumpernickel bread for the gravlax, if you decide to make it.)

One final note: When laying the buffet for a large party, don't set out all the food at once, especially if the buffet will be "in operation" for several hours. You want the buffet table to remain fresh and attractive-looking throughout, so hold part of each side dish in reserve. Charge one of your servers with the task of keeping an eye on the buffet, tidying the table and replenishing the serving dishes as necessary.

Honey-Mustard Glazed Ham with Pineapple

We make no apologies for this extremely traditional recipe. There's a reason that glazed hams are eternally popular: They're great.

1 fully cooked ham, about 12 pounds
whole cloves
1 cup honey
1 cup yellow mustard
1 fresh pineapple or 1 (20-ounce) can pineapple rings
maraschino cherries

Preheat the oven to 325° F. With a sharp knife, remove any skin from the ham, but leave the fat, trimming it if necessary to create a smooth surface. Score the fat in a diamond pattern, making cuts that penetrate into the meat (¼ to ⅜ inch deep) and that are about 1 inch apart. Insert whole cloves at the intersections of the cuts, pushing them in as deep as they will go without breaking. Place the ham in a roasting pan.

Mix the honey and mustard in a small mixing bowl until well blended. (This is a perfect opportunity to use old honey that has crystallized. Heat it over low heat until it melts, then mix with the mustard.) Using a pastry brush—preferably one made of silicone—brush the entire exposed surface of the ham, cut and fat sides, with the glaze.

Bake the ham for 20 minutes per pound (that's about 4 hours for a 12-pound ham), brushing on more glaze at intervals of 45 to 60 minutes. Watch carefully during the last 2 hours of baking to make sure that the ham does not scorch. If it seems to be cooking too fast on the surface, lower the heat to 275° to 300°.

If using a fresh pineapple, core it and cut it into rings following the method explained on page 123; reserve the juice. If using canned pineapple, drain the rings and reserve ¼ cup of the juice.

About 45 to 30 minutes before the end of the cooking time, remove the ham from the oven. Carefully arrange pineapple rings and maraschino cherries over the top and sides of the ham, securing the fruit with toothpicks. Mix the pineapple juice with the remaining glaze and brush over the ham and fruit. Return the ham to the oven to finish cooking. Check the ham often during this final stage, brushing on more glaze every 10 to 15 minutes until all the glaze has been used.

At the end of the cooking time, remove the ham from the oven and let stand for 15 minutes before serving. Carve part of the ham and place these slices as well as the rest of the ham on a platter. Set the platter on the buffet table along with a carving knife, so that guests can carve additional ham for themselves, as needed.

Brined and Roasted Turkey

Brining a turkey before roasting it need not take an excessive amount of time. Here's a turkey recipe that can *mostly* be accomplished (while you're doing everything else!) on the day of your party. Make the brining liquid the day before, however. Note that you'll need a lot of refrigerator space—or a large cooler—for the brining. (Note, too, that you should *not* stuff a brined bird.)

1 turkey, 12 to 20 pounds

FOR THE BRINING:
2 gallons water
2 cups dry, un-oaked white wine

1 large onion, coarsely chopped
4 large cloves garlic, crushed
1½ cups kosher salt
½ cup sugar
2 bay leaves
1 tablespoon black peppercorns

FOR THE ROASTING:
1 lemon, quartered
4 cloves garlic, crushed with the blade of a knife
8 large fresh sage leaves
4 sprigs fresh rosemary
2 sprigs fresh thyme
¼ cup olive oil or melted butter

Make the brine: Begin the brine in the late afternoon or early evening of the day before the party. In a large pot, combine the water, wine, onion, garlic, salt, sugar, bay leaves, and peppercorns. Bring to a boil, stirring until the salt and sugar are dissolved. Remove the pot from the heat and let cool to room temperature, then place the pot in the refrigerator to chill overnight.

Brine and roast the turkey: The next day, rinse the turkey and place it in a pot or other vessel just large enough to hold it. Pour the cold brine over the turkey to cover. Cover and refrigerate for 4 to 6 hours, turning one or more times to ensure even brining. (If you don't have enough refrigerator space, place the vessel in a cooler with ice or icepacks to keep the brining liquid chilled.)

Preheat the oven to 350° F. Remove the turkey from the brine, rinse it, and pat it dry. Put the lemon, garlic, and herbs in the cavity. Brush the skin with the oil or melted butter. Insert a meat thermometer into the thickest part of the breast, being careful not to place it next to a bone. Set the turkey in a V-shaped rack in a roasting pan, and roast for 12 to 15 minutes per pound, until the thermometer in the breast registers 170° to 180°. (Smaller turkeys require 12 minutes per pound; larger turkeys more time.) Check every hour or so, basting with the pan juices. The skin should brown nicely. If it does not, increase the oven temperature to 425° F during the last 20 to 30 minutes of roasting.

Let the turkey stand for 20 to 30 minutes before carving. Carve part of the turkey and place these slices and chunks as well as the rest of the turkey on a platter. Set the platter on the buffet table along with a carving knife, so that guests can carve additional turkey for themselves, as needed. Accompany with a bowl of cranberry relish (recipe follows).

CRANBERRY RELISH WITH MANDARINE NAPOLÉON

Don't think of this deeply spicy cranberry relish as a holiday-time dish only. It's a heavenly accompaniment to turkey at any time of year. (Use frozen cranberries when the fresh berries are out of season.)

1 pound cranberries, fresh or frozen
2 whole allspice berries
1 cinnamon stick, broken into a few pieces
14 whole cloves
a ½-inch cube of peeled fresh ginger
¼ teaspoon freshly grated nutmeg
1 cup sugar
½ navel orange or large juice orange
2 tablespoons Mandarine Napoléon liqueur

Rinse and drain the cranberries. Place the spices in a tea ball or cheesecloth sachet. In a large saucepan, combine the sugar with 1 cup of water, place the tea ball or sachet containing the spices in the pan, and bring to a boil, stirring until the sugar is dissolved. Add the cranberries. Squeeze the juice from the half-orange into the pan, then add the rind (with the pulp). Reduce the heat to medium-low and, stirring occasionally, simmer until most of the berries have burst, about 10 minutes for frozen berries (slightly longer for fresh berries). Add the liqueur and stir well. Remove the spices from the pan, but leave the orange. Pour into a serving dish, burying the orange in the relish, and let cool. When cool, cover with plastic wrap and refrigerate until serving.

GRAVLAX

The fish in this traditional Scandinavian dish is cured with a mixture of salt, sugar, and herbs. Our version adds a decidedly *non*-Scandinavian liquor—tequila—to the curing ingredients. It is essential to obtain the freshest, highest-quality salmon for gravlax. When examining the salmon, make sure that the eye is clear and the smell is clean. Have the fishmonger clean and fillet the fish for you. Note that you must begin curing the gravlax at least two days—and preferably longer—in advance of the party.

1 whole salmon (6 to 7 pounds), filleted
½ cup kosher salt
¼ cup superfine sugar
¼ cup finely chopped cilantro (leaves and small stems only)
¼ cup finely chopped flat-leaf parsley (leaves only)
¼ cup finely chopped fresh chives

¼ cup finely chopped fresh dill (leaves only)

2 tablespoons white tequila

2 tablespoons finely grated lime zest

2 teaspoons coarsely ground black pepper

Remove the dark, oily meat from the skin sides of the fillets and discard. Turn the fillets over and carefully bone them. Rub your finger down the center of each fillet to be sure you have removed all the bones.

Lay out two long pieces of aluminum foil (each about 3 feet long) on a work surface. On top of each of these, lay a piece of plastic wrap of the same size.

In a small bowl, mix the salt and sugar together well. Carefully sprinkle one-quarter of the mixture on the center portion of each piece of plastic wrap, covering an area the size of one of the fillets. Lay one fillet atop the salt and sugar mixture on each sheet of plastic wrap. Sprinkle the rest of the salt and sugar mixture on top of the fillets, coating each fillet as evenly as possible. Seal the plastic wrap and then the aluminum foil to enclose the fillets tightly. Set these packages on a large tray, jelly-roll pan, or baking sheet with sides. Refrigerate for at least 8 hours and up to 2 days.

Carefully unwrap the fillets, transferring them to a work surface and discarding the plastic wrap as well as liquid that may have collected in the tray. If any of the salt mixture has not been absorbed into the fish, quickly rinse it off and pat the fillet dry. If liquid has collected in the foil, rinse and dry it before returning it to the baking sheet. Arrange a new piece of plastic wrap on each piece of aluminum foil.

In a small bowl, mix the chopped herbs. Rub the fillets all over with the tequila. Center the fillets on the sheets of plastic wrap, then sprinkle each with the lime zest, pepper, and herbs. (They should be thickly coated.) Rewrap the fillets tightly. Put both fillets back on the tray, then set another tray on top with at least 5 pounds of weight. Refrigerate for at least 6 and up to 24 hours.

When ready to serve, carefully unwrap the fish and cut each fillet at an angle into paper-thin slices using a long, thin, sharp serrated knife. Arrange the slices on a serving tray, accompanied by thin-sliced pumpernickel or dark rye bread (or rye crackers), a bowl of sour cream, and a bowl of cucumber relish (recipe follows).

CUCUMBER RELISH

1 large sweet onion (such as Vidalia), diced
1 cucumber, peeled, seeded, and diced or thinly shaved with a vegetable peeler
½ teaspoon salt
½ teaspoon sugar
1 teaspoon olive oil
½ teaspoon cider vinegar

Bring a pot of water to boil. Place the diced onions in a sieve and blanch in the boiling water for 1 minute, then immediately plunge into a bowl of ice water. Drain thoroughly on paper towels.

Place the onion and cucumber in a medium-size bowl, sprinkle with the salt and sugar, and toss. Cover and let stand for 2 hours, then drain and transfer the onion-cucumber mixture to serving bowl. Add the oil and vinegar and toss. Serve at room temperature.

VEGETABLE TERRINE

A homemade veggie terrine (a.k.a. vegetable mousse) is a work of art: It'll dazzle your friends' eyes—and their taste buds. Like any great work of art, however, it takes time and effort to make. Its long baking time includes a stint in a bain-marie (water bath); see the Technicalities sidebar on page

117 for instructions. If you've looked at our recipe for devils on horseback (page 336), you know that we admire the finishing sauces made by the Roland Food Company. Roland's Spicy Chipotle sauce—puddled around the terrine on the serving platter—is a fantastic accompaniment.

Special equipment: traditional terra-cotta terrine (glazed on the inside), about
   8½ by 5 by 3 inches)

1 quart vegetable stock
1 pound parsnips, peeled and sliced into ½-inch coins
1 pound carrots, peeled and sliced into ½-inch coins
2 (10-ounce) packages frozen peas
¼ teaspoon fresh ground nutmeg
¼ teaspoon crushed fennel seeds
½ teaspoon dried chervil
freshly ground white pepper
salt (optional)
3 large egg yolks
3 large egg whites
herbs and vegetable "flowers," for garnish (optional)
butter for greasing the terrine
Roland brand Spicy Chipotle Finishing Sauce (optional)

In a large saucepan, bring the vegetable stock to a boil. Add the parsnip coins to the boiling stock and cook until just tender (begin testing with a fork after 5 minutes). Remove the cooked parsnips from the stock with a slotted spoon, draining as much liquid from them as possible before transferring them to a food mill. Pass the parsnips through the mill into a bowl, and set the bowl of parsnip puree aside to cool. (One pound of parsnips should produce 2 scant cups of puree.) Clean the mill thoroughly.

   Repeat the same procedure, using the same stock, for the carrot coins and then for the peas, cleaning the mill after each use. (It will save time if you cook the carrots while pureeing the parsnips and the peas while pureeing the carrots.) Note that the vegetables should be cooked in order by color, from lightest (parsnips) to darkest (peas), and that each puree should be placed in its own bowl.

Add the nutmeg to the parsnip puree, the fennel seed to the carrots, and the chervil to the peas. To each puree, add fresh ground white pepper to taste, and mix. (This recipe probably won't require salt, because of the saltiness of commercial vegetable stock, but you may want to taste the purees and add a pinch of salt to each, if needed.)

Separate the eggs, dropping each yolk into a separate small glass or bowl. (The whites can all be put in the same steel bowl, for whipping.) Once the purees have cooled, add 1 yolk to each, and mix each thoroughly.

Beat the egg whites until stiff peaks form. Add one-third of the beaten whites to each puree. Using a wooden spoon or rubber spatula, gently fold the whites into each puree until the color and consistency are even.

Preheat the oven to 375° F, and set water on to boil for the bain-marie. Lightly butter the inside of the terrine. Cut a piece of parchment paper so that it can be folded to fit snugly inside the terrine, covering the bottom and the two long sides. (It's OK if the short ends of the terrine are left uncovered.) Place the parchment paper in the terrine and lightly butter its surface.

Beginning with the parsnips and then following with the carrots and, finally, the peas, carefully spoon each puree into the terrine, creating layers about 1 inch deep. With the back of the spoon, smooth each layer—creating as even a layer as possible—before adding the next layer. (Again, the order of the vegetables is important: the densest puree—the parsnips—must go on the bottom, and the least dense—the peas—on the top.) Discard any excess puree.

Lightly cover the terrine with aluminum foil, set in a bain-marie, and bake for 30 minutes. Remove the foil and continue to bake in the bain-marie for another 20 minutes. Then carefully remove the bain-marie from the oven and set the terrine directly on the oven rack, continuing to bake for another 30 to 40 minutes, until a knife inserted into the center of the terrine comes out clean. (It's OK if the top of the terrine browns slightly, but don't let it burn.)

Let the terrine cool for at least 30 minutes. Carefully loosen the short ends of the terrine (not lined with parchment paper) with a knife before turning the terrine out onto a platter. Remove the parchment paper and allow the terrine to cool completely, about 1 hour, before gently but tightly covering it in plastic wrap and refrigerating.

Remove the terrine from the refrigerator 1 hour before you lay the table. Decorate with herbs and with floral shapes cut from carrots and red bell peppers, if desired. (See the drawing on the previous page.) If you wish, create a "moat" of Spicy Chipotle Finishing Sauce on the platter, surrounding the terrine.

Note that the terrine can be made a full day in advance of the party. It will yield about thirty thin slices.

Black-Eyed Peas

The key to sensational black-eyed peas (a favorite party side dish, especially during the holidays) is long, slow cooking. (The peas—a kind of bean, really—should be reduced to a fairly thick, lumpy paste by the time this dish is done.) Do *not* add salt to this dish; the large quantity of commercial chicken broth used will make the black-eyed peas plenty salty enough.

6 (15½-ounce) cans black-eyed peas
4 tablespoons extra-virgin olive oil
4 large shallots, minced
1 quart chicken broth, plus more as needed
⅓ cup amontillado sherry
2 tablespoons dried herbs du Provence
2 teaspoons hot chili sauce
2 tablespoons sun-dried tomato paste

Drain the black-eyed peas. Heat the oil a large, heavy-bottomed saucepan or medium-size Dutch oven, add the shallots, and sauté over medium heat until they soften and become translucent, 3 to 4 minutes. Add the black-eyed peas, broth, sherry, herbs, chili sauce, and tomato paste; stir; and bring to a boil over medium-high heat. Immediately reduce the heat to low and simmer uncovered, stirring occasionally, for 3 to 4 hours, until the beans have partly disintegrated to form a thickish, creamy paste. After the first hour, check the pot frequently, adding more stock and stirring when necessary to prevent the beans from burning. When the beans have cooked, turn off the heat and cover the pan; reheat briefly—again adding more broth, if needed—before serving.

Orzo-Asparagus Salad

We know. At this point in culinary history, most pasta salads should *be* history. But the rice-shaped pasta called orzo makes for a pasta salad that's at least half a step off the too-well-trodden path.

1 pound orzo
2 tablespoons extra-virgin olive oil
2 pounds fresh asparagus (about 40 spears)
2 cups heavy cream
2 cups grated Parmigiano-Reggiano
3 cups cooked ham, cut into ½-inch cubes
½ cup diced red bell pepper
½ cup chopped scallions (white and green parts)
½ teaspoon freshly ground black pepper
½ teaspoon salt

Boil the orzo until al dente, 11 to 13 minutes. Drain and transfer to a large mixing bowl. Drizzle with the oil and stir to coat. Set aside.

Trim the tough, woody ends from the asparagus spears. Steam them until bright green and just tender, about 4 minutes. Immediately plunge them into ice-cold water. When cool, drain the asparagus and cut into ¾-inch lengths.

Add the asparagus and the remaining ingredients to the orzo and gently mix until well integrated. Cover and refrigerate until serving.

Ramona's Dinner Rolls

Full disclosure: For a big party, we sometimes (well, often, actually) resort to the dinner rolls that the Pillsbury Doughboy has so painstakingly prepped and deposited in our grocer's dairy and frozen food cases. But we feel *just awful* doing so, since homemade rolls are so much better. This recipe, a standard in Ramona's repertoire, produces rolls that are the quintessence—the veritable Platonic Form—of the dinner roll.

1 cup very warm (not hot) milk

2 tablespoons sugar

2 tablespoons vegetable oil or melted butter, plus more for greasing your hands and the pan

1 egg

1 tablespoon (1 envelope) dry active yeast

about 3 cups bread flour (or unbleached all-purpose flour)

½ teaspoon salt

additional butter or oil for greasing hands and pan

In a large mixing bowl, combine the milk, sugar, oil (or melted butter), and egg, breaking the egg and stirring well. Add the yeast, stir, and let stand for 5 to10 minutes, until bubbles from the yeast cover most of the mixture's surface.

Add enough flour (about 2½ cups) to form a sticky, slightly soft dough. Gather the dough into a ball. Sprinkle more flour into the bowl and knead the dough with greased hands until all the flour is incorporated and you can form a fairly elastic ball that does not stick to your (greased) fingers. (Do not leave any bits of dough stuck to the sides of the bowl, as they will dry out and make hard lumps in the rolls.) Grease the dough ball, cover the bowl with a cloth, and leave in a warm place until doubled in bulk, 30 to 60 minutes.

Grease the inside of a 9" × 13" × 2" baking pan. Punch down the dough and divide it into quarters. Divide each quarter in half, and divide each of these eighths into three pieces. With well-greased hands, roll each into a ball. Place the dough balls in the pan, not touching, in a pattern four rows wide by six rows long. (Make sure the rolls are well greased when they go in the pan.) Set in a warm place until the rolls expand to fill the pan, 45 to 75 minutes.

Preheat the oven to 350° F. Bake the rolls for 20 to 30 minutes, or until the tops are golden brown and the rolls sound hollow when tapped smartly with a fingertip. Let stand for 5 minutes. Break apart and serve hot.

DESSERTS

Setting out the desserts (and coffee) is a signal that the party is drawing to a close—and that it's time for you, the host, to quit working and fully join in the goings-on, just before they end! (Now that's what we call bitter *and* sweet!)

Clear the buffet table and use it as the platform for your dessert selection. (Don't forget to include cream and sugar for the coffee—and do serve decaffeinated as well as regular coffee.) In the following pages, we offer three dessert possibilities, but don't limit yourself to these when choosing which desserts to serve. Among other desserts to consider, elsewhere in this book, are maple-walnut biscotti (see page 45), lemon curd bars (page 103), ginger-oat snaps (page 161), meringues with chocolate (page 164), Aunt Babe's cake (page 179), and flan Napolitano (page 251).

MEXICAN FLOURLESS CHOCOLATE CAKE

Mexican chocolate differs from other chocolates in that it's spiced with cinnamon. (Abuelita and Ibarra are popular brands of Mexican chocolate, which is typically sold in hexagonal cartons, each containing six three-ounce tablets of chocolate.) This flourless cake rises higher than many such confections; the center—once the baked cake has cooled and settled—has a dense, custard-like texture.

9 ounces (3 tablets) sweet Mexican chocolate

¼ cup (½ stick) unsalted butter, plus more for greasing the pan

2 tablespoons brewed espresso

2 tablespoons Kahlúa or other coffee liqueur

2 tablespoons confectioners' sugar

¾ cup blanched, sliced almonds, plus additional for garnish

9 large eggs, separated, at room temperature

⅛ teaspoon salt

⅓ cup granulated sugar

whipped cream

In the top of a double boiler over barely simmering water, melt the chocolate with the butter. Stir until smooth, then stir in the coffee and Kahlúa. Set aside and let cool to room temperature.

Preheat the oven to 350° F. Grease a 10-inch springform cake pan and thoroughly coat the inside with the confectioners' sugar. Sprinkle the bottom of the pan with the almonds, coating it evenly.

In a large mixing bowl, beat the egg whites together with the salt until soft peaks form. Gradually add the granulated sugar, continuing to beat until stiff peaks form. In a separate large bowl, beat the egg yolks until thick and lemon-colored, about 5 minutes. Fold the chocolate mixture gently into the egg yolks, then fold the yolk mixture into the egg whites.

Pour the batter into the prepared pan, tilting the pan to distribute it evenly. Bake for 30 to 40 minutes or until the edges of the cake are puffed and firm, but the crusted center of the cake is just barely set. Transfer the cake to a wire rack and let it cool completely, 45 to 60 minutes, before releasing the springform. Gently slide the cake from the bottom of the springform pan onto a cake platter. Serve with whipped cream sprinkled with more almonds.

Gingerbread with
Cointreau Crème Chantilly

Simple gingerbread makes a wonderful dessert throughout the fall and winter. (And if you're lost in the woods of party preparation, you can make the gingerbread a day ahead, wrapping it tightly once it's cooled.) Topping it with Cointreau-laced crème chantilly transforms gingerbread into a grownup treat that Hansel and Gretel wouldn't recognize.

FOR THE GINGERBREAD:

3 cups all-purpose unbleached flour

2 teaspoons baking soda

1 teaspoon salt

1 teaspoon ground ginger

1 teaspoon ground cinnamon

¼ teaspoon freshly grated nutmeg

¼ teaspoon ground cloves

1 cup (2 sticks) unsalted butter, softened

1 cup sugar

2 large eggs

1 cup molasses

1 cup warm milk

FOR THE CRÈME CHANTILLY:

1 cup heavy cream

1 tablespoon sugar

1 tablespoon Cointreau

2 teaspoons finely grated orange zest

thin slices of orange, cut into small wedges, for garnish (optional)

Make the gingerbread: Preheat the oven to 350° F. Grease and flour a 9" x 13" x 2" baking pan. In a medium-size mixing bowl, whisk together the flour, baking soda, salt, and spices. In a separate large bowl, cream the butter and sugar together until fluffy. Add the eggs one at a time, mixing after each addition. Add the molasses to the egg mixture and stir; then add the milk, stirring again. Add the flour mixture and stir until smooth. Pour the batter into the prepared pan, tilting the pan to distribute it evenly. Bake for 40 to 45 minutes, until a toothpick inserted in the center comes out clean. Let stand for at least 15 minutes, then cut into pieces about 2 inches square. (Makes about 20.)

Make the crème chantilly: In a medium-size mixing bowl, beat the cream together with the sugar until stiff peaks form. Gently fold in the Cointreau and orange zest.

Top each square of gingerbread with a dollop of crème chantilly. If desired, garnish each with a small wedge of sliced orange.

PUMPKIN CUSTARD

Ramona and James crave custards and puddings. This one's sensational for holiday-time parties. Like many custards, it's baked in a bain-marie; see the Technicalities sidebar on page 117 for instructions.

2 cups heavy cream
1 cup sugar
½ cup canned pumpkin
9 large egg yolks
½ teaspoon ground cinnamon
¼ teaspoon freshly grated nutmeg
⅛ teaspoon ground allspice
⅛ teaspoon ground cloves
⅛ teaspoon salt
Granny Smith apples, thinly sliced, for garnish

Preheat the oven to 325° F. Boil water for the bain-marie. In a separate, medium-size saucepan, mix together the cream, sugar, and pumpkin and heat over medium-low heat until the mixture begins to steam. Meanwhile, lightly beat the egg yolks together with the spices and salt in a large mixing bowl. Slowly pour in the hot pumpkin mixture, continuously stirring as you do so. Strain the mixture through a sieve into a souf-

BAR ASSOCIATIONS

YOUR SIGNATURE HERE

Serving a special mixed drink, a party punch, or (in the winter) a mulled wine can enhance a party and put a distinctive stamp—your personal signature—on the event. We close this (long!) chapter—and this book—with just a few recommendations for special cocktails, some relatively simple party punches, one mulled wine (a mulled port, actually), and one final beverage suggestion (on page 369) that we strongly urge you to obey.

For additional ideas, do check out *Drinkology: The Art and Science of the Cocktail*. (The Lemon Drop, on page 255 of that volume, was a stupendous hit at one of Ramona and James's "research" cocktail parties.) *Drinkology* also supplies general advice on preparing, serving, and garnishing punches (pages 351–353).

In the mixed-drink recipes that follow, we provide instructions for making individual drinks as well as for batches that can be prepared ahead of time and chilled until the party begins.

KEY LIME CAIPIRINHA

The Caipirinha (kai-puh-REEN-yuh)—a muddled combination of limes, sugar, and the cane-sugar spirit called cachaça (kuh-CHAH-suh)—has the reputation of being the "national drink" of Brazil. We were reminded of just how good Caipirinhas are when

flé dish. Cover the top tightly with aluminum foil, and set the soufflé dish in a bain-marie. Bake for 40 to 50 minutes, until a knife inserted in the center comes out clean. Let cool completely. Serve in small bowls, garnished with thin slices of Granny Smith apples. (To prevent the apple slices from rusting, briefly dunk them in a solution of two cups water and the juice of one lemon. Pat them dry before adding to the custard.)

the Brazilian bartender at one *Drinkology EATS* bash insisted on being able to offer his country's signature drink to our guests. (We happily obliged.) More recently, we've discovered a new brand of cachaça that makes our taste buds samba. Called Leblon, it's briefly aged in cognac casks after distilling, which impart an aroma that's fruity and slightly vanilla-like. Poured over sugar-muddled key limes, it makes a drink that's pretty, delicious, and oh-so potent.

2 key limes, halved
2 tablespoons superfine sugar
2 ounces Leblon cachaça

Place the key lime halves in a double rocks glass and mash them with a muddler or the back of a teaspoon. Sprinkle the sugar on the mashed-up limes and muddle until the sugar has dissolved. Fill the glass with ice cubes and pour in the cachaça. Stir.

To make a pitcher of Caipirinhas, use 2 dozen key limes, halved. Place the lime halves in a nonreactive bowl and mash them. Add 1½ cups superfine sugar and muddle until the sugar has dissolved. Transfer to a glass or ceramic pitcher, pour in 1 (750ml) bottle of cachaça, and stir. Refrigerate for at least 2 hours, stir again, and pour into ice-filled double rocks glasses. (Makes about 12 drinks.)

POMEGRANATE MARTINI

 Pomegranate Martinis (which, taxonomically, are about as close to the original Martini as a pomegranate is to an olive) have become as popular in the last few years as the Cosmopolitan was in the 1990s. (*Plus Ça Change* Dept.: The drink closely resembles a Cosmo in both color and flavor.) Our recipe, we think, strikes the right balance of tart and sweet. If pomegranates are in season (October and November), consider garnishing the drink with a few fresh pomegranate seeds rather than the lemon twist. (Do rim the glass with the twist, however.)

⚜ lemon twist
2½ ounces lemon-flavored vodka
½ ounce pomegranate juice
¼ ounce fresh lemon juice
½ teaspoon grenadine
½ teaspoon simple syrup

Rim a chilled cocktail glass with the twist. Combine the remaining ingredients in a mixing glass, with ice. Stir, then strain into the cocktail glass. Garnish with the twist.

To make a pitcher of Pomegranate Martinis, pour 1 (750ml) bottle lemon-flavored vodka into a glass pitcher. Add ¾ cup pomegranate juice, ½ cup fresh lemon juice, 2 tablespoons grenadine, 2 tablespoons simple syrup, and half a dozen ice cubes. Stir and refrigerate for 3 to 4 hours before serving. Stir again before pouring into chilled cocktail glasses, each rimmed and garnished with a lemon twist. (Makes about 10 drinks.)

BROOKLYN MANHATTAN

 James, who lives in Brooklyn, is an apologist for his borough, and he never tires of pointing out that the Manhattan (his favorite cocktail) was invented—in 1874—for a party given by Lady Randolph Churchill (Winston's mum), who at the time resided in Brooklyn Heights. (That Lady Churchill's party was held at the Manhattan Club, in Manhattan, is, for James, merely an inconvenient detail.) At one *Drinkology EATS* bash, we served up batches of "Brooklyn Manhattans"—which, in truth, approximate the original Manhattan's recipe. As first concocted, the Manhattan called for *rye* whiskey—not the bourbon or Canadian blended whisky with which the drink is usually made today. So our so-called Brooklyn Manhattan (made with rye) is actually the Ur *Manhattan* Manhattan. Go figure.

2 ounces rye whiskey
¾ ounce sweet vermouth
¼ teaspoon maraschino cherry syrup (from the jar)
2 dashes Angostura bitters
♂ maraschino cherry

Combine all the liquid ingredients in a mixing glass, with ice. Stir, then strain into a chilled cocktail glass. Garnish with the cherry.

To make a pitcher of Brooklyn Manhattans, pour 1 (750ml) bottle rye into a glass pitcher, add 1 cup plus 2 tablespoons sweet vermouth, 3 ounces maraschino cherry syrup, 8 or so dashes Angostura bitters, and half a dozen ice cubes. Stir and refrigerate for 3 to 4 hours before serving. Stir again before pouring into chilled cocktail glasses, each garnished with a maraschino cherry. (Makes about 12 drinks.)

BUDDHA PUNCH

On to the punches. We shall resist commenting that this one is a foretaste of Nirvana. (Or, rather, we shall not.) The combination of Riesling, rum, Cointreau, and Champagne (and other stuff) is certainly refreshing—it's a great summer punch—but we can find no explanation for this punch's having been named for the Enlightened One.

2 cups dry or semi-dry (*halbtrocken*) Riesling, chilled
1 cup light rum, chilled
½ cup Cointreau, chilled
1 cup orange juice
½ cup fresh lemon juice
½ cup simple syrup
4 or 5 dashes orange bitters
1 (750ml) bottle brut Champagne or other good brut sparkling wine,
    chilled
1 orange, thinly sliced

Place a cake of ice in a chilled punchbowl, and pour in the Riesling, rum, Cointreau, juices, and simple syrup. Shake in the bitters and gently stir. Carefully pour in the Champagne and garnish with the orange slices. (Makes about fourteen 4-ounce servings.)

CHAMPAGNE-COGNAC PUNCH

Simple, sweet, fizzy, pretty, and *potent*.

> 1 cup cognac, chilled
> 1 cup Cointreau, chilled
> ½ cup simple syrup
> ½ cup maraschino cherry syrup (from the jar)
> 2 (750ml) bottles brut Champagne or other good brut sparkling wine, chilled
> 1 liter club soda or seltzer, chilled

Place a cake of ice in a large chilled punchbowl, and pour in the cognac, Cointreau, simple syrup, and maraschino cherry syrup. Stir gently. Carefully pour in the Champagne and club soda. (Makes about twenty-six 4-ounce servings.)

SANGRIA BLANCA

 The Spanish punch called sangria is most often made with red wine; using white wine instead produces a light, refreshing drink suitable for summertime parties. (For a party of twenty, make at least two pitchers' worth.)

> 1 lemon, cut into 4 or 5 thick slices
> 1 lime, cut into 4 or 5 thick slices
> 1 orange, cut into 4 or 5 thick slices
> ½ cup Cointreau
> 1 (750ml) bottle of fruity Spanish white wine, such as Verdejo or Albariño
> 1 tray of ice cubes

Place the citrus slices in a large glass or ceramic pitcher and pour in the Cointreau. Carefully muddle the fruit and liqueur, smashing the fruit slightly. Add the wine and ice cubes and stir. Refrigerate for 1 to 2 hours before serving.

A variation: Substitute 2 large, very ripe peaches (pitted, peeled, and cut into wedges) for the citrus fruit. Place them in the pitcher, pour in the Cointreau and wine (do *not* muddle), add the ice cubes, stir, and refrigerate for 1 to 2 hours before serving.

The Original Bishop (Mulled Port)

 This book's companion, *Drinkology*, contains a recipe for a cold red-wine cocktail called the Bishop. It's a fine drink, but the original Bishop (which dates back several centuries) was a hot drink made from the fortified red wine known as Port—further fortified with cognac. (Apparently, the drink was called the Bishop because its deep red color resembles that of a bishop's robes.) Here's a recipe for this heady and powerful wintertime drink.

6 oranges
dark brown sugar
6 dozen or so whole cloves
3 cinnamon sticks
4 (750ml) bottles good ruby Port
2 cups cognac

Preheat the oven to 350° F. Rinse the oranges in water and immediately roll them in brown sugar to coat. Stud each orange with about 1 dozen cloves. Place the oranges on a baking sheet with sides and bake until the juice begins to ooze from the oranges, about 15 minutes. Transfer the oranges to a large, nonreactive pot (do *not* use an aluminum pot) and add the cinnamon sticks, Port, and cognac. Stir gently, and heat the mixture over medium heat until it steams. Do not allow it to boil. Carefully pour the mixture into a large, warmed, heat-proof bowl. Ladle into heatproof mugs. (Makes about twenty 6-ounce servings.)

AFTER THE PARTY'S OVER

After the break of dawn? No matter how late (or early) it is, do not send yourself to bed without the following prophylactic nightcap. It will help ameliorate your hangover (and quiet your barking dogs).

2 tablets ibuprofen
1 large glass of water

Place the ibuprofen tablets in your mouth. Wash them down with the water. (Try to drink the whole glass of water.) Plan on sleeping in the next day, and do not set your alarm.

Bottoms up. Sweet dreams. Goodnight.

CHAPTER ELEVEN

Hangovers and Leftovers

SOME AFTER-THE-PARTY SUGGESTIONS

We think there ought to be a name for the mood that envelopes the host on the day after a bash. "Post-party depression" is clever (well, slightly), but it doesn't really capture the complete complex of emotions and sensations. The mood we're talking about is an emotional-physical cocktail that's composed of more than just the trepidation you feel at the monumental cleanup job that awaits you and your dismay for getting a hangover after all those promises you'd made to yourself not to overindulge. It also incorporates a fair measure of self-satisfaction (assuming, that is, that the party went off well) and of relief that the whole thing's finally over—and that, after days of doing nothing but party prep, you can begin your reentry into normal life.

A TRUTH NOT UNIVERSALLY ACKNOWLEDGED

First, though, you want to do something about that hangover. The hangover is certainly as ancient an aspect of human experience as is intoxication—and it's doubtless true that people have been devising and recommending hangover cures ever since the sun so mercilessly rose on the morning after the first-ever drinking party.

Now, we hate to tell you this, but there doesn't appear to be any such thing as a real, scientifically verifiable hangover remedy—aside, that is, from sleep, fluids (plenty of 'em, to remoisten your alcohol-dehydrated system), and time. Sure, most drinkers have favorite ways of doctoring themselves up after a bender, but that such "cures" seem to work for those who swear by them is probably the result of a personal, idiosyncratic placebo effect. The one kind of intervention that demonstrably *does* relieve some of a hangover's symptoms—we mean the time-honored "hair of the dog that bit you" approach—is nothing more than a delaying tactic. If you have a drink when you're hungover, you'll probably feel somewhat better—until the effects wear off, at which point the repressed will vengefully return.

Having apprised you of the bad news, *Drinkology EATS* can offer some slender comfort. Although the hangover cure per se remains perpetually beyond drinkers' tremulous grasp, there are a few foods that seem—emphasis on the *seem*—genuinely to offer some minor relief, at least to some people. One of these foods is the humble egg, which contains a chemical compound, called cysteine, that may help your liver recover from the assault it suffered when you had a few drinkie-winkies too many. The other is the equally humble banana, which, because it's so laden with the essential electrolyte potassium, will help restore the metabolic balance that, by drinking too much, you quite literally pissed away. (Alcohol is a powerful diuretic.) With the proviso that neither is a full-fledged cure, we present two recipes—for scrambled eggs and a banana frappé—that may help lighten your morning-after burden. (If your hangover is so bad that the mere thought of food makes you want to retch, don't try to eat. Drink as much water—or, if you can keep it down, fruit juice—as you can, and go straight back to bed.)

JAMES'S SCRAMBLED EGGS

The secret to this recipe—which produces scrambled eggs that are fluffier and more deliciously eggy than the ordinary kind—lies entirely in the cooking technique. The method is akin to that used in many French restaurants, but James has been making scrambled eggs this way for so many years that he dares claim it as his own. The recipe makes two servings.

Special equipment: Small nonstick frying pan; nonstick whisk

4 eggs
salt and freshly ground black pepper to taste
2 tablespoons unsalted butter

Place two small heatproof bowls in the oven and preheat it to the "warm" setting. Beat the eggs well, adding salt and pepper as desired. Melt the butter in a small nonstick frying pan over medium heat. Pour the eggs into the pan and begin slowly stirring with a nonstick whisk. After a few seconds, remove the pan from the heat while continuing to stir. After a few more seconds, return the pan to the heat and continue to stir. Repeat this procedure—taking the pan off the heat and putting it back on, stirring all the while—until the eggs form glistening curds. When the eggs have set but are still soft and slightly wet, transfer them to the warmed bowls. Serve with buttered toast or English muffins.

Banana Frappé

You'll find this simple, healthful shake to be restorative even when you *aren't* feeling hangover-shaky. If your blender is not capable of grinding up ice cubes, crush the ice before adding it to the carafe.

1 cup whole or reduced-fat milk
1 ripe, medium-size banana, cut into chunks
½ teaspoon vanilla extract
pinch of freshly grated nutmeg (optional)
2 ice cubes

Place all the ingredients in a blender and blend until smooth, about 1 minute.

Meat and Bones

To conclude this book, we thought we'd offer you what some Southerners call a lagniappe: a little something extra. Our lagniappe consists of three recipes that might help you deal with the party leftovers—assuming you have some leftovers from the baked ham and/or roasted turkey that graced your main buffet table. The recipes—a mousse, a soup, and a glorified à la king–style dish—all fall squarely into the category of "comfort foods." (After all your hard work, you're certainly going to need some comforting.)

Ham Mousse with Sherry

Not only does this recipe give you something to do with at least some of your leftover ham, but the mousse would make a wonderful cocktail party dish in its own right. The flavors meld beautifully, but it is exceedingly rich, and a little goes a very long way.

1 envelope (1 tablespoon) unflavored gelatin
¼ cup cold water
8 ounces cream cheese
1 (10¾-ounce) can condensed cream of mushroom soup
¼ cup amontillado sherry
1¼ cups cooked ham, chopped
1 tablespoon chopped fresh chives
1 cup mayonnaise
⅛ teaspoon sweet paprika
¼ teaspoon freshly ground white pepper
fresh parsley sprigs
lemon slices

Lightly butter a 4-cup ring mold. Soften the gelatin in the cold water. Place the cream cheese, mushroom soup, and sherry in a large saucepan and heat over medium-low heat, stirring frequently until the cream cheese has just melted and the mixture is smooth. Remove from the heat and add the softened gelatin, stirring well. Place the ham in a food processor and pulse until finely chopped. Add the ham, chives, mayonnaise, paprika, and white pepper to the cream cheese mixture and stir until thoroughly incorporated. Pour the mixture into the prepared mold and refrigerate for 2 to 3 hours, until set. Turn out onto a large serving plate and garnish with the parsley sprigs and lemon slices. Serve with leftover baguette slices that have been lightly toasted.

RAMONA'S SPLIT PEA SOUP WITH HAM

There's no better use for a leftover ham bone than to make a split pea soup. Here's Ramona's recipe:

1 pound green split peas
1 ham bone, meat attached
1 large onion, coarsely chopped
1 large carrot, diced
1 stalk celery, diced
2 large cloves garlic, crushed
2 tablespoons tomato paste
2 teaspoons salt (or to taste)
½ teaspoon freshly ground black pepper
½ teaspoon Coleman's dry mustard
¼ teaspoon ground sage

In a colander, rinse the peas, picking out any foreign objects. Place the peas in a large pot with the remaining ingredients, add about 3 quarts water, and bring to a boil. Reduce the heat to low, cover, and simmer until the peas are so soft that they fall apart when gently stirred, 2 to 3 hours. The soup should be slightly thick—but not pasty. Check the pot occasionally to make sure that it is not becoming too thick. If so, add more water and stir. If, on the other hand, the soup remains too watery after several hours of cooking, take the lid off the pot and let the soup simmer uncovered until it gains the right consistency. When the soup is finished, remove the ham bone, pull off the meat, and chop it for garnish. Reserve the bone.

The soup may be refrigerated after cooling and reheated the next day (and the next day, and the day after that—up to nine days old, in fact). Place the bone back in the pot before refrigerating—and leave it in the pot when reheating the soup. (The more often the soup is reheated, the more gelatin from the bone will leach into the soup, improving the flavor.) Each time you reheat the soup, add more water to return it to the proper consistency.

JAMES'S TURKEY À LA KING

James sometimes hankers for classic diner/deli food—Salisbury steak, hash 'n' eggs, Reuben sandwiches. (You get the picture.) One day several years back, he found himself yearning for a mess o' turkey à la king, and this recipe resulted. He strongly feels that the turkey cubes, celery slices, and carrot cubes ought to be cut as uniformly as possible, to approximate the look of something prepared in a school cafeteria. (The recipe, which serves four, works as well with chicken as with turkey.)

1 cup whole milk
½ cup chicken broth
2 tablespoons cornstarch
5 tablespoons unsalted butter
2 stalks celery, cut into ¼-inch slices (about 1 cup)
1 large carrot, cut into ⅜-inch cubes (about 1 cup)
4 ounces cremini mushrooms, sliced
2 tablespoons amontillado sherry
2 cups roasted turkey breast, cubed
¼ cup canned pimientos, cut into ¼-inch squares
½ cup frozen peas (not thawed)
salt and freshly ground black pepper to taste

In a small saucepan, combine the milk, chicken broth, and cornstarch, whisking until cornstarch is dissolved. Add 2 tablespoons of the butter and heat over medium heat, whisking frequently, until this white sauce thickens. Do not boil. When moderately thick, remove the pan from the heat and set aside.

Insert a steamer basket in a large saucepan, fill with water to the level of the basket's bottom, and heat over high heat. When the water boils, place the celery and carrots in the steamer basket, cover, and steam until the carrots are just tender, 6 to 7 minutes. Transfer the celery and carrots to a bowl and set aside.

In a heavy-bottomed saucepan or small Dutch oven, melt the remaining 3 tablespoons of butter. Add the mushrooms and sauté over medium heat, stirring occasionally, until the mushrooms have softened and begun to release their liquid, 2 to 4 minutes. Add the sherry, stir, and cook for 1 minute more. Add the white sauce, celery, carrots, turkey, pimientos, and peas, salt, and pepper and stir. Continue to cook over medium-low to medium heat, stirring occasionally, until the mixture is heated through and the peas are done, 5 to 10 minutes. Serve over rice or egg noodles.

Indexes

INDEX OF EATS

Chantilly, crème, 360–61
cheddar-parmesan ice-box crackers, 40–42
cheese: apple-Camembert wedges, 89; beer and cheese fondue, 169–71; blue, 182; bruschetta with two cheeses, 321–22; cheddar-parmesan ice-box crackers, 40–42; for cocktail parties, 302–3; feta compli, 323–25; herbed cream cheese, 149; nutted-cheese sandwiches, 137–38, 160; quesa fresca with salsa verde, 235; soufflé, 116, 119; spicy parmesan crisps, 42; Stilton dips, 33; stuffed dates, 328; ugly bread, 320–21
cheese straws: garlic, 299–300; herbed, 298–99. See also puff pastry twists
chicken: cocktail kebabs, 51–52; cubes with mole, 232–33; and tarragon salad, 144
chicken liver: devils on horseback, 336–37; mousse with currants and Madeira, 313–16; mousse with sage, 312–13
chicken wings, 61–64
chickpeas. See hummus bi tahini
chiles: stovetop roasting of, 226; toreados, 227
chips: potato, 31–32; sweet potato, 32
chocolate butter cream glaze, 181
chorizos with salsa verde, 234
cinnamon-cocoa cocktail nuts, 297
coated nuts, 18–23, 296–98
cocktail sauces, 69–70
compote, dried-fruit, 95–96
cookies: ginger-oat snaps, 161; lemon curd bars, 103–4; maple biscotti with walnuts and star anise, 45–47; meringues with

chocolate, 164–65; peanut butter bars, 164
corn: salad, 214–15; tortillas, 235–38; winter succotash, 196–97
cornbread, Maryland-style, 197–98
crab: about, 187–88; grades of meat, 207; imperial, 210–11; puffs, 207–8; seasoning with Old Bay, 204; softshell, 211–13; soup, 208–9
crackers, 40–42; for cocktail parties, 303–4
cranberry relish with Mandarine Napoléon, 348–49
cream cheese, herbed, 149
cream scones with currants, 157–58
crème Chantilly, 360–61
crudités, 304–9
crumpets, 97–99
crystal cocktail nuts, 296–97
cucumbers: for crudités, 305; cucumber relish, 351; cucumber sandwiches, 136, 139
curried salt, 28
curried shrimp salad, 146–47
custard: flan Napolitano, 251–52; pumpkin, 361–63

date bread, 93–94
dates, stuffed, 328
dessert: Aunt Babe's cake, 179–81; buñuelitos, 248–50; dried-fruit compote, 95–96; flan Napolitano, 251–52; fresh peach chiffon pie, 219–20; gingerbread with Cointreau crème Chantilly, 360–61; ginger-oat snaps, 161; Lady Baltimore cake, 198–201; lemon curd bars, 103–4; meringues with chocolate,

164–65; Mexican flourless chocolate cake, 358–59; not-your-grandmother's ambrosia, 121–22, 124; peanut butter bars, 164; pumpkin custard, 361–63
deviled eggs, 317–20
devils on horseback, 336–37
dinner rolls, 356–58
dips: "caviar," 33–34; hot artichoke, 309–10; Mexican-style guacamole, 230–31; nopalitos, 228–30; spinach, 310; Stilton-mayonnaise, 33; Stilton–sour cream, 33. See also salsas
dried fruit: for cocktail parties, 303; compote, 95–96; stuffed dates, 328

East meets West wings, 63
egg-mayonnaise topping, 331
eggs, about, 24–25; deviled, 317–20; as hangover remedy, 371; hard boiled, 26–28; marbled tea, 147–48; pickled, 29; poached, 101–2; rarebit, 99–100; salt mixes for, 28; scrambled, 372; shirred, 93
English muffins. See crumpets

fennel, and carrot quiche, 112–13
feta compli, 323–25
finger foods. See appetizers, canapés, crudités, hors d'oeuvres, snacks
finger sandwiches. See tea sandwiches
fish: anchovy butter, 85; ceviche, 241; gravlax, 349–51; rustic salmon-roe canapés, 88–89; salmon salad, 144–45; smoked trout canapés, 341–42
flan Napolitano, 251–52
flavored salt mixes, 28

scallions, for crudités, 307
scallops, ceviche with, 241
scones, cream, with currants, 157–58
scrambled eggs, 372
seafood: anchovy butter, 85; angels on horseback, 191; ceviche, 241; crab imperial, 210–11; crab puffs, 207–8; gravlax, 349–51; Maryland crab soup, 208–9; oysters on the half shell, 64–70; oyster stew, 191–93; pan-fried oysters, 193–94; rustic salmon-roe canapés, 88–89; salmon salad, 144–45; shrimp cocktail, 74; shrimp and crème fraîche filling, 333–34; shrimp puffs, 340–41; shrimp salad, 146–47; smoked trout canapés, 341–42; softshell crab sandwiches, 211–13
shellfish. *See* crab, oysters, scallops, shrimp
shirred eggs, 93
shrimp: cocktail, 74; and crème fraîche filling, 333–34; puffs, 340–41; salads, 146–47; steamed, 70–73
shucking oysters, 66–67
smoked trout canapés, 341–42
snacks: buffalo "chips," 49–50; cheddar-parmesan ice-box crackers, 40–42; cheese straws, 298–301; chicken cocktail kebabs, 51–52; chicken wings: 61–64; french fries, 34–37; garlic bread popcorn, 43; hard-boiled eggs, 26–28; meatballs, 56–61; nuts, 18–23, 296–98; oysters on the half shell, 64–70; pickled eggs, 29; pork saté, 52–53; potato chips, 30–32; spicy parmesan cheese crisps, 42; steamed shrimp, 74;

sweet potato chips, 32. *See also* canapés, dips, hors d'oeuvres
snow peas, for crudités, 308
softshell crab sandwiches, 211–13
soufflé, cheese, 116, 119
soup: Maryland crab, 208–9; oyster stew, 191–93; split pea with ham, 374–75; yellow split pea, 171–72
spicy parmesan cheese crisps, 42
spicy tartar sauce, 195
spinach dip, 310
split pea soup: with ham, 374–75; yellow, 171–72
spreads. *See* dips, sandwich spreads
squash, for crudités, 306
starters. *See* appetizers, canapés, dips, hors d'oeuvres, snacks
steak roulades, 337–39
steamed shrimp, 74
stewed tomatoes, 195–96
Stilton-mayonnaise dip, 33
Stilton–sour cream dip, 33
stovetop roasting (of chiles and tomatoes), 226
string beans: for crudités, 307–8; haricots verts with Dijon mustard dressing, 120–21
stuffed dates, 328
succotash, winter, 196–97
summer shrimp salad, 147
Swedish meatballs, 56–59
sweet glazed pecans, 19–20
sweet mint butter, 148–49
sweet potato chips, 32

tamales with shredded pork and chile filling, 243–47
tapenades, 81–83; mushroom, 310–12
tarragon-chicken salad, 144
tartar sauce, spicy, 195
tea breads and cakes: cream scones with currants, 157–58;

crumpets, 97–99; Madeira cake, 159
tea eggs, marbled, 147–48
tea sandwiches, 135–47, 160
terrine, vegetable, 351–54. *See also* mousse
tomato and herb filling, 334
tomatoes: for crudités, 307; fried, 213–14; salsa cruda, 227–28; salsa roja, 247; stewed, 195–96; stovetop roasting of, 226; vinaigrette, 103
tortillas: corn, 235–38; canapés, 328–31. *See also* chalupas
trout canapés, smoked, 341–42
turkey: à la king, 376–77; brined and roasted, 346–48
twice-cooked brussels sprouts, 178–79

ugly bread, 320–21

veal. *See* Swedish meatballs
vegetables: Alice B. Toklas's mushroom sandwich spread, 142–43; black-eyed peas, 355; carrot-fennel quiche, 112–13; carrot-ginger sandwich spread, 143; carrot rolls, 323; chiles toreados, 227; cucumber relish, 351; cucumber sandwiches, 136, 139; feta compli, 323–25; fresh corn salad, 214–15; German potato salad, 176–77; guacamole topping, 330; haricots verts with Dijon mustard dressing, 120–21; hot artichoke dip, 309–10; jicama canapés, 231–32; Maryland fried tomatoes, 213–14; Mexican-style guacamole, 230–31; mushroom filling, 334–35; mushroom tapenade, 310–12; nopalitos dip, 228–30; nopalitos salad, 242–43; onion

marmalade, 155; orzo-asparagus salad, 356; radish sandwiches, 140; red cabbage with apples, 177–78; red-leaf lettuce salad, 112; refried beans: 238–39; roasted beet sandwich spread, 141–42; spinach dip, 310; split pea soup with ham, 374–75; stewed tomatoes, 195–96; tomato and herb filling, 334; tomatoes vinaigrette, 103;

twice-cooked brussels sprouts, 178–79; watercress sandwiches, 140–41; white asparagus with hollandaise sauce, 94–95; winter succotash, 196–97; yellow split pea soup, 171–72. *See also* crudités, salsas

vegetable terrine, 351–54

walnuts, hot and spicy, 20. *See also* boozy spiced nuts, ginger orange nuts

water bath (bain-marie), 117–18
wax beans, for crudités, 307–8
white asparagus with hollandaise sauce, 94–95
white bean spread, 84–85
wings, chicken, 61–64
winter succotash, 196–97

yellow split pea soup, 171–72
yogurt. *See* chicken cocktail kebabs, smoked trout canapés

zucchini, for crudités, 306

INDEX OF DRINKS

ABOUT THE AUTHORS

JAMES WALLER is the Brooklyn, New York–based author of *Drinkology: The Art and Science of the Cocktail*, and its companion volume, *Drinkology WINE: A Guide to the Grape*, both published by Stewart, Tabori & Chang.

RAMONA PONCE is a caterer, food stylist, and costume designer; she lives in Manhattan. Both James and Ramona like to eat and drink—and they much prefer doing so in the company of friends.

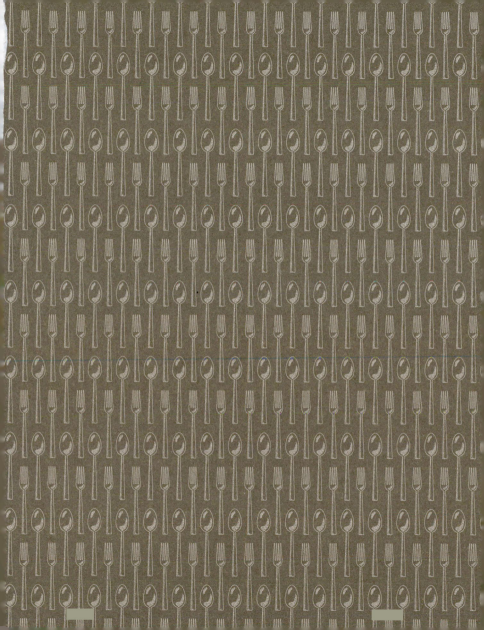

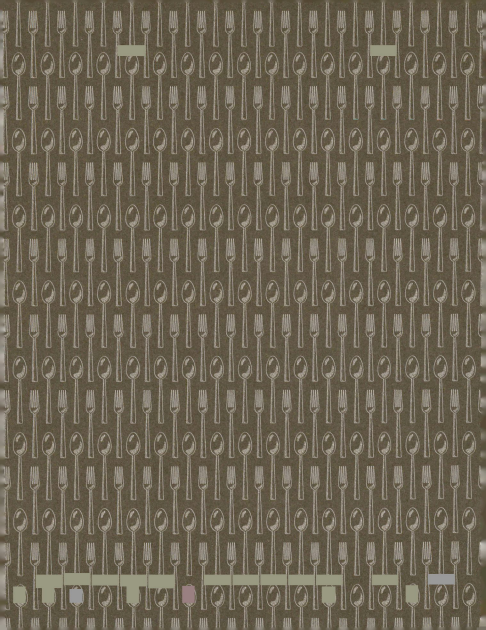